D1707946

The Days We Danced

The Days We Danced

The Story of My Theatrical Family

from Florenz Ziegfeld to Arthur Murray and Beyond

Doris Eaton Travis

with Joseph and Charles Eaton
as told to J.R. Morris

Marquand Books
Seattle

Library of Congress Control Number: 2003110849
ISBN: 0-8061-9950-4

Distributed by
University of Oklahoma Press
1005 Asp Avenue
Norman, OK 73019

Frontispiece and page 6: Doris Eaton in the *Ziegfeld Follies of 1919*
Page 10: Doris at age sixteen in the *Ziegfeld Follies of 1920*
Page 119: Reproduced with permission of *The Dance Magazine*

Edited by Jennifer Harris
Proofread by Barbara R. McGill
Designed by John Hubbard
Color separations by iocolor, Seattle
Produced by Marquand Books, Inc., Seattle
   www.marquand.com

Printed in Canada by Friesens

CONTENTS

INTRODUCTION

On Saturday, May 9, 1992, the University of Oklahoma conferred on Doris Eaton Travis a Bachelor of Arts degree with distinction. She was eighty-eight years old and had been a part-time undergraduate for twelve years. In her senior year, she was selected as the outstanding history major and was initiated into Phi Beta Kappa. That same year, she danced an impeccable soft-shoe to the song "Mandy" in the School of Music's *Broadway Gala*. It was the same routine she had performed over seventy years before, as understudy to Marilyn Miller in the *Ziegfeld Follies of 1919*, when she was fifteen years old.

From the age of seven, Doris was in and out of school, appearing with her brothers and sisters in stock company productions in Washington, D.C., and Baltimore, and later on the road. At the age of twelve, she and her sister Mary made their first appearance on the New York stage in leading roles. Her formal schooling ended in New York with the completion of the eighth grade in 1918. That was the same year she joined her sister Pearl in the *Ziegfeld Follies* for the road tour. She claimed she was sixteen then and gave her name as Doris Levant, using Pearl's married name in the hope that those who looked after the welfare of children would not discover that she was only fourteen. For the next two years, she would be a specialty dancer with the *Follies*, and soon there would be five Eaton children with Ziegfeld credentials: Pearl, Mary, Doris, Joseph, and Charles. No other family in the twenty-five-year history of the *Follies* had such representation. From 1918 to 1923, there was always an Eaton in the *Follies* cast, and throughout the twenties, the Eatons were well known in show business circles. While Joe went away to college, Pearl, Mary, Doris, and Charlie stayed busy on Broadway or on the road, with their mother, the remarkable Mamie Eaton, always nearby.

While Mary became the biggest star, they all had successful careers in show business before talking pictures, radio, and the Great Depression changed everything for theatrical people. Those were the historic forces that emptied legitimate theaters, destroyed "the road," killed vaudeville, and put a great many performers on the streets. Beginning in 1936, Doris went on to a second successful career with the Arthur Murray Dance Studios, where she became

copartner of the first Murray franchise outside of New York. With her partner, Cy Andrews, she operated ten studios throughout Michigan, and after
they dissolved their partnership and Doris took over the franchise in 1948,
she opened eight additional studios. Hers was the nation's largest franchise
chain of dance studios in the country under the Arthur Murray banner. She
was joined there in 1940 by her brothers, Joe and Charlie, and together they
made Detroit the national center for Latin dances—the rhumba, the samba,
the tango, the mambo—teaching dance teachers from all over the country.
In 1968, after thirty years in Michigan, she retired, along with her husband,
Paul Travis—a successful inventor and manufacturer of automotive parts—and
moved to a horse ranch in Oklahoma to raise quarter horses.

She had two unfulfilled dreams: to get a college education and to tell
the story of her remarkable theatrical family. So, while helping Paul run the
ranch, she started the twelve-year odyssey toward her college degree. In the
years that followed her graduation, she thought more and more about telling
the story of her family, and in 1995, she asked whether I would help her with a
book about the Eatons. I had been one of Doris's professors and had become
a friend of both Paul and Doris. She even taught me how to do country-and-
western dances, not to mention the fox-trot and rhumba and all those others.
I agreed to help with the book, and in January of 1996, Doris (at ninety-two)
and Charlie (at eighty-five) and I started talking about the Eaton family, consulting brother Joe (at eighty-eight) by telephone at his home in Troy, Michigan. We were blessed with a great array of scrapbooks that Doris had kept over
many years, including those of Pearl and Mary, who were no longer living. We
were also greatly aided by the discovery of some of sister Pearl's reminiscences
written forty-five years earlier and a host of letters written by the eldest sister,
Evelyn, many of which answered some perplexing questions about events that
took place when Doris and her brothers were too young to recall or simply
not in a position to know. When necessary, we went to various reference books
to check facts, confirm dates, resolve conflicts, sharpen memories, correct
sequences, and reconstruct certain events.

The story is told by Doris, but the telling really became a family affair,
with Joe (who died in December of 1998) and Charlie involved from the
beginning. Other family members—whose lives were often written about in
newspapers and magazines, and whose own writings, letters, pictures, and
memorabilia were available—helped to complete the story. As with any family,
there are successes and there are sorrows, and it was our aim to tell the whole
story. The Eaton family is exceptional not only because they experienced so

many exhilarating achievements, but also because they endured more than their share of heart-wrenching tragedies and disappointments. The surviving members of the family were as candid and frank in revisiting the past as memory can allow, and their story is a fascinating one. So what follows are the memories—wonderful and poignant—about an extraordinary family whose experiences virtually span a century. Along the way, some light is shed on a unique period in the history of show business in the United States. There has never been another time like it, and there never will be.

J. R. Morris

PROLOGUE

The twenty-year period from 1911 to 1931 was a time of great success for my brothers and sisters and me. We started in show business as children in Washington, D.C., and grew into seasoned and talented performers, acting, dancing, and singing. We were originally called "The Seven Little Eatons," although only five of us actually performed. When we arrived in New York, the Broadway producers liked us, and they continued to use us as teenagers and young adults. For years, we had no problem finding jobs. It was up, up, up. No one cautioned us about the downside of show business.

In the twenties, we became known as "The Eatons of Broadway," with four of us appearing at the same time in four different theaters on that fantastic isle of Manhattan. During that precious moment in time, we enjoyed the rewards of our collective success and shared the friendly company of Broadway's elite.

In truth, we were a family of innocents that had been launched into the sophisticated theatrical world of New York, and we never gave much thought to what tomorrow might bring. After 1929, when the depression came and theaters closed and jobs disappeared, it seemed that no producer in the theatrical world wanted any of us any more. I watched us rise and fall, not quite realizing what was happening. None of us did until it became painfully clear. We frantically searched around for a few barren years, looking for opportunities that never came. The emotional burden of rejection—along with the practical concerns for rent and food—was overwhelming. It was difficult to face the bitter truth that we were in fact out of show business. Our world suddenly turned bleak, and in the years that followed, an incredible succession of tragedies struck our family.

Of the seven Eaton children, one got lost along the way in alcohol and drugs; one was found murdered in her apartment; one died of an overdose of pills; one died alone, with unmitigated fury and grief in her soul; one lived a long and good life and died with the stalwart courage of a soldier, doing whatever needed to be done, without complaint and regardless of the stress on his health; one lives with unused capacity to create artistic play, a born comedian never having reconciled being out of show business. I alone, for whatever reasons, emerged from that dark cloud to enjoy a continuing life of success and happiness.

How did it all happen? How did it happen that by 1936, three of us were living together in a tacky one-room apartment in an old brownstone on Eighty-sixth Street in New York with our rent six weeks in arrears, depending each month on the twenty-five dollars that brother Joe sent us from his Civilian Conservation Corps (CCC) camp in California? How was it that our family of innocents rose to such acclaim and celebrity on the Great White Way and then stumbled and fell into oblivion? How was it that I, of all the Eatons, survived show business, built a prestigious chain of dance studios in Michigan, struggled through a successful although rocky marriage of fifty years, became a millionaire, and now live a comfortable and busy life on an 880-acre ranch in Oklahoma?

Now, seventy years after our exit from show business, I am the only Eaton left who can tell the story of my beloved and tragic family. My purpose in writing this book was twofold. First, to whatever extent I could, I wanted to rescue my family from the oblivion into which they fell after having played a significant role in the musical theater of the twenties. They deserve to be remembered and to share a place in theatrical history. Second, I wanted to sound a warning to young and talented people drawn to acting, singing, or dancing that one thing has not changed over the years about the world of show business. In the words of Saint Matthew, "Many are called, but few are chosen." Show business is a tough, harsh world in which the failures far outnumber the successes. Too many starry-eyed youths in schools of music and drama fantasize about their futures with excitement and determination with too little awareness of the hazards and pitfalls that await them.

Remember that you work in show business only when someone lets you work. No matter how great your talent might be, you must be chosen to perform. The hard reality of this becomes clear when the aspiring performer is sitting in an agent's office with ten or so other desperate people, all hoping for the "one job" in the "one show" going into rehearsal. Rejection is much more common than acceptance. Even for those who achieve initial success and enjoy a certain recognition, there comes a time—sooner or later—when the producers are looking for something new and different. After a few years of being gloriously in the public eye, your face is old news, and you are shoved aside. It happens to the stars and gypsies alike, and too few are prepared for any other life.

The popular song "New York, New York," by John Kander and Fred Ebb, carries the sentiment of love and fascination that many headed into show business experience: "If I can make it there, I'll make it anywhere." But this is just hope and dreaming, and although there is nothing wrong with that, it is not practical or realistic. The problem is that only a comparative few actors and actresses can "make it anywhere." When careers never get off the ground or are ended too quickly, few are prepared to do any other type of activity. Many starve in mind and body. I recall that one of the brightest stars of the *Ziegfeld Follies* eventually had to ask the Ziegfeld Girls' Club for money to pay her rent. There are too many contemporary examples of this.

This is what I call the dark side of show business, and it is real and persistent, generation after generation. The final curtain does come down, and the lights go out. There is no more music, applause, or opportunity. With my family, that curtain fell long before we were ready, and certainly before we had the foresight and the know-how to land on our feet. Some of my family felt they could not live without show business, and they never recovered from their grief and sense of loss. The profession of the theater is like a trap—very easy for some to fall into, and very difficult to get out of because the enticement is blinding and numbing to our sensibilities.

This pessimistic note is not intended to discourage young people from developing their talents to the fullest capacity and pursuing the entertainment profession in all the richness of its opportunities. Movies, television, radio, Broadway, regional theaters, recordings, all offer a range of unprecedented opportunities. Nevertheless, it is important to have thought through some appealing alternatives if show business doesn't work out or ends too soon. It is important to look beyond the present moment and not be mesmerized by the thought, "This will never happen to me." The odds are that it will.

For those of you just trying out your tap shoes, ballet slippers, vocal chords, or musical instruments, I hope this story of my beautiful, wonderful, tragic family will furnish insight and inspiration—as well as a certain wariness—for the future that awaits you. My experience in show business convinced me that the world of entertainment is a wonderful road to artistic achievement and inspiration if one is well prepared to cope with the slings and arrows of the business. Perhaps observing the lives of those who have gone before can be a useful part of that preparation. This is our story. It is also the story of my long love affair with my husband, Paul Travis, who became the most important person in my life.

Doris Eaton Travis

The seven Eatons

Clockwise from left:
Robert (fourteen), Joseph
(five), Evelyn (sixteen),
Pearl (twelve), Mary
(nine), Doris (six),

and Charles (two).

CHAPTER ONE

GETTING STARTED

The summer of 1911 was a pivotal time for the Eaton family. Although we did not suspect it at the time, our quiet lives on Rhode Island Avenue in Washington, D.C., were about to be forever changed. We were scarcely aware of the important political and social events around us. William Howard Taft was in the middle of his term as the twenty-seventh president of the United States. The Supreme Court was busy dismantling the big monopolies of Standard Oil and American Tobacco. The women's suffrage movement was gaining steam, with several states already having granted voting rights to women. Carrie Nation's death in June ended her zealous efforts for prohibition, but the movement would go on and eventually culminate in the Volstead Act.

The parlor song of the day was twenty-three-year-old Irving Berlin's first big hit, "Alexander's Ragtime Band." The ragtime music craze was at its height. Vaudevillians and the dancing schools were incorporating ragtime music into their dancing, and even social dancers had begun to "rag" the popular two-step. Berlin's song combined ragtime with the popular song style of the day, and its success made him famous worldwide. I was only seven years old at the time and could not have imagined that in just seven more years I would be shaking hands with Irving Berlin on the stage of the New Amsterdam Theater on Forty-second Street in New York City!

What really mattered to the Eatons in the early summer of 1911 was that *The Blue Bird* was coming to town. Nathaniel Roth, agent for the Shubert Brothers, was in Washington preparing for the arrival of the road company production of that popular play, which had been the Shuberts' biggest hit in New York the previous season. Its author, the Belgian poet and playwright Maurice Maeterlinck, won the 1911 Nobel Prize for literature, adding enormous prestige to the Shuberts' production.

In those days, it was common practice to hire local people to add to the cast of touring plays, and only the principals traveled from city to city. Roth needed twenty or more children from the area to add to the cast of *The Blue Bird,* so he placed an ad in the *Washington Post* announcing auditions at Washington's Belasco Theater.

My eldest sister, Evelyn, read the ad, and while she was too old at seventeen to try out herself, she grew very excited about the opportunity it presented for her three sisters—Pearl, Mary, and me. Pearl was twelve, Mary was ten, and I was seven. We had all been studying dance at Miss Cora Shreve's Dancing School and had appeared in the little recitals she did now and then to show off her pupils. My two younger brothers, Joseph and Charles, were too young, and my older brother, Robert, who was fifteen, was decidedly uninterested. Evelyn had a passion for the theater. Before we left Norfolk, Virginia, for Washington, D.C., when Evelyn was eleven or twelve, Aunt Rose Stevens, Papa's sister, had taken Evelyn to the professional theater with her several times. This began a fascination for the theater and show business that developed in her like a virus—one that eventually blighted her whole life. Although never striving to perform herself, she was the one who started us Eatons on our show business journeys. She reaped some personal fulfillment in the theatrical successes of her own children years later, but at this moment, at seventeen, she was aglow with ambitions for her sisters and brothers.

Evelyn's room was plastered with pictures of actors and actresses cut from magazines, and she was always directing Pearl, Mary, and me in some kind of make-believe performance. Even before I was old enough to remember, we would put on shows for the rest of the family and charge five pins for each person to attend. When it was warm, we would entertain in the backyard, and if the other family members didn't like what we did, they would throw dry leaves at us.

That wonderful backyard is one of my clearest memories of those early years when we lived on Rhode Island Avenue. The yard extended all the way to the street that ran behind our house, and I can recall standing there, watching the brightly colored, horse-drawn fire wagons coming up the street from the station just two blocks away, the bell clanging and two mighty horses galloping along pulling the wagon. I will never forget the sound of those horses' hooves, in perfect coordination with one another pounding out a steady rhythm as they came dashing down that street. Maybe that sound embedded in my early youth had something to do with my becoming a tap dancer in later years, pounding out varied rhythms on the stage with my own "dainty" hooves.

Evelyn saw that with the coming of *The Blue Bird,* there was an opportunity for us to be on the stage with real professionals from New York. So she asked Mama if she could take us to the Belasco Theater for the tryouts. Mama said, "Well, I guess the only thing bad that could happen is that they won't get picked. So if you want to do it, it's okay with me."

While Evelyn's efforts initially got us into show business, Mama too was strongly drawn to the theater. I remember Mama saying that as a small girl she wanted desperately to go to the theater and eventually become an actress, but her parents—who were very religious and straitlaced—would never even permit the subject to be discussed. They were leaders in the Methodist Church in Portsmouth, Virginia, and my grandmother was a national officer in the Woman's Christian Temperance Union. The only exceptions they ever made about performing were for Mama to give recitations at church socials or school activities.

According to W. O. Saunders, Mama's cousin, who wrote an article about her for *Collier's* in 1925, she was the star elocutionist in the public schools and well known for her dramatic ability. He also wrote, "Mamie was a wild young thing—not a bad girl . . . she was full of fun and laughter and mischief, and she liked to kick up her legs. . . . She was a romping, frolicking, reckless kid with the prettiest legs and the greatest wealth of curly blond hair in Portsmouth."

He also wrote that on one occasion, Mamie (although her given name was Mary, everyone called her Mamie) brought home a paperback romance novel, which had been loaned to her by a girlfriend, and Mama's mother was so upset with the book that "the evening was spent in family prayers." Her parents didn't really know what to do with her, and when Mama was sixteen, she ran away with Papa, and they went to North Carolina and got married. In spite of her adventurous and fun-loving rebel nature, she loved and respected her parents and never let any of us children get involved in professional theater until after their deaths.

In my scrapbook, there is a clipping from 1929, when we were all in Hollywood, in which Mama is quoted by Robin Coons, who had a syndicated column called "Hollywood Lights and Sounds":

No, I didn't tell [my children] they must go on the stage. I don't believe in forcing one's children into a profession. But I think they inherited the urge. Mr. Eaton was talented musically, and . . . I hope they inherited some dramatic ability from me. . . . I simply encouraged them. Gave them music and dancing lessons, took them to plays, let them take part in dramatic productions—but even that was after my own parents had died. Whenever the girls had a new dress, they would try it on before the mirror, and dance around in it. We talked about the theater all the time.

Early dancing school days

Mary

Doris

Charlie

Joe

Later dancing school days

Pearl

Mary and Doris

Left to right: Mary, Doris, Avery
Grant (our cousin), Joseph, and
Charlie

Doris and Mary

In Norfolk, where we had lived until I was three years old, Mama had taken us to various dramatic and musical programs at church or school functions. Mama later said that Mary sang her first song in public before she was three, a little song called "I Don't Want to Play in Your Yard." On the rare occasion when Mama took us to a play at a local commercial theater, she wouldn't dare tell her folks where we had been. Had Mama's folks lived long lives, we probably would never have gone into show business.

My two younger brothers, Joe and Charlie, clearly remember Mama saying that she wanted to see all seven of her children in show business and wanted them to become famous. Looking back now, it seems clear to me that she really did want us in the theater, although I can't remember her talking about it. Maybe she avoided saying those things to us girls early on because she did not want us to say anything in front of her folks. I certainly don't remember feeling any pressure from Mama to dance, sing, or act. She was never stern or demanding, always loving and supportive, and maybe skillful in guiding us gently in the way she wanted us to go.

On the other hand, it was clearly Evelyn who was relentless and controlling in her efforts to see us all succeed as entertainers. It was always Evelyn— perhaps as the instrument of Mama's ambitions—who talked to us incessantly about performing. It had been Evelyn's idea to take us to Miss Shreve's dancing school, and it was she who convinced Miss Shreve to take us as students even though we couldn't afford to pay the full price. Evelyn took us to our lessons, saw to it that we practiced, and coached us about our routines for the dance recitals. And it was Evelyn who took us to the Belasco Theater to try out for *The Blue Bird*.

At the tryouts, Mary and I were selected for specific roles, and Pearl was selected as one of the extras in the group scenes. There would be eight performances a week for two weeks. We were each to be paid fifty cents a performance, and that meant that altogether we would earn an additional twelve dollars a week for the family. Since Papa's wages were pretty low, that sounded like a lot of money to us, and it all went into the family pot, with a modest allowance for us three girls. For years to come, that would be the family practice, and it built a strong sense of mutual responsibility within the family that served us well over the years.

Mary and I didn't have speaking parts in *The Blue Bird*. We were in a scene called "The Palace of Night," and I was a child sleeping between the paws of a great lion statue in an unreal, dreamlike garden. As a matter of fact, my character's name was Sleep. The stage was bathed in moonlight, with stars flickering in the background, and children dancing and flitting about. All I had to do was lie still and keep my eyes closed. Mary had some similar role, so it wasn't very taxing on either of us. Neither was it as thrilling or special as one might think. Being on the Shubert stage seemed a natural progression from performing at Miss Shreve's. The difference now was that we were getting paid! Probably only Evelyn sensed that this could be the opening wedge for the theatrical careers she envisioned for us.

Mama had to arrange for us to be out of school whenever that was necessary. Of course, in those days it was not unusual for children to work during all or some of the school hours. Mama was always with us at the theater, and that would be the case for many years to come. She was the one who dealt with Nathaniel Roth, and over time, she developed a good relationship with him and with the Shubert organization. The Shuberts were the largest theatrical management organization in the country, owning over seventy theaters and holding management contracts with many more. That good relationship with the Shuberts would be very helpful to us Eatons a little later on.

After *The Blue Bird,* we were hired by the Poli stock companies in Washington, D.C., and Baltimore for several productions over the next three-to-four-year period. Poli was one of the largest chains of theaters and stock companies in the country, concentrated primarily in the East. Zefferino Sylvestro Poli was an Italian immigrant who built his first vaudeville house in 1892 and just kept building until he was a major force in the entertainment business. (He reversed his initials and became known as S. Z. or Sylvester.) The stock companies typically consisted of a group of eight actors: the leading man and woman, two second leads, two character actors, an ingenue, and a juvenile. Others were added from the local community as needed for a particular play.

Our first play for Poli was *Mrs. Wiggs and the Cabbage Patch,* which included, along with us three sisters, five-year-old brother Joe in the cast. Mary had a one-line speaking part, which always brought down the house: "Many are cold, but few are frozen." Mary received seven dollars a week; the rest of us received four dollars each. We followed *Cabbage Patch* with *Little Lord Fauntleroy,* with Mary in the title role and me as Dick the Bootblack. Twenty or so years later, the part of Dick in the movie version was played by Mickey Rooney, who coincidentally would also get the movie version of the role of Andy Hardy, a role originated by my brother Charlie in 1928 on Broadway in a play called *Skidding.*

The local stock company managers at the Poli theaters soon knew that if you needed three or four or more children, you could call Mama Eaton and get them all at one place. The sex of the child didn't matter. You could put

Stock company days:
Little Lord Fauntleroy

Mary as Little Lord Fauntleroy

Doris as Dick the Bootblack

Mrs. Wiggs and the Cabbage Patch

Mary, Doris, and brother Joe

Pearl

pants on the girls or dresses on the boys and that worked just fine. When Joe appeared as a girl, he was often listed in the program as Josephine. In a play called *Seven Sisters,* five of the sisters were Pearl, Mary, Joe, me, and a cousin named Avery, who was living with us at the time. Avery's mother (Mama's younger sister) was disabled from epilepsy and living in an institution. Avery's father was away in the navy, so she lived with us for a few years before going to a Catholic boarding school in New York.

Joe, with his beautiful blond hair, was a doll, and he did not seem to mind masquerading as a girl. Largely because of Mama's practical attitude from the very beginning, we approached performing with a kind of no-nonsense ethic—we did whatever the part required. It was our job. Years later, when Joe was at the University of Pennsylvania, he was the leading lady in the Mask and Wig Club's all-male productions. He was smashing in his roles for three years, but that ended Joe's theatrical career. He had had enough of performing.

We were often referred to as "The Seven Little Eatons," even though Evelyn and Robert, the two eldest, were not performers and Charlie was just a baby during the Washington years. We ranged in size like stair steps, and one writer said we were like a "fairy stepladder." He went on to say, "Each looks more like a Raphael cherub than the other." One critic said he suspected that whenever the Eaton children were in the cast, they added angels with wings to the script just because the audiences loved to see us that way. We all had some shade of blond hair and blue eyes. We girls had long curls, and it was our good fortune that audiences found us "adorable." Mary recalled years later that she got one part in Washington simply because of her beautiful honey-blond hair. We had arrived at the theater too late to try out for the cast of some play, but when the director saw Mary's beautiful hair, he said, "I can use her. I don't have anyone with hair like that!"

We did Christmas musicals and several dance programs, and we became seasoned troupers, going back and forth between the stock companies in Washington, D.C., and Baltimore. When we were in Baltimore, we spent the nights at a boarding house—Mrs. Pizer's boarding house—where there was good food and comfortable beds. We would spend one week in rehearsals, then do the play for a week, and then return to Washington. Between plays, we would go to school, take dancing lessons, and practice on the broken-down piano we had at home.

Papa (whose name was Charles Henry Eaton) really was a natural musician. He could play on the piano any tune he could hum, although he could not read music. Both Mary and Charlie could do the same thing, playing by ear, and also Pearl to some extent. But I never could, although I did learn to read music, and in time, I could play pretty well with the music in front of me. Joe also studied music, beginning at age six, and he learned to play the piano quite well. It seems that we always had a piano of one kind or another wherever we lived, and someone was usually playing it. And if Papa wasn't playing, he was singing—there was always music in the house.

Papa did this funny clownlike shuffle step across the room that made us all laugh. We called it "Papa's step," and before Charlie was even two years old, he would try to imitate Papa doing that step and we would all fall down laughing at him. We knew Charlie was a born entertainer even before he could speak a sentence clearly. We had fun entertaining each other, and someone in the house was usually singing or dancing about. New songs of that time like "I Want a Girl Just Like the Girl That Married Dear Ol' Dad" and "Oh You Beautiful Doll" were fun to sing and easy for Papa to play.

After moving from Norfolk, when Papa took a job with the *Washington Post* as a linotype operator, we first lived in a small house on New Jersey Avenue, but after Joe and Charlie came along, there wasn't room for seven kids. So we moved to a larger, two-story house at 1408 Rhode Island Avenue, and that is where we lived most of the years we were in Washington. When we started making money from Poli, we could live a little more comfortably. Papa had made only eighteen dollars a week when he worked as a printer for the *Norfolk Landmark,* and he made twenty-eight dollars a week at the *Washington Post.* My brother Robert, who was eight when I was born, sold newspapers, and he contributed about two dollars a week to the family pot. My Uncle Bobby (Mama's little brother)—when he came to live with us temporarily and earned his money working on a Washington tour bus—gave about three dollars a week to the pot. With my cousin Avery there, that meant eleven people in the house. It had not been easy to make ends meet in such a large household.

Papa was a master of borrowing from Peter to pay Paul. He would take the gas money and pay the milk bill. Then, before they cut off the gas, he would take the grocery money for the gas company. And when the rent man started knocking on the door, all the other creditors were put on hold. He didn't seem to worry about this constant juggling game. He wasn't the worrying type, but Mama was. She would get exasperated because Papa wasn't as frugal as she thought he ought to be. She bought all the groceries and cooked for all of us, so when there was no money for food, Mama was upset and frustrated.

I am sure that Mama was greatly relieved when we started having a little extra money coming in from the stock companies. The money went into a pot that Mama controlled, and it was easier then for her to make ends meet and keep food on the table for eleven people. Around the house, Mama pretty much ran things. She was continually busy cooking or cleaning or doing laundry. She worked terribly hard. I recall seeing her so many times coming up out of the basement into the kitchen with a heavy scuttle of coal for the stove, looking tired but never slowing.

If she was not busy with other chores, she was busy sewing. She made all of our clothes, and that was a never-ending task. It was very important to her that we always look clean and well-dressed, and that required her constant effort. I remember her giving us younger children baths in a big wooden tub in the kitchen of that first house on New Jersey Avenue. The adults used a bathroom on the third level of the house, where the plumbing did not always deliver hot water. So we were bathed in our basement kitchen, always with little homilies about cleanliness and looking nice.

Mama couldn't do it all by herself, so Evelyn was drafted to assist her in all the household chores, including taking care of the smaller children. To me, Evelyn was a teacher. She and I shared a bedroom in the big house, and in our talks—even at my young age—she was always concerned about my education and would tell me of its importance to my future life. While she was still in high school, she would work late into the night on household chores and then study under a gas lamp after we all had gone to bed. Later she dropped out of high school to take a stenographer's course, and I remember reading letters to her so that she could practice her shorthand. Years later, I learned that Papa had insisted that Evelyn leave school to help Mama in the house, and in retrospect, I can understand how unfair and regrettable it was that Evelyn's desires and ambitions were subjugated to her role as Mama's helper. It affected her whole life.

Pearl, Mary, and I were in school when we were not in shows, and we were not much help around the house, even though each of us had chores to do. When she was a teenager, Pearl would often clash with Evelyn, and they would have some stormy arguments—mostly because Evelyn disagreed with whatever it was that Pearl was doing or contemplating, as when she dropped out of high school. But Pearl had her own mind and was determined to do her own thing—whatever it was.

Papa worked at night and slept during the day, but he gave all of us children a good deal of attention. He was playful and fun loving, typically affectionate and easygoing. He was for the most part deferential toward Mama, but there were times when they would disagree and argue about things. Papa would sometimes lose his temper. When he was upset, he would get red in the face and rail against the object of his anger. On occasion, he would take his anger out on the boys if they gave him good reason. Both Joe and Charlie remembered being thumped roughly on the head by him, or spanked with his hand—never with a belt or paddle. I can recall him unleashing his temper on Robert when he was a rebellious teenager and he just wouldn't do what Papa told him to do. As early as fourteen, Robert had started drinking and staying out very late, and that was often the cause of great concern with Mama and Papa. On one occasion, Papa got very physical, slapping Robert around. But I think that never occurred again.

With us girls, Mama dished out whatever discipline was required. She was soft and gentle, but proper behavior and good manners were very important to her. She had the ability to communicate volumes in a single withering look, without ever opening her mouth. She could be quite disapproving in that way, but it was not in her manner to use a heavy hand or be strident or aggressive in a physical way. What passed for a spanking was a quick slap on the bottom, and that was that. Mama had no mean part to her, and we all wanted to please her. It was always crystal clear how she felt and what she believed. In some ways, she fit the stereotype of the chubby, lovable, and jolly person. Although she would really hate being called fat, she always had a problem with her weight. Mama was less than five feet tall, and she never controlled her weight very well in those earlier years.

Mama had inner strength, and over the years, she would show that she had the courage of her convictions. She was game for almost anything that wasn't vulgar or demeaning, and she could be playful and spirited. Even in tough times, her outlook was basically positive, brightened by a lively sense of humor and a wonderful laugh. She could express herself with grace and clarity, and that would prove to be a great asset when she started negotiating jobs for her brood. The theatrical managers liked dealing with her and knew that she could be counted on to have her children at the right place, at the right time, and under control.

There was never a doubt among us children that Mama was motivated by a strong and abiding love for us—a love that never faded throughout her life. We knew she would look after us, and we always felt safe and protected with her around. Her affection and thoughtfulness set the atmosphere for our family life. She could envelop us with big bear hugs, and we all knew we had the best mother on the planet.

Stock company days

DORIS EATON

Of the well known Eaton family of children, famous to the American stage Little Doris will play the part of "*Mary Ann Heath*" in SALOMY JANE at the Temple next week. She will be remembered by playgoers as playing the principal childpart in THE BLUE BIRD, and you will recall her clever work of last week in the part of "Bobby" in ALIAS JIMMY VALENTINE. This clever little actress will be seen in other plays produced by THE TEMPLE PLAYERS. The management trusts that mothers will not neglect to have the little folks at home visit the Temple during next week to witness the very clever performance of America's foremost child-actress.

NEXT WEEK
THE TEMPLE PLAYERS
PRESENT
PAUL ARMSTRONG'S
Beautiful Western Drama
SALOMY JANE
Founded upon the Fascinating Romance of the Sierras by
BRET HARTE

Who has been recognized throughout the English-speaking world as a story-teller and poet unrivaled in his field. His Western tales, in addition to interest as work of fiction, have an historical value, in giving the best picture in all our literature of the conditions of life in the far West fifty years ago.

In this artistic and vivid portrayal of a life that has passed away, Bret Harte stood alone, and rendered a unique service to the American Literature.

JOSEPH EATON

the youngest of the Eaton family will play the part of "Anna May Heath" in SALOMY JANE. This clever little juvenile actor made his first appearance in arms at His Majesty's Theatre in London, in THE BLUE BIRD, and has played seventeen different child parts in as many different stock productions. Both Joseph and Doris are accompanied from New York by their mother and a governess and four hours every day are devoted to study. The balance of their time is spent in a few moments recreation and playing the parts they are cast for with a true likeness of the well-seasoned actress and actor.

While Mama was not moralistic, she was deeply spiritual. Her brother-in-law, Kel Grant, who was Avery's father and an officer in the U.S. Navy, gave her a copy of *Science and Health with Key to the Scripture,* by Mary Baker Eddy, the founder of the Christian Science Church. Mama became deeply involved in the teachings of that church, and we all went to the Christian Science Sunday school—except for Papa, who never showed any interest in the church or in studying Christian Science.

Evelyn's Sunday school teacher, Jane Locker, and her sister, Lucille, became close friends to us. Jane Locker was also a Christian Science practitioner. When my brother Joe had infantile paralysis at age six, Mama called Jane Locker to help her through the ordeal. She was a wonderful help to Mama. When she visited Joe in the big second-floor bedroom in the house on Rhode Island Avenue, Mama would let me stay in the room. Because we all saw her quite often for several weeks, we began to call her "Aunt Jane." I loved to listen to her telling us about God being there with us and that all was well.

As we grew into adulthood, some of the members of the family would call Aunt Jane for spiritual help periodically, but none of us pursued the study regularly. When I had reached a very desperate moment, in an effort to find myself and a life more worthwhile, I began to turn to conscientious study of the Bible and the writings of Mary Baker Eddy, with sincere attempts to follow the spiritual guidelines set forth in those teachings. I have been able to work through many agonizing moments in the succeeding years. Aunt Jane became a spiritual guide to me. I still have some of the beautiful supporting letters she wrote to me through the years.

When it was decided that the family would move to New York, Aunt Jane suggested to Mama that Joe stay in Washington, D.C., with her and her sister for the school term until we had gotten settled. Charlie was too young for school and too young for Mama to leave with Aunt Jane, so Joe was the only one who remained in Washington. This became the pattern for Joe for several years, staying with Aunt Jane during the school terms and spending the summers with us in New York. This way, his formal education was not interrupted, as ours was. When he reached high school, the family was well established in show business, and he came home with us permanently. As it turned out, Joe was the only one in the family to graduate from high school on schedule and go directly on to college.

The Locker sisters' father lived with them. He was a veteran of the Civil War (on the Confederate side), and he told stories of the war that Joe found fascinating—so much so that he developed strong interests in all things military. As a child, Joe began collecting toy soldiers, which in time would become a joint hobby with Charlie. Together, they eventually collected over 100,000 lead toy soldiers. (The entire collection is still intact in the care of my brother Joe's son, Joe Jr., filling several shelves in the basement of his home in Michigan.) Many of the soldiers came as gifts from famous showbiz friends. Douglas Fairbanks Jr., who also collected lead soldiers, often visited the boys when we were living in Hollywood just to see Joe and Charlie's collection. He said that it was one of the best and largest collections in the country.

Joe loved the Lockers, and rather than being disappointed at being left behind, he basked in the love they showered on him—free of having to compete for attention with six brothers and sisters or to endure the ordeal of being out of school and on the road year after year, as Charlie and I did. As a consequence, Joe developed a kind of personal stability—a solid, healthy personality—that over the years would prove to be the exception rather than the rule within the family.

For a time, Charlie stayed involved with Christian Science. He remembers going alone to the Christian Science church in New York when he was ten or eleven. At that time in his life, he seldom missed going to church on Sunday and Wednesday. Because of his acting jobs, he wore his hair bobbed, and he was often the target of New York toughs, who would pick on him on his way to and from church. A friend of the family taught Charlie how to box so that he could defend himself. He could move well on his feet (which also made him a good dancer), and soon he no longer feared the hostile encounters because he had become quite a fighter.

◖ ◖ ◖

I never understood the relationship between Mama and Papa. From the time I was old enough to remember, there was not a lot of affection or closeness between them, and as Joe put it, "They just didn't get along." While they were both affectionate and loving toward us children, I can never remember them being that way to each other. They had seven children together, and obviously there had been a time when they had been very much in love. Maybe after the seventh child Mama said enough is enough, and in the years that followed, they would grow farther and farther apart.

I wish now that I had learned more about their relationship: whether they stayed together because they loved us children but not each other, or whether there was something specific—some incident or problem—that pulled them apart. While I don't really know, I suspect it was just a slow growing away from each other. And as our jobs in the theater took Mama away from home more and more, over a period of several years, they simply lived separate lives. It is symbolic of this distance between them that Papa is buried in California and Mama in Virginia, far apart from each other. That is sad but true.

Over the years, as we all developed as entertainers and matured in the entertainment world, Papa remained unchanged. He was never comfortable in the glib and worldly company of Broadway folks. While he was very bright, he was not well educated, and he felt much more at home among the craftsmen in the newspaper plants, where he spent most of the nights of his life. Even when he wasn't working, he would hang out there.

My fondest memories of Papa are of the times he would take Mary and me for a weekly outing. On his payday, which was every Friday, we would go with him to pick up his pay envelope, then go to the five-and-dime store for a nickel bar of candy, and later go to see a silent movie. I remember how we loved to watch the great siren Theda Bara rolling her eyes and grimacing at the camera in her highly emotional expressions. Mary and I even then thought being an actress would be something wonderful.

Papa would also buy himself a cigar, which he would save to smoke on Sunday, and after we started earning extra money with Poli, he would have two cigars. Sunday was the only day he smoked, but he did chew tobacco while he worked on the printing press. He chewed tobacco until the day he died.

A few years later, instead of Mary and me, it would be Joe and Charlie he took with him on outings. He particularly liked to go to Glenn Echo amusement park in Washington; and after the family moved to New York, he would take Joe and Charlie to Palisades and Coney Island. Papa enjoyed play even when he didn't have work. That's just the kind of man he was.

It was during our time on Rhode Island Avenue that I remember Papa and Evelyn talking to Mary and me about Santa Claus and that it was about time for him to come down the chimney to leave presents for us kids. They said there were so many of us that Santa would have to bring his elves to help out. We had a double fireplace, opening on both the first and the second floors, and Evelyn went up to the second floor and was making chirping elf-like noises into the chimney so that we would believe Santa and his helpers were on the way. But a light went on in my head, and Mary and I snuck upstairs and saw Evelyn at the fireplace making her elf sounds. We snuck back downstairs, and when Evelyn returned to the parlor, I cried out, "There is no Santa Claus!" Somehow it really got to me that the two of them had teamed up to deceive us. The fact that I remember that event so vividly indicates its impact on me. That would not be the last disillusionment in my life, but it was clearly a profound one.

During the Christmas season of 1914, Mary and I did a stock company show called *Our Cinderella,* and the *Washington Post* critic wrote that "Mary and Doris Eaton danced the Pavlowa gavotte, which proved they were the peers of any child dancers seen in Washington in years." A few months later, James Thatcher, the Washington manager of the Poli stock company, received permission from the Shubert Brothers for a local production of *The Blue Bird.* He hired Mary and me to play the two principal roles of Tyltyl and Mytyl. Those were long and demanding parts for kids our age, and we worked very hard getting ready for the opening. I remember Evelyn helping us with our lines, and we would go over them, over and over. They also cast Pearl in a minor role. For the two-week run in Washington, the business was phenomenal, and Mary and I received great notices for our performances. During the run, Nathaniel Roth came to see the play. He told Mama that the Shuberts were thinking about a revival of *The Blue Bird* and that he had recommended that Mary and I be hired for the leads. The revival would involve about four months on the road, followed by a run in New York. He added that he did not have the final say and it would be necessary for us to go to New York to try out for the producers. While he couldn't guarantee that we would be hired, he felt certain that we would be. In those days, there was no pay for rehearsals or for the transportation to tryouts, but Mama—knowing nothing of New York or where the money was coming from—readily agreed to go. She was confident that we would be hired and be successful.

God knows what conversations might have gone on among Mama, Papa, and Evelyn after that proposal, because Mary and I would obviously miss several months of school and family life would really be disrupted. The final decision was that Mama would take us all, including little Charlie, and Evelyn would stay home to take care of Papa, Robert, Joe, and cousin Avery. Pearl simply would not let us go without her.

Evelyn had great love and respect for Mama, truly idolized her, and I am sure that she agreed to this arrangement, concealing the awful disappointment she must have felt. I am certain that she had often dreamed of getting this kind of opportunity for herself, and now she was being denied even the vicarious satisfaction of traveling with us. It would be many years before I realized just how painful this episode was for Evelyn.

Mama borrowed $200 from her brother in Norfolk and packed up a lot of canned goods and her sterno stove in a trunk. On the last night of *The Blue Bird* in Washington, there was a big farewell party for us at the theater, with oyster stew and crackers and all kinds of cakes and pies. The next day, a big crowd of family and friends gathered at Union Station to see us off. Mama was

Stock company production of *The Blue Bird*

Mary as brother Tyltyl; Doris as sister Mytyl

truly brave to set out like that, knowing nothing of New York. She had merely been told to get a hacker (a cab driver) at Pennsylvania Station to take us to the theatrical rooming-house neighborhood in the west Forties, where we could find a place to stay. Taxis had only recently appeared on the streets of New York, and you could ride a mile for fifty cents. As soon as we got situated, we were to contact the Shubert Brothers to arrange an audition.

When the train pulled out of Union Station for New York, none of us realized the profound changes that would soon come to our family.

CHAPTER TWO

FROM PEARL'S NOTEBOOK

A great many years after we made that fateful trip to New York and long after the death of my sister Pearl in 1958, I discovered among her things some writing she had been doing during the forties, apparently in the hopes of having it published. To my knowledge, she never published anything, but I found her account of that early time and her close friendship with Volga Hayworth to be revealing—revealing of Pearl as well as of those rare and exciting days. In 1917, Volga Hayworth married the famous Spanish dancer Eduardo Cansino, and they had a daughter, Margarita Carmen Cansino, whom the world would later know as Rita Hayworth. At the time that Pearl wrote the following reminiscence in the mid-1940s, Rita Hayworth was Columbia Pictures' biggest star—the "sex goddess of the forties"—and one of the most popular pinup girls of World War II. Pearl's account also captures the aura of that first epic trip to New York:

On the first day of school in 1914, I met Volga Hayworth. A wonderful friendship began and did not end until thirty years later, with the untimely death of Volga on January 15, 1945. It was our freshman year and we were assigned to the same classes. Our mathematics teacher, Mr. Finkle by name, was also our homeroom teacher, and he was something out of this world. He was handsome, blond, with a marvelous physique, and, praise heaven, he had a good sense of humor. He loved caramels, and Volga and I always made sure that we had caramels to give him. He would walk around the room chewing them, and trying to give us math problems. The pupils would all laugh at him, but his warmhearted manner and his charming banter made everyone relax—and remain untrained. We learned nothing about math.

Volga and I made our best grades in English and dramatics classes. It was during rehearsals of a play called *Secret Service* that we got better acquainted and found to our mutual delight that we dreamed about being in the theater. Volga wanted to be a Sarah Bernhardt, and I envisioned myself as being in a musical extravaganza—since I was studying dance and could dance pretty well.

In our family backgrounds, no one had been in the theatrical world. Both our dads were printers—but the difference was that Volga's dad owned the printing establishment and my dad was a printer for the daily newspaper. Believe me, there were vast differences in our home lives. There were six in the Hayworth family and there were nine of us Eatons, plus an orphan cousin and a hypochondriacal uncle. Financially we were miles apart. Volga's family was well off, and my family barely managed from week to week. But spiritually we walked arm in arm, Volga and I, and the dreams we conjured up were enough for a hundred adolescents.

The local stock company was our chief source of thrills. The usual high school activities—dances and picnics and such—were fun, of course, but we fancied ourselves more sophisticated than that. We usually treated our boyfriends shamefully, because of this sense of superiority that we had. Sometimes I would ask Mama for twenty-five cents for school supplies, and we would save up the money and then ditch school to go to the stock company matinee. Finkle didn't seem to mind, and after all, with our future planned in the theater, it seemed more important than math, for heaven's sake.

Well, when summer came, we hightailed it to the Poli stock company and applied for jobs. My brothers and sisters and I had done some work for Poli, so they were not unfamiliar with me. The director liked us, and after we applied for what were called "atmosphere" jobs—extras, really—Lady Luck smiled on us and we were hired. We had small parts all summer, and by the end of summer we felt ready for Broadway.

So what! We had to go back to school. But we really had a brainstorm. Thoroughly convinced that we had what it takes—with that vast stock company experience under our belts—we began to plan secretly to run away to New York. We started saving money for railroad fares, and we filched canned goods from our parents' larders and hid them in an old trunk in my cellar. Then one day, in an unguarded moment when our exuberance showed itself in overly loud conversation, Mama heard us and surmised what was up.

We confessed all to her. And Mama, bless her heart, was her usual understanding self, so instead of berating us, she just gave us a sensible pep talk, and promised that as soon as we finished high school, she would help us to realize our ambitions. She talked with Volga's mother, and they concluded there wasn't any harm in our pipe dreams. So we weren't punished in any way.

But wait! They weren't pipe dreams. We continued to appear in Poli's stock company plays and continued to get experience. And then when Mary and Doris starred in *The Blue Bird,* Volga and I were in the play as "hour girls" who came walking out of this big clock and danced a lively routine that everyone seemed to like. Well, Mary and Doris were sensational in their roles, and the Shuberts wanted them to come to New York to try out for a new road company production that would also play in New York.

Mama told Volga's mother that she would look after her, so we two could try out for the play. God in heaven, our dreams had come true!

Things happened so fast that when I think of those first thrills, knowing we were going to New York, I get dizzy all over again. Getting packed . . . having a big farewell party at the Poli Theater . . . leaving Union Station with all our friends and family there to say goodbye—the train ride to Pennsylvania Station, searching for a place to live, and finding a real theatrical rooming house on West Forty-fifth Street, exploring the streets for stores and delicatessens. . . . Mama becoming a wizard in cooking on her little sterno stove . . . and then at last the rehearsals with the New York company.

We went on the road, and regardless of the hardships we endured—all the one-night stands and one-horse towns—it was heaven to us. We played some of the big cities of course, Pittsburgh and Indianapolis and several others. But it didn't matter, Volga and I thought it was all . . . elegant. We were actresses and come what may, we knew it was all for the sake of our art. Sixteen weeks later, we were back in New York. And all the way, Mary and Doris had been hailed by the critics as remarkable little actresses.

Then a stunning thing happened. J. J. Shubert talked to Mama and said that he had nothing at the time for Mary and Doris, and advised Mama to take them back to Washington and put them in school and have Mary study ballet. When Mama reported this to us, she seemed sad and disappointed, then she looked at Volga and me and spoke the most exciting words I had ever heard: "But," she said, pausing for effect, "Mr. Shubert wants you two to report to the Winter Garden Theater next Monday for rehearsals with the chorus. It's the new Al Jolson show."

Can you believe it?

CHAPTER THREE

SEARCHING FOR THE BLUE BIRD

Mary and I made our New York debut in the revival of *The Blue Bird,* during the 1915–16 season. But, to be honest about it, it was not on Broadway or anywhere near Broadway. It was at a Shubert Theater up on 106th Street. It didn't make any difference to us, it was still New York. We were experienced performers by that time—having played Indianapolis, Detroit, Cleveland, Rochester, Philadelphia, Pittsburgh, and a host of small and nameless towns. Audiences everywhere seemed to enjoy the play, and we had become very confident in our roles. It had been a wonderful adventure, and the Shuberts declared the tour a great success—it filled the theaters, and the reviews were laudatory. Mary and I received high praise for our acting and for being "adorable."

In the play, Mary was Tyltyl, a boy, and I was Mytyl, his younger sister. The play is a lovely fairy tale about life, death, and the search for the blue bird of happiness through an enchanted world of make-believe. All ages seemed to like it, from children to grandparents. *The Blue Bird* was not really a children's play (although the Shuberts referred to it as such). It was written as a serious work of art, but the dreamlike qualities of the play made it possible for children to enjoy it on one level, while a more sophisticated audience could enjoy it on quite another. That was the beauty, as well as the popular appeal, of Maeterlinck's play. If the mysteries and secrets of life were beyond your contemplation, you could enjoy the simple story of a boy and his sister searching through a fantasy world for a blue bird to help cure the sickness of a sad little girl.

The play opens with the son and daughter of a poor woodchopper being tucked into their trundle beds on Christmas Eve. After the parents go to bed, the children go to the window to observe with envy the holiday festivities in the home of their rich neighbor. A fairy, Berrylune, enters the cottage and demands that the children find for her "grass that sings" or "a bird that is blue." The latter, she says, will bring happiness to mankind and health to a sickly little girl. When the children agree to look, the fairy places a cap on Tyltyl's head. In the center of the cap is a large, wonderful diamond. When the diamond is turned, many entrancing transformations take place—the walls of the cottage turn opal; utensils come to life; and Cat, Dog, Fire, Water, Bread, Light, Milk, and Sugar become animated speaking comrades. The Hours—twelve dancing girls (two of whom were Pearl and Volga)—trip laughing from an old grandfather clock, and while the children marvel at all of this, the window magically opens and invites them to begin their journey.

Mary and I loved the play and never tired of encountering its interesting characters night after night—the personifications of Light, Time, Night, Sleep, Death, Maternal Love, Fire, Water, Trees, and Animals. There were a great many changing scenes and an effective use of light and other stage effects to produce a dreamlike quality. There was also a small orchestra playing theme music (mostly Debussy) and accompanying the several dances.

When Tyltyl and Mytyl return home from their search and unhappily admit to the sick girl's mother that they did not find the blue bird, she tells them that her daughter would be very happy to have the turtledove that is in a cage in the cottage of the boy and girl. On going to the cage, they discover that the dove has changed to a beautiful blue color. While they are celebrating finding the blue bird—as Dorothy found happiness in Oz, right in her own backyard—the bird gets free and flies away. They dissolve into tears, but Tyltyl, regaining his composure, announces with confidence that they will catch it again. He (Mary) steps to the front of the stage and speaks directly to the hushed audience in a clear voice: "If any of you should find him, would you be so very kind to give him back to us? We need him for our happiness, bye and bye." Curtain. Thunderous applause.

From the very beginning, Mama never let us get carried away by all that on-stage enchantment and the adulation of audiences. In the blatantly practical sense that seemed to dominate our family, we knew it was a way of earning our livelihood. Perhaps because of starting so young, I never became much impressed with the romanticism of the theater or thought of it as a way of expressing myself as an artiste or anything like that. It was simply a job, and if you could have fun doing it, that was great. But when it wasn't fun, you still did it, because that was what you did! As Mama said a hundred or more times, "Don't get conceited. Remember someone can always take your place."

For the four-week run of the play in New York, Papa and Evelyn came up from Washington and brought Joe. Both Charlie and Joe were given roles among the large number of children in the cast. It was the only time that all five of us would appear on the same stage at the same time. Charlie—at the age of four—was one of the "unborn children" waiting in the Kingdom of the Future to become a blessed event for some lucky couple. The children were covered with only pale blue chiffon ribbonlike drapes and were barefooted. Air blowing across the stage lifted the drapes in a waving, surreal way that created an otherworldly ambiance. Charlie, who really became quite a comedian later on, got his first big laugh one performance when he appeared among the other children without much chiffon and with a conspicuous pair of oversized black shoes on his feet. I don't think he ever got over the wonderful sound of an audience laughing. It was a debut that the family never stopped talking about.

In the years that followed, there were three efforts to make a movie of *The Blue Bird,* but none of them really succeeded. The first was a silent film made in 1918, then a 1940 version was made that starred Shirley Temple (in what was probably her worst film), and finally in 1976, a star-studded version was made in Leningrad—as the first detente movie in a joint effort with the Soviets —that starred Elizabeth Taylor, Jane Fonda, Ava Gardner, Cicely Tyson, and Robert Morley. Even with that terrific cast, the movie was a disaster and earned back only a small fraction of its cost. At least the Soviets paid for half of it.

The movies did not succeed, I think, because they failed to capture the childlike innocence, freshness and purity of Maeterlinck's play. Even after all these years, I can still feel the special aura of that *Blue Bird* production. To Mary and me, night after night, the charm and innocence and wonderment were fresh and real. We felt it anew every performance. We believed it and lived it. And, of course, we were so young and innocent and pure ourselves that it gave the play a special quality that was never captured on film. More sophisticated and seasoned actors might bring greater theatrical skill, but they could not bring a child's innocent belief in that fairy-tale world.

We did not know it then, but that was the beginning of the end of our innocence, as the family would soon plunge into the harsh world of show business. Starry-eyed, provincial, and determined, Mama would lead us into that world, armed only with her undaunted confidence in our talent and her willingness to devote herself totally to our success. We were completely unprepared for the risks and hazards ahead, and we could not foresee the tragic finales that would be played out by some of our beloved family members. But in 1915, we were blissfully and naively on our way, and it was *The Blue Bird* that had brought us to that pivotal moment and transformed our family and our lives. Looking back on that time, I cannot escape the poignant and nostalgic hold that fateful play had on me. It was for me a life-changing masterpiece.

Pearl, who was always more cynical (and probably more sophisticated) than Mary and I were, did not like the play in the way we did. Pearl seemed worldly even as a teenager, and she thought *The Blue Bird* was overly sweet and silly. That is perhaps the prevailing view of the play today, which—to my knowledge—hasn't been staged in many years, but I prefer to remember it my way—as a wise and philosophical work. (Perhaps the Walt Disney people will attempt it one day as an animated film. It seems made for Disney. As a matter of fact, the singing and dancing kitchen utensils in *Beauty and the Beast* seem right out of *The Blue Bird.*)

After the play closed, J.J. Shubert told Mama that there was nothing else at the moment for Mary and me but that he wanted to put Pearl and Volga in the Winter Garden chorus for *Robinson Crusoe, Jr.,* the new Al Jolson show. Shubert advised Mama to put Mary and me back in school and get Mary into ballet lessons. But Mama was not resigned to Mr. Shubert's pronouncement about nothing being available for Mary and me. She knew there were a lot of other theatrical managers and agencies. Someone would have work for us. Indeed, the Poli folks had many stock companies throughout New England, so Mama felt confident that we should move to New York and capitalize on the reputation we had developed in *The Blue Bird.*

Evelyn encouraged Mama in her decision to move to New York, and of course, Mary and I thought it would be wonderful. Pearl was already determined to stay there. Papa said, "Well, the stage is going through this family like the measles, so we might as well go on to New York." That is what everyone wanted to hear, so in 1916, the decision was made to move. Joe went to stay with Aunt Jane Locker, and Robert just took off for New York on his own. I don't remember the details about Robert's reaction to the move, but he would no longer live with the family. He was twenty years old, and he found work as a bellman in a New York hotel. From that time on, we would see him only at unpredictable intervals, usually when he was "between jobs."

By 1916, Pearl, Mary, and I had become the primary breadwinners for the family, and we had gone from fifty cents a performance in that first *Blue Bird* to earning a great deal more money than Papa. It would be that way throughout the rest of Papa's life. At different times, each of us became the chief breadwinner—first Pearl, then me, then Mary. When her ballet studies ended, Mary started earning more than all the rest of us put together.

Immediately following the close of *The Blue Bird,* we returned for a brief period to Washington and to the apartment on Willard Avenue that Papa had rented after we had left to do *The Blue Bird* on the road. It was a small apartment, and I remember that Mary and I slept in the attic on a pallet. Before the final move to New York, we did one play for Poli at the Baltimore stock company. It was called *Jimmy Valentine*. The character Jimmy Valentine was a safecracker, and in the play, he had to break open a safe to get me out. (Today, I haven't the foggiest memory of how my character ended up in the safe). When he got the door open, I came tumbling out, almost lifeless from suffocation, and was scooped up in the arms of the actor Lowell Sherman (as Valentine). Later, Sherman was featured in David W. Griffith's great movie, *Way Down East,* which starred Lillian Gish. He was a fine actor who looked after me as if I were his daughter. He was a very nice man and one of the strengths of the Baltimore stock company.

Many years later, when I was starring in the *Hollywood Music Box Revue* and we were on the road in San Francisco, I noticed in the paper that Lowell Sherman was appearing there in some show, and I learned that we were staying in the same hotel. So I gave him a call and told him who I was. We had a friendly chat, and he said in a somewhat cozy voice, "Why don't you come to my room?" I said, "Oh, no, thanks, I just wanted to say hello." That was the last I ever talked with him. While I still thought of him as a kind of father figure, he no longer seemed to regard me as the little girl to be protected. Oh, well—that's showbiz too.

Following the move to New York, we continued to work for Poli stock companies, traveling to Rochester, Hartford, and other cities doing such plays as *Prince Chap, Salomy Jane,* and *On Trial,* which was the first play by the young playwright Elmer Reizenstein, who would change his name to Elmer Rice. He won the Pulitzer Prize some years later for *Street Scene. On Trial* had been one of the outstanding hits of the 1914 Broadway season, and now, two years later, it offered me the most serious dramatic role I had yet played. I was about twelve (although all the newspaper articles called me ten), and I had a major scene on the witness stand with very dramatic dialogue. I had to cry while I spoke. James Crain, the leading man and another nice guy, would always hold me in his arms after the performance to help me get back to normal.

At that time, my role models in show business were all serious, dramatic actresses. The story was told in my family that when I was just learning to speak, I was taken to the theater in Norfolk, and the following day, I put on one of my Mama's hats and pulled a tablecloth over my dress and proclaimed in lispy speech, "I want to be a show lady." The show lady I had seen the night before was in a melodrama called *Ten Nights in a Barroom.* If Mama's parents had known that, it would have required a very long prayer session.

My scrapbook reveals that at the time I was doing *On Trial,* I made the following statement to a reporter for a Rochester newspaper: "I'm going to be an

emotional actress and do big things on the stage. I don't want any light dancing and musical comedy—they are what Mary likes, you know. What I want
to be is a Modjeska, a Mary Anderson, a Maude Adams. I just adore Maude
Adams! Don't you?" As it turned out, dancing and musical comedy were what
I ended up getting paid to do, and Maude Adams's parts rarely came my way.
That was all right with me because it did not take long for me to discover that
dancing was my real love and it was what I did best. Perhaps if I had stayed
focused on dramatic acting, my career would have taken a different turn. Or
maybe I wouldn't have had a career at all. Anyway, Pearl, Mary, and I all had
successful careers because we were dancers. We sang and acted also, but our
dancing is what got us the jobs.

Although we had no way of knowing it when we made the move to New
York, we would soon be caught up in Broadway's golden age. When we first
arrived there, moving into a modest flat on Eighth Avenue not far from the
theater district, we saw new theaters being constructed all around Broadway.
By 1920, there were over fifty legitimate theaters in the Times Square area, and
each year, there were scores of new theatrical productions—dramas, comedies,
revues, musicals—and the number would continue to increase throughout the
twenties, reaching an all-time peak before the decade's end. Of course, many
of those shows didn't last very long, and as soon as one closed, another was
preparing to open. Most theaters would house several productions each year,
because long runs were exceptional. If you could get a hundred performances
out of a show, it was a hit.

What was unique to that time was the importance of "the road." It was the
lifeline for the theater because there was a huge demand for live entertainment throughout the country. Before radio and talking movies, there was an
abundance of work in live entertainment for actors, singers, and dancers. And
for the producers, it was the road that frequently made the difference between
a profitable and an unprofitable production. In the 1916–17 season, there
were ninety-five legitimate New York productions on the road. One of the
Shubert brothers referred to New York as the theatrical manufacturing center
of America. Just as Pittsburgh shipped steel, New York shipped entertainment
to the rest of the country.

The New York of that time was vastly different from what it would soon
become. It was not then a city filled with skyscrapers and traffic. Most of the
taller buildings around mid-Manhattan were only six to eight stories. There
were some skyscrapers scattered throughout the city—the Woolworth Building
with sixty floors being the tallest—but they were not close together, and there

was an openness to the city. You could see the sky, and you didn't feel hemmed in. Automobiles had not fully taken over the streets. People were just getting accustomed to moving about in cars, and the electric streetcars were still very much in evidence. Horse-drawn carriages were still around, but not for long. Ten years later, taxis would be everywhere in the Times Square district, and busses would have replaced most of the streetcars.

The subways, of course, had been in operation for many years. Times Square got its name the year I was born—1904—when the subway station opened in Longacre Square where the Times Building stood and the station was named for the building. The district did not have all those blazing lights and flashing neon signs of later years. Neon would not come about until the late twenties. Most of the signs were still gas-lighted and were not so bright and obtrusive. In my memory, everything about New York in those early days was muted, softer, easier on your senses. And, of course, it was certainly less congested. I loved everything about the city in those days. It was infinitely interesting. As Larry Hart wrote in his "Manhattan" lyric, "The city's a wondrous toy." That's the way it seemed to me at twelve.

Although our Eighth Avenue flat was modest, everything around us seemed orderly and well kept. We had very little room when one of us was not on the road, and Pearl, Mary, and I often slept in the same bed. The whole experience was so much of an adventure that we never complained.

We had a great fascination with the Broadway theaters, and in time, we would get to know almost all of the legitimate houses in the area. Each seemed to have its own personality, and they were beautifully designed, opulent palaces that offered their own magnificence along with the show—all for three dollars or so a ticket.

Those familiar theater names remain for me part of the nostalgic poetry of Broadway: the Apollo, the Belasco, the Lyceum, the Garrick, the Globe, the Selwyn, the Empire, the New Amsterdam, the Knickerbocker, the Winter Garden, the Ritz, the Palace. To be in any one of them as an entertainer meant that you had achieved a certain kind of success, and if you were merely in the chorus—well, you were that much closer to having your name on the marquee. Hopes and dreams are what kept show folks going, and Broadway overflowed with tales of triumphs, which you remembered, and bitter disappointments, which you tried to forget.

We didn't have a lot of room in our flat for seven people—Mama, Papa, Evelyn, Pearl, Mary, Charlie, and me—but quite often some of us were on the road working with the Poli stock companies, so we were able to get by in the limited space. In the beginning, Pearl was bringing in the best income for her Winter Garden work, and she was essentially supporting us all. Papa got a part-time position working at the *New York World,* first as a linotype operator and then later as a proofreader, but he couldn't get a full-time job. Although Papa was a strong union man, he blamed the union, with its insistence on local seniority and local priorities, for preventing him—at least initially—from getting full-time work. As it turned out, never again in his life did he have a regular full-time job, although he was only forty-two at the time we moved to New York. I think his failure to get full-time work was a blow to his self-esteem and might have accelerated the process of distancing Papa from a central role in the family.

Papa went to work about six in the evening, because they put together the morning newspaper at night, and even though he was only part-time, he never arrived back home until the early morning hours. He loved to play cards, and he often played penny-ante poker with others at the newspaper plant. It was hard for any of us to know how much he was working and how much he was playing cards. He was always a night person, and he slept during the day. Years later, after he was no longer employed even part-time, he would still go to the newspaper plants or the union office at night to visit with the workers and play cards. There was a sense of mystery about Papa's nightlife and that will never be resolved. I think now that I did not know Papa really well, although I loved him very much.

Papa also enjoyed the role of being a voluntary advisor on labor-management affairs, and some of his time was spent just hanging out and pontificating with the blue-collar boys. Papa, even though he did not have a good education, was bright and had a wide range of knowledge, as well as strong opinions. And while for the most part he was not an assertive guy, he could be a tough-minded negotiator and a wise counselor when called upon. That helped him later, when he represented Mary as her agent.

If Papa found pleasure at the paper plants, Mama's pursuits were all directed toward us children and our budding careers. She had no life other than being mother and mentor. Mama had never been a shrinking violet, but neither was she aggressive. She simply knew how to relate to people and how to communicate pleasantly and effectively, always with good humor and infinite patience. She never hesitated to tackle things she did not know a lot about, and she did so with a quiet strength and unusual physical endurance. She made the rounds of all the theatrical managers, often sitting for hours in waiting rooms just to be told to come back the next day. But she would not

"Mamie," our beloved mother

Our first Christmas in New York, 1916

Left to right: Mary, Papa, Pearl, and Doris

give up in her efforts to find jobs or to just get our names planted in the minds of the managers. She had the gift of gab and a charming personality that made her popular with the managers and with show folks generally. When she wasn't looking for jobs for us, she was backstage at the theater or on the road with one or more of us. None of us under eighteen traveled without Mama or Evelyn being along. Evelyn played a role similar to Mama's, and she too got to know all the managers. I think Mama typically listened to and followed Evelyn's advice about jobs and opportunities. Evelyn seemed very much aware that once you begin in show business, it takes a dogged and unrelenting effort to keep your career going, and Evelyn could be very pushy. While she may have lacked some of Mama's charm, she was so well-informed, clever, and articulate that she could present a convincing case on behalf of her siblings. She would have made a great theatrical agent.

As soon as we had arrived in New York, Mama enrolled Mary in the Theodore Kosloff ballet school, as Mr. Shubert had suggested. Mary had shown a great deal of talent for ballet when she studied in Washington, and it was really her great love. I remember when Mary was about eleven, the great Anna Pavlova was appearing in Washington with Mikhail Mordkin and the Imperial Russian Ballet Company. Mary said that when she saw Pavlova dance, "It changed my life." Mary was determined to meet her, so we went to the stage door, but we were stopped by a guard who told us rather harshly to leave. Anna Pavlova was just approaching the door, and she heard Mary's request and the doorman's brusque denial. She greeted us warmly and to our great delight invited us to her dressing room. She was a slender and delicate lady, with dark eyes and dark hair. Not beautiful, but she handled herself with such grace and expressiveness that she was extremely attractive. She did not speak good English, but she was friendly, gentle, very dignified, and seemed genuinely interested in us. It was a terrific thrill for Mary, and she always said that Pavlova was her first inspiration. Mary once said that Pavlova made her realize how naive the instruction was that she had been receiving and she knew that she must have great teachers to realize her potential.

Indeed, Mary went on to study with some truly great teachers: Theodore Kosloff, Adolf Bolm, and Ivan Tarasoff. Ballet was just becoming popular in the United States, and Mary was fortunate to study with three of the best teachers in the country. And throughout her show business career, she never stopped studying. She had that driving passion for ballet that seems to characterize all great ballerinas. As it happened, Mary would not make her mark in classical ballet but rather as the première danseuse in the *Ziegfeld Follies*.

Mama, Joe, Charlie, and I were on the road through most of the summer of 1916, with Joe and me doing child parts in several different plays throughout New England. Each appearance with a stock company meant being away from home for about two weeks—typically there were five or six days for rehearsals and eight performances in the following week. When the curtain came down, we would head for home, unless we had another booking somewhere else. Most often, there was enough time between shows to return home, go back to school, work on our dancing, or whatever. We did far more stock company work than Mary or Pearl because Mary was busy with her ballet studies and Pearl had become a fixture in the Winter Garden chorus, often as understudy to the lead dancer. In the years to come, Pearl often went on the road with New York companies, but she did no stock work after we left Washington.

During our stay in any one place, we had time to meet the "locals," learn something of the city, and often be entertained by the friendly members and supporters of the stock company. Stock companies were so important to the townspeople that visiting performers were really given celebrity treatment. Everyone seemed to know who we were. Mama was so comfortable in meeting new people and in new situations that we always seemed to feel at home. It was important too to Mama that we look nice, because the townspeople took an interest in us and in the other traveling actors.

Sometimes we would stay in a boarding house, sometimes we would stay in a hotel, and sometimes we would have a small apartment. Mama always made sure that it was a clean place in a nice part of town. And she also made sure we got plenty of rest, good food, and time to study our lessons. Stock company work was all-consuming, hard work, and the goal of every stock actor was to get to Broadway. Most of the successful actors and actresses on Broadway had paid their dues on the road. Of course, after the twenties, when movies and radio had become so popular, most of the year-round stock companies just disappeared. A few summer stocks survived, but the road, as we knew it in those early days, would just disappear forever.

In 1917, six-year-old Charlie and I were in the New York cast of *Mother Carey's Chickens*. We toured the eastern parts of the country before opening in New York for about four weeks, and after the New York run, we were back on the road, altogether spending almost a year in the cast. Unlike the stock companies, with the touring company there were a lot of one-night stands. Sometimes we would arrive in a place on the train in the morning, do the show that evening, and get on another train to go to the next location. We hardly saw the towns in daylight.

I suppose that is why so many of my memories of being on the road are of traveling on trains at night. I can recall looking out the train window at the dark landscape, the lights of small towns and lonely farmhouses in vast shadowy fields, rivers and lakes shimmering in the moonlight. Sometimes a blanket of snow covered everything and gave a strange ghostlike beauty to the passing scenery. Now and then, when the train stopped, we would watch and listen to the huddled groups outside, under the yellow lights of the station house. To my child's mind, it seemed as if we were traveling through strange and unknown lands, far away from the home and friends we had known.

In hot weather, it was even better to travel at night because, in those days before air conditioning, trains could be oppressively hot. You had to open the windows to get some air, and dust, grit, and soot would come in with hot wind. I remember some miserable days in July and August when we thought we would die on hot afternoons. When we ate our lunch, it was hard not to get grit in our mouths, and it seemed like there was sand in the food. But most of the time, we kids could find ways to make the time go by. We would visit with the other passengers, and we loved to tell them about ourselves—proud that we were performers on the road and eager for them to make a fuss over us.

We traveled in sleeping cars when the distances between the cities were long so that we would be rested the next day and ready to perform. When we did stay over in a city, Mama always arranged hotels or rooming houses for us, and she carried the ever-present sterno stove along with her to prepare our meals in our room. Mama could do wonders with that little sterno stove. She took great care of us, and having good food and a good night's sleep was an important part of that care. I remember that we decided to eat in a cafeteria in Cleveland once, because we had never been in a cafeteria—a rather new innovation in food service. We filled our trays and walked to our table, and I recall Mama—who felt awkward carrying the food tray in front of her—saying, when she finally got to the table, "Good Lord, I felt like a blind mule walking across the room." After that, Mama never did like to go to cafeterias.

During those days, I missed a lot of school. Mama always had lessons for me to do. Every day on the road, I studied grammar and read a good deal. It was really like being home-schooled (or train-schooled) a good part of the time. I missed a lot of the normal experiences that are a part of growing up. But every time I returned to school after an extended absence, I was able to catch up quickly with what was going on, and where the three R's were concerned, I seemed to be at the level of the better pupils in my class.

Things got off to a very fast start for Pearl, with her immediately going into *Robinson Crusoe, Jr.* Al Jolson had made his Broadway debut in the Shuberts' opening production in the new Winter Garden and played only at that theater for several years. That opening show was called *La Belle Paree,* and Jolson appeared in blackface to sing a song that reflected the mindless racism of the time, "Paris Is a Paradise for Coons." That's hard to believe, but it is true. There was a lot of racism in the show business world. Jolson didn't make a very big splash in that first performance, but nevertheless he stayed with the blackface. Soon he was the most important star the Shuberts had. He had risen quickly to become the dominant personality on Broadway—"The World's Greatest Entertainer"—and it was said that "the Shuberts may run the Winter Garden but Jolson owns it."

It was an exciting first appearance for Pearl, and during that run, the whole family would get acquainted with Al Jolson. Pearl would do another show with Jolson, and ten years later, I would appear in a principal role with him in the stage version of *Big Boy.* Jolson had come out of minstrel shows and vaudeville, and he had that electrifying presence with audiences that few could ever match. His plays were usually flimsy concoctions just to get him on stage, and that was true of *Robinson Crusoe, Jr.* It was all Jolson.

Even on Sunday nights, when the regular show was not presented, Jolson performed special concerts at the Winter Garden, and they were well attended by theatrical managers and performers who had Sunday night off. Several acts from other shows would also be featured in the concert. Jolson would come on stage about 9:30 and tell jokes and sing late into the night.

Not long after Pearl had started at the Winter Garden, she became friendly with one of the other chorus girls who was about her age—seventeen or eighteen. One night, the friend was sent a note by a young man inviting her to a party after the performance, and he suggested that she bring Pearl along. At first Pearl said no, that she didn't have the proper clothes and also that she didn't think her mother would approve. The friend suggested that they take a cab to Pearl's flat, where she could change and ask Mama whether she could go, which they did. Even though Mama told Pearl she did not want her to go, Pearl decided—as if it were her declaration of independence—that she would go anyway. She had always been something of a rebel and strong willed, and now she was earning more money than anyone in the family, so she decided she was her own boss. It really surprised and hurt Mama that Pearl would defy her. It turned out to be the defining act in Pearl's coming of age.

From that time on, Pearl assumed grown-up status and became increasingly independent, making her own decisions and judgments, living her own life. Mama was not one to argue or plead, and she was never demonstrative with her pain and disappointment. Although her relationship with Pearl changed, her love for her did not.

Pearl's work in the chorus was appreciated by the Shuberts, and after a run of several weeks in the Jolson show, she moved on to the Shuberts' next production, the 1916 edition of *The Passing Show,* at the Winter Garden, starring Ed Wynn and Florence Moore. Pearl was made understudy to one of the principals, and Evelyn was also hired for the chorus. It would be her only appearance on the musical stage. She quickly learned that it was not her thing. She was more comfortable in promoting her sisters than in performing herself.

This annual Shubert revue, *The Passing Show,* had become a long-standing effort to compete with the splendor of Florenz Ziegfeld's *Follies.* While it never really came close in its beauty and elegance, it was a durable and entertaining effort year after year and quite profitable for the Shuberts. In some ways, it was more daring than the *Follies,* with the costumes often more revealing. Evelyn didn't really like that. She was far too self-conscious and shy, and she was uncomfortable being stared at in what she regarded as a seminude state. She never felt as attractive as her sisters and often said, "I'm the ugly duckling who never turned into a beautiful swan."

So when Pearl went on the road with *The Passing Show,* Evelyn did not. She decided to get married to a boy she had been serious about in Washington, Bob Mills. She had been about ready to announce her engagement when we left Washington, but she put it off to come with the family to New York. Her marriage ended her short showbiz career as a performer, but it was not long before she was involved again as an unrelenting stage mother with her own children—and a self-appointed advisor to her unappreciative sisters.

I think a great deal of Evelyn's behavior was motivated by her underlying sense of inferiority when compared with her sisters. Maybe to cover that up, she had a tendency to be bossy and demanding. That did not go over well, and conflicts developed from time to time with both Pearl and Mary. Their relationship with Evelyn would become strained and eventually distant. Nonetheless, Evelyn—who over the years became quite sophisticated and discerning about the ins and outs of the theater—would continue to give Mama and the rest of us advice or useful information. And while Mama was more tolerant than my sisters, Evelyn often came across as so opinionated and demanding that she was often ignored.

Years later, I learned that Evelyn had been harshly punitive to Joe and Avery in Washington, when the rest of us were on the road. Joe recently recalled the time when he and Avery had received very bad grades on their report cards and so decided to sign each other's cards on the parent line. When Evelyn found out what they had done, as punishment she said she would give them a spanking every evening for three evenings in a row. On the third evening, Joe begged her not to spank him again, and she did not. That experience certainly diminished the love that Joe had for Evelyn. Not long before his death, Joe recalled being in Child's Restaurant in New York with Avery while Evelyn was relating to Mama how bad the two children had been while Mama was on the road with the rest of us. Mama, in her unmistakable disapproving look, conveyed to Joe how disappointed she was in him. It was hard to say which of Joe's feelings were stronger—his guilt for disappointing Mama or his contempt for Evelyn.

To me, Evelyn was truly a second mother, and I loved her very much. Of course, there were times when Evelyn's frustrations and disappointments in her life made her hard to get along with. She was often moody and suffered from the age of twelve with severe migraine headaches (as Papa also did), and her discomfort was often expressed as anger and crankiness.

In addition, Evelyn was so protective and sacrificial with regard to the family that even her best efforts to be helpful were often too strident and narrow-minded. At times, she would be openly critical of Pearl and Mary, especially with regard to their social behavior. If they smoked a cigarette or had a cocktail, Evelyn would object in an overbearing and moralistic way. She felt that there was no excuse for drinking, and it had no part in the idealism that she nourished for us all. She would tell them that they were on their way to hell, and while her admonitions did not alter their behavior, it did create a tension between Evelyn and my other sisters that persisted throughout their lives. (Too bad they didn't listen to her, since alcoholism would later be their downfall.)

Drinking and smoking never appealed to me, so I had no confrontations with Evelyn on that score. The two of us remained close throughout her life. I was fortunate to have spent a lot of time with her when traveling on the road, and I absorbed many of her ideas about enriching one's life through study and discipline. She always tried to get the best, the beautiful, and the good out of every small opportunity.

Evelyn never lost her strong interest in show business; she simply lived it out vicariously through us and through her own children. In time, she would have three children—Edwin, Evelynne, and Warren—who would all have pretty good careers in show business, primarily as featured and supporting players during their childhood and adolescent years. Once Evelyn appeared on Broadway in a nonspeaking role, holding her infant daughter, but she spent much of her life being the off-stage stage mother.

After she and Bob Mills were married in 1917, they moved for a short while to St. Louis. Because Evelyn could not stand to be so far away from the showbiz involvement of the family, they returned to New York within a year. Bob would struggle for years trying to get established in the insurance business in the New York area, and it was obvious that the move to New York was not a good career move for him. Like Mama, Evelyn was more in control of things than her husband, and she appeared to rule the roost. Bob seemed very patient with her, but the conflicts between them were building, and their relationship was increasingly charged with anger. All of her energies went into working on behalf of her own children's careers in show business.

When *The Passing Show* was in Washington, Pearl went on for the principal and received very good reviews as a hometown girl. A critic wrote, "She dances . . . in a whirlwind Apache number . . . she dances extraordinarily well and does not disguise her manifold charms." This road trip would prove eventful for Pearl in more ways than one, because she met a young violinist named Harry Levant, who was in the orchestra of the road company. He would go on to become a highly successful Broadway conductor, and his little brother, Oscar, would achieve musical fame of his own ten years later. Pearl and Harry fell in love, they were married on the road, and Pearl became pregnant. I am not sure of the order in which all of that took place, but it would have a definite impact on the family, with both Pearl and Evelyn now married.

The year I was enrolled in the sixth grade, we were on the road quite a bit. After Evelyn returned to New York, she would occasionally take Mama's place and travel with Charlie and me. I remember that when Charlie and I were doing *Mother Carey's Chickens,* Evelyn accompanied us on several trips, while Mama took care of Evelyn's baby boy Edwin. I loved traveling with Evelyn because she was so curious and inquisitive about everything. And I never resented her constant admonitions and directions the way my sisters did. She always planned well so that we could see the major tourist attractions in each city, and we never had a wasted moment. It was Evelyn who insisted that we read, read, read—a practice that proved to be of great help to me over the years.

Pearl and Harry moved into an apartment on Fifty-first Street, although Harry continued to travel a great deal with various shows. We all felt that Harry was a good guy and genuinely liked him, but it was not a marriage that would endure. While they were together, Oscar spent a lot of time with them and was very fond of Pearl. He loved her wit and intelligence, and later he would play piano for her when she taught tap dancing in a Broadway studio. According to the biography of Oscar Levant by Sam Kashner and Nancy Schoenberger, *A Talent for Genius: The Life and Times of Oscar Levant,* Pearl paid him one dollar an hour for playing, but he would have done it for free to be with Pearl. They wrote, "Her quick wit and intelligence dazzled Oscar, and the dance studio was frequently visited by Pearl's sister, Mary Eaton, whose appearance that year in *Kid Boots* [1923] had made her one of Broadway's darlings." They also suggest that Oscar's interest in George Gershwin started as he played "(I'll Build) A Stairway to Paradise" at one of Pearl's dance lessons.

Mary and I were taking piano lessons during this time. When Oscar came to our apartment to practice on Mary's baby grand piano, which was painted in the style and color of Louis XIV, he would often check my progress and would give me some education in classical music. These were wonderfully interesting interludes in my learning experience. Of course, just about the time I had mastered a short piano composition, away I would go on the road again. I never had any illusions about becoming a great pianist. I was a hoofer—all the way.

Oscar became a more frequent visitor to our apartment during the late twenties, and Mama always treated him like a member of the family. By that time, Harry had gained great stature as a Broadway conductor, and it was often said that having Harry Levant as musical conductor guaranteed the success of a musical.

Harry's marriage to Pearl produced a lovely daughter, who was named for me, Doris Levant. We all called her Dossie and showered her with affection and attention. Since Pearl always lived near us, Dossie was often surrounded by doting relatives. After they were separated, Harry would come to visit Dossie through the years, but only rarely did he socialize with anyone else in the family.

Very quickly after giving birth in 1918, Pearl got herself back in shape, wanting to get back to work as soon as possible. I must say she did a great job of it and was even more beautiful afterward. She had a great figure with beautiful legs, and was back on the stage dancing in no time. Happily, there was a lot of work waiting for her.

Not long after Mary started studying ballet with Theodore Kosloff, she was hired to do a solo dance in a show called *Follow Me,* which starred Anna Held, who had once been the common-law wife of Florenz Ziegfeld. (It has been said that they were married in Paris, but my understanding is that they never really had benefit of a legal ceremony.) It was Anna who gave Ziegfeld the idea for the *Follies*, patterned after the *Folies Bergère* in Paris. Unfortunately, Mary was forced to leave the cast of *Follow Me* when it was discovered that she was not yet sixteen. A performer had to be sixteen to work legally in a musical, and Mary was only fifteen. But it was a good start for her in building her reputation as a beautiful "toe dancer," which is what all the entertainment writers called her.

As soon as Mary reached that magic age of sixteen, she would replace Pearl as the primary breadwinner for the family, and over the years, her generosity would continue to raise the quality of life for Mama and Papa. Even when Charlie and I joined Mary and Pearl on the Broadway stage and were able to do our share, Mary was earning more than all three of us put together. It was as though she had "star" written all over her from the very beginning. Throughout her show business career, she remained very generous not only to Mama and Papa, but also to the rest of us Eatons.

CHAPTER FOUR

BROADWAY GOES TO WAR

The United States went to war against Germany in 1917. Although President Woodrow Wilson's request that Congress declare war was very controversial (some called it "Wilson's War"), show people were very supportive, and there was a great deal of patriotic fervor. Everyone looked for ways to help in the war effort, with benefits and bond sales and special events for soldier boys.

There were dozens of new songs spawned by the war: "Au Revoir, but Not Good Bye, Soldier Boy," "Bring Back My Daddy to Me," "Good Bye Broadway, Hello France," "I May Be Gone for a Long Long Time (Hitchy-Koo)," "When Yankee Doodle Learns to Parlez Vous Francais," and the most popular of the war songs, "Over There," by George M. Cohan. Even some flag-waving patriotic songs written years before the war, especially Cohan's "Give My Regards to Broadway" and "It's a Grand Old Flag," became identified with World War I. Several of the favorites would be sung by groups around campfires for years to come: "Pack Up Your Troubles in Your Old Kit Bag," "K-K-K-Katy," "There's a Long, Long Trail A-Winding," and "Till We Meet Again." Manhattan was alive with such music. It was like show folks were fighting the war with their songs, and Woodrow Wilson continually expressed his appreciation to entertainers for their patriotic support.

Soon after war was declared, Mary danced at the Belasco Theater in Washington in an Adolf Bolm ballet called *Intime*. President Woodrow Wilson was in the audience with a great many dignitaries and political leaders. Mary's dance was called the "Butterfly Dance," described in the program as "a little butterfly awakened from its slumbers; it flitters from blossom to blossom and falls to sleep again." A critic writing in the *Washington Post* called it a flawless performance, describing Mary as "adorable"—an adjective that seems held over from our childhood days. That same show played the Booth Theater in New York, and Mary's dancing stole the show. It was hard to remember that she was only sixteen, because she had developed into a truly talented dancer. Ballet had certainly given her the kind of exposure that most newcomers pray for, and it was the show-stopping artistry of her dancing that later led to her first huge break in show business.

That was not Mary's first time to perform for Woodrow Wilson. At the Poli stock company in Washington, both Mary and I performed before President Wilson several times. He had a Friday night box, and when we were in the show, we always waved at him during curtain calls and he would wave back. Later on, his daughter Eleanor Wilson sent me some flowers and a complimentary note after a performance of *Rackety Packety House,* in which I played a stern duchess. A great many years later, when I was a college student studying the history of that World War I period, I said to my teacher, Professor Paul Glad, "I bet you'll never have another student who performed before Woodrow Wilson." Of course, he agreed. Most of his students had been born a half-century after the Wilson years.

Later Mary had a dancing role in a patriotic show called *Over the Top,* with the lovely Justine Johnson and Ed Wynn at the Forty-fourth Street Theater Roof. The show, which had only a brief run, introduced the dancing of the brother-sister team Fred and Adele Astaire, in their first appearance on Broadway. Fred was only eighteen then, but he and his sister, who was two years older, had been dancing all over the East Coast in vaudeville houses. They were a big hit even if *Over the Top* was not. Mary had a solo dance number that attracted attention and critical praise. Mary was so beautiful and elf-like that she made a stunning appearance on stage, and she had developed the ability to do repeated pirouettes as she circled the stage. It is common in ballet today, but at that time, no one had seen such virtuoso "toe dancing" on Broadway. At the end of her second circle of pirouettes, she would whirl off the stage into the wings, where a stagehand with strong arms was waiting to catch her. It became an argument among the stagehands at each performance as to whose turn it was to catch "our Mary." This "stunt" became her trademark as a ballet dancer.

I remember about this time that Mary was also appearing at some swanky nightclub—I think it was the Cabaret des Artistes up on 125th Street—in which she stood alone in the balcony and sang "Roses of Picardy," a beautiful song imported from London. I recall listening to her, so proud and moved that I almost wept. She sang so beautifully you could feel the impact she had on the hushed audience. She received a tremendous ovation, and the whole audience seemed teary eyed. Mary always looked so delicate and beautiful, and her voice—while not big and strong—had a lovely melodic quality.

The war came home to the family when Robert joined the army in the summer of 1917 and was sent to Europe. Even though Robert lived apart from the family and we did not see him very much, no one could resist loving him

Robert, our brother who wanted nothing of show business, lived most of his brief life apart from the family.

At age five

During World War I

At age twenty-five

and fearing for his safety. He seemed more serious, maybe more mature as he left for military training, and Mama and Papa both felt that he might gain from the discipline and responsibility of being in the army—if he just did not get hurt. And as it turned out, we had every reason to be fearful. Robert was in the battle of the Marne and Chateau-Thierry with the Twenty-third Infantry. He saw a lot of action in what were very bloody battles. Fortunately, he survived without a scratch—at least, physically. Later, when he could talk about it, Robert told us that he had had the terrible job of assisting in the gathering of bodies of dead American soldiers and identifying them. For him, it was a traumatic and haunting experience that he had a difficult time overcoming—if indeed he ever did. In those days, we didn't know about post-traumatic stress syndrome. "Shell shocked" was the popular phrase. In retrospect, I think his war experiences adversely affected Robert for the rest of his life.

Of course, we were all happy and relieved when he returned from the war, and we could take down from a front window the special banner with his picture that had hung there signifying a family member was in the American Expeditionary Force. Our big surprise was that Robert brought home with him a lovely Belgian bride named Jean. It gave Papa and Mama renewed hope that Robert would settle down, and for a time he did. He and Jean worked as maintenance staff in a large apartment building for a while and then started providing domestic services—cooking, cleaning, chauffeuring, butlering, whatever came along. They were quite successful for several years following the war.

Pearl in 1918 was a specialty dancer (still at the Winter Garden) in *Sinbad,* another show written for Al Jolson, and once more he was a huge success. Three of his greatest hits were included (interpolated actually from earlier origins or added after the show had been running): "Swanee," "My Mammy," and "Rock-a-bye Your Baby with a Dixie Melody." It was a good break for Pearl because she was out of the chorus and in a featured dancing role in a major production. She had established a name for herself as a first-rate dancer, and she was rarely out of work. Although throughout her career she would not have her name in lights the way Mary did, she would become well known as a dancer and choreographer. I found in her scrapbook that she capitalized on her greater exposure in *Sinbad* by doing magazine advertisements for Stillman's Celebrated Freckle Cream ("Forget the sun—Have your fun!"), as well as a number of other endorsements as she achieved at least minor celebrity status.

I was determined to complete the eighth grade. Because of the stock company work I had been doing during the regular school year, it was necessary for me to go to summer school in 1917 and 1918 to complete the eighth grade requirements. My skills were pretty good. Evelyn had kept me reading book after book, and in the long hours between shows and traveling on the road, we talked about what we were reading. I had read every novel of Charles Dickens, and I read *Oliver Twist* three times. I read Louisa May Alcott, Booth Tarkington, Victor Hugo, Bullfinch's *Age of Fable,* and a host of others. I remain forever grateful to Evelyn for the great influence she had on my learning. In school, I was able to compete very well with my classmates, and in the summer of 1918, I finished the eighth grade. There was never a thought about going on to high school, because a week after I completed the eighth grade, I was on the stage in the *Ziegfeld Follies.*

After Evelyn and Pearl were married and no longer living with us, we moved from the Eighth Avenue flat to an apartment at the far north end of Manhattan on 213th Street. It was near an area of tenements called Inwood, where a large number of Jewish and Irish immigrants lived, but where we lived was not a crowded area. Our apartment building was surrounded by open fields, trees, and bushes, and there were always children playing in the area. For some reason, there were huge piles of rocks in one of the fields, great to climb around on and jump from one rock to another.

It took about forty-five minutes to get to the theater district on the train. (George M. Cohan could have written his song "Forty-Five Minutes from Broadway" about Inwood, but he actually wrote it about New Rochelle. Anyway, it became a kind of theme song for us while we were living so far up there.) I remember we were living there when Pearl came to stay with us to have her baby, which she did at home in that apartment. She and Dossie lived there with us for a while afterward, because Harry was on the road so much. In time, they got an apartment of their own on Fifty-first Street near Ninth Avenue.

We had moved so far away from the theater district to get cheaper rent. Our income at that time was not yet large, and we were struggling once again to make ends meet. With Pearl being married, we had lost one source of income, and Mary was not yet making large salaries. I was back in school, Papa was working only part-time, and Mama was back once again at the terrible task of stretching pennies.

I have never forgotten those long, hot train rides every day to get to summer school—which was in the midtown area—and then back home again.

Fortunately, I always had books with me and spent the time reading. Reading made those daily trips at least tolerable.

By the summer of 1918, we had thankfully moved back to the midtown area, and I could walk to school. We took a larger and much more convenient flat at 330 West Fifty-first Street, just off Eighth Avenue, an easy walk to the theaters and a block away from where Pearl and Harry had an apartment. Our flat was small and confining, but it was great to be near the theater district—and my school. There were all kinds of shops and delicatessens nearby, as well as restaurants and clubs for late-night refreshments after the theater.

During the summer months, Joe came from Washington to live with us and Papa would take Joe and Charlie to Palisades amusement park in New Jersey. They would go four or five times during a summer, although they would sometimes go to Coney Island after the subway was extended there in 1920. They preferred Palisades because the operators—the Schenck family—were heavily involved in vaudeville and knew a lot of show folks. They always gave the Eatons complimentary passes for free rides. The boys loved the Big Racer, which was the roller coaster, and they rode repeatedly while Papa would usually hang out with one of the Schencks. Actually all of us liked going there, riding on the giant Ferris wheel or the carousels, the loop-the-loops and shoot-the-chutes. It made for a great outing.

In spite of the difficult times we were having financially in 1918, we all remained optimistic. Our apprentice years were behind us, and our professional lives were about to take a turn for the better. My turn came earlier than expected, because—with Pearl's help—I was soon to become the youngest girl in the *Ziegfeld Follies*.

CHAPTER FIVE

THE ZIEGFELD YEARS

Pearl had the biggest break of her career when she was selected to dance with the chorus of the *Ziegfeld Follies of 1918,* opening at the New Amsterdam Theater on June 18. The show starred Eddie Cantor, Will Rogers, W. C. Fields, and two of Ziegfeld's discoveries, Lillian Lorraine and Ann Pennington. It would be the last *Follies* for the beautiful Lillian Lorraine, whose first had been in 1909. It was well known that Lillian Lorraine had a long love affair with Flo Ziegfeld, an affair that was now at its end. Ann Pennington—who would later popularize the dance known as the "black bottom"—would also leave the *Follies* after 1918, but would return in the twenties to do two more shows for Ziegfeld. Also this was the first *Follies* for the beautiful Marilyn Miller—who like Pearl and Evelyn had danced in the Shuberts' *The Passing Show.* She would become Ziegfeld's biggest star within a few years and a close friend of the Eatons.

When Pearl was hired by Ziegfeld, the whole family was jubilant. We all knew that for a young dancer, to be selected for the *Follies* was the best thing that could happen for her career. Ziegfeld's glittering productions were in a class by themselves, and although others tried to mimic them, they could not match Ziegfeld's flair and style and willingness to spend money to achieve true elegance. He understood youth and beauty and sensuality—that was his special domain. For many years, he personally interviewed and hired all the prospective Ziegfeld girls. He was unique, and the special quality of his productions has stood the test of time.

Pearl was hired for two reasons: she had beautiful legs, and she was a terrific tap dancer. Ziegfeld soon discovered that she was very intelligent and possessed a lot of showbiz know-how. It was a tribute to her ability that at only twenty years of age she was given the additional job of assistant to the highly talented Ned Wayburn, Ziegfeld's famous director who staged the *Follies* dance numbers for many years. For Pearl, it was an important start on her way to becoming a successful choreographer and dance director. She learned a great deal over the next four years from Ned Wayburn and later went on to do dance directing for another highly successful producer, Charles Dillingham. I have always thought that Pearl was happier on the production side than she was on stage, although she never really admitted that, and she did keep performing throughout the twenties.

Billy Schroeder, Ziegfeld's affable stage manager for many years, liked to tell the story of walking down Forty-second Street with Flo Ziegfeld, when Ziegfeld's attention was obviously focused on the legs of the young lady walking in front of them. Ziegfeld never missed a pretty pair of legs. He said, "Any girl with legs that beautiful ought to be in our show." To which Billy replied, "She is, Mr. Ziegfeld. That's Pearl Eaton." Later Ziegfeld met everyone in the family and always treated us with great kindness and respect. We all were aware of the rumors about his incessant sexual escapades with Ziegfeld girls, but he never made a pass at any of us, and we could not have been treated better.

That 1918 *Follies*, coming at the time of World War I, had a patriotic theme throughout, including a rousing opening with the "Star Spangled Banner." There was a notice on each seat explaining that the boys appearing in the chorus "were not slackers," but had been exempted from the draft for one reason or another. The last scene in Act One was one of those gigantic tableaux with the beautiful show girls in every imaginable war-related attire (but not too much attire), from nurses and orphans to wounded soldiers, dying "Huns," and grenade-throwing Yanks fighting beside the French. A single file of fully clad girls standing high above the scene waved the flags of the allies, with bare-breasted Kay Laurell standing proudly in the center representing the Spirit of France. When the curtain fell, the applause was deafening. Kay Laurell became identified with those naked-above-the-waist poses in the grand tableaux created by Ben Ali Haggin. There was a loophole in the law that allowed girls to be naked on stage if they did not move. And that was incentive enough to inspire those spectacular and provocative tableaux. The story was that Ziegfeld asked for a volunteer to be naked above the waist, and Kay Laurell was the first to consent. Hers became the most revealed breasts on Broadway in that era.

It has often been said that Ziegfeld never really understood humor, although it was always one of the essential ingredients of the *Follies*. He couldn't recognize a joke until someone else laughed. He never knew why people laughed at W. C. Fields, Will Rogers, Bert Williams, or Fanny Brice. And he never hired any of these people himself, at least not initially. He often rehired them when he learned the kind of response they got from audiences or he had personally become very fond of them (as was the case with Will Rogers and Bert Williams). It was the very gifted Gene Buck, who wrote skits and lyrics and scouted talent for Ziegfeld, who discovered the funny performers from vaudeville and burlesque. After all, the *Follies* were actually vaudeville raised to its highest form.

The *Follies of 1918,* filled as it was with war-related material, included that now-famous song of Irving Berlin, "Oh! How I Hate to Get Up in the Morning," which was interpolated from an earlier Berlin show. In those days, that was a common practice—to borrow songs that had been used in other shows or, in some cases, new songs from Tin Pan Alley, the Manhattan district where most of the popular songs were published. As you walked through the area, you could hear the tinny sounds of pianos being thumped by aspiring composers trying out new songs. And there was always specialty music written for the big chorus scenes that were the hallmark of Ziegfeld's *Follies.*

In one of Wayburn's spectacular production numbers involving Pearl, there were as many as forty-eight chorus girls on the stage at once, all dressed as aviators, with wonderful sets by the talented Joseph Urban, Ziegfeld's designer since 1915. Urban was actually an architect, but he proved a perfect creative partner in bringing the dazzling color, originality, and grandeur to the Ziegfeld stage. Ziegfeld's genius, I think, was not only in his eye for beautiful show girls, but also in his ability to choose the right creative talent to bring his vision to the stage. He was the best in the business at doing that.

While Pearl's association with Ziegfeld would last for five years, she never became a principal in the *Follies.* Pearl could never light up the stage in the way Mary could. She was an excellent dancer with good showmanship and wonderful comedic ability. But she was a better ensemble dancer than a solo performer. She danced for two years in Ziegfeld's *Nine O'Clock Revue,* a nightclub act on the garden roof of the New Amsterdam Theater, which was not continued after 1919. Her longest Ziegfeld association (through 1922) was with the popular *Midnight Frolics,* which was also on the New Amsterdam Roof. The *Frolics* were a little racier, the costumes more revealing and the humor a good deal less inhibited than the *Follies.* The same stars were typically involved, particularly the comedians, such as W. C. Fields, Will Rogers, and Fanny Brice. It was a good showcase for Pearl's dancing as well as her dance direction. The *Frolics* had two shows a night. Initially, the cover charge was $2 for the first show and $3 for the second show. (The latter was raised to $5 in a few years.) The food served on the New Amsterdam Roof had the reputation of being the best of any New York nightclub. By any cabaret standards, the shows were lavish productions. The *Frolics'* principals (who were *Follies'* stars) received $700 per week, and the chorus girls averaged between $50 and $75. Pearl received $75 initially and then later was increased to $125, as her responsibilities increased. For one of the shows, she taught Will Rogers a little dance routine, which he worked very hard to perfect. No one had ever seen him dance like that before, and when he performed the routine the first time, he stopped the show. Pearl loved Will Rogers and called him the nicest and most generous man in show business.

One day during the preparation of the 1918 *Follies* for its road trip, Pearl asked me if I wanted to go with her to a rehearsal. Mama said that I could, and so I asked Mary whether I could wear one of her long dresses. At fourteen, I was still wearing my dresses at the knee, while the style for women was to wear them halfway between the knee and the ankle. Mary loaned me a dress, and I really dressed up for the occasion, makeup and all, and off we went. While Pearl and I were sitting on a bench during a break in the rehearsal, Ned Wayburn—a tall, rotund figure with little, round, thick-lensed glasses and a jaunty golf cap on his head—came over to where we were sitting. It was hard to imagine Wayburn as a dancer, because he was quite obese, but he could still move with grace and style. I noticed him eyeing me intensely, and he asked Pearl who I was. When he learned that I was Pearl's sister, he said, shaking his head in bewilderment, "I can't believe it. She looks enough like my wife to be her twin sister." Then he asked Pearl, "Can she dance?" And Pearl told him, "Yes, she can dance very well." So he asked me—right then and there—if I would like to join the cast of the *Follies* for the road show, and of course I said yes. However, Pearl told Mr. Wayburn that I was only fourteen years old and that Mama would not want me to go. Mr. Wayburn came back with, "You tell your mother she can travel with Doris just like one of the members of the company. We will pay her travel expenses. I would like for Doris to understudy Ann Pennington." So after consultation with Mama and the family, we accepted the offer. The next day was Friday, the last day of summer school, completing the eighth grade. I came home at noon, put on Mary's dress again, gathered some practice clothes, went to the Amsterdam Theater, and began rehearsing with the other "new" chorus girls—and I was in the *Ziegfeld Follies.*

At fourteen, I was the youngest girl in the *Follies,* but no one asked any more questions about my age, and I didn't volunteer any information. Because the Gerry Society for the Prevention of Cruelty to Children would not allow children under sixteen to perform in musical productions, I simply became sixteen overnight and changed my name to Doris Levant, taking Pearl's married name. (The following year, I changed it to Lucille Levant to make it different from that of Pearl's daughter, Doris. When I was sixteen, I changed back to my actual name.)

So Mama and I went on the road with the summer *Follies*. The road show was a four-month deal, with a month in Chicago; a week in each of several other major cities, like Kansas City, St. Louis, and Cleveland; and always two weeks in Philadelphia. As Mr. Wayburn promised, I became understudy to the star Ann Pennington. Ann—whose nickname was Tiny because she was so petite—had been in several *Follies,* but this one would be her last for a while. She left to dance in *George White's Scandals,* in which she starred for several years before returning to the *Follies* in 1923. I never went on for her in that road tour of 1918, although I came very close once, even had her costume on, when she came rushing in late, and I had to make a very quick change.

The road company was an elaborate logistical affair. We had two railway cars—one for the company and another for all the scenery and costumes. There was a kind of informal class system on board, with the big name stars usually being in a group by themselves. As the newest kid, traveling with my mother, I never engaged in any give-and-take with the established cast. But that summer and fall was a great experience for me, and I gained important confidence on the stage. I knew I could hold my own with the other dancers, even attracting some flattering comments from critics and other cast members. In Chicago, the critic Ashton Stevens wrote, "Mine eyes are yet dim with the luminous elfin beauty of a little girl named Doris Levant." How about that!

I was thrilled to be rehired for the 1919 *Follies*. Mr. Ziegfeld, himself, hired me. To me, that particular *Follies* was his greatest *Follies* of all—not because I was in the show, but because of the great cast and memorable music. The cast included Eddie Cantor, Billie Dove, DeLyle Alda, Johnny Dooley, Ray Dooley, Van and Schenck, Bert Williams, and Eddie Dowling. The music was by Victor Herbert and Irving Berlin. That year, Irving Berlin wrote the never-to-be-forgotten "A Pretty Girl Is Like a Melody." It was sung by the tenor John Steel and has become the signature song for the name *Ziegfeld Follies.*

That was the year Marilyn Miller took over as Ziegfeld's singing and dancing star. She was sensational, and she became the apple of Ziegfeld's eye for the next few years. She received great notices in New York, and when we played Chicago, one critic said of Marilyn, "[She] danced and whirred like a beauteous slim pink hummingbird." I was thrilled when I was made her understudy, and there were two occasions when I went on for her when we were on the road.

Also in the 1919 *Follies,* the great Bert Williams made his final *Follies'* appearance. Ziegfeld had initially hired Bert Williams, the gifted black comedian, in 1910, and it was highly unusual to have "colored" performers appearing in an otherwise white production. As a caricature on the fact that he was black, Williams wore blackface, just like the white performers in the minstrel scenes, and he affected the voice and mannerisms associated with being a "Southern darky." He was a master of pantomime, storytelling, and putting over a song. "Nobody" was his signature song, which was supposed to be sung with "mock solemnity," but you had the feeling with Bert that his solemnity was never mock. Someone once said, "He was the funniest man I ever saw, and the saddest man I ever knew." The undercurrent of pathos that was always a part of him is reflected in his song:

> When life seems full of clouds and rain,
> And I am filled with naught but pain,
> Who soothes my thumping, bumping brain?
> Nobody!

Bert often stopped the show with his sheer artistry. Around the turn of the century, he had built a reputation as a "cakewalker," doing the dance that had its origin during slavery. The cakewalk was originally a dance contest among a group of slaves, with the winner receiving a cake as the prize. Over the years, the dance became standardized as a high-kicking, strutting routine that could bring the audience to its feet when done by a master like Bert Williams. In the eight *Follies* in which he appeared, he never shed his blackface makeup, which is a pity and a sad comment on the racism of the time. Although he was a masterful showman and everyone loved him, he could not ride up to his hotel room in the regular elevator. As a "colored man," he was required to use the freight elevator. And he was not allowed to eat in the hotel dining room. No wonder there was always that undercurrent of pathos in his humor. He once observed, in talking about the Jim Crow absurdities of that time, that after the change came (as he predicted it would), the new generations would never believe that such practices actually existed. I lived to discover that he was right. The young people of today are incredulous that such bizarre practices could have taken place. I am forever glad I had the privilege of meeting him. He was a wonderful human being, very bright and well-informed. His lonely hours were filled with reading. He left the *Follies* after the 1919 edition, and died in 1922 at the age of forty-seven, while on tour in the musical comedy *Under the Bamboo Tree*. In my estimation, he was one of the greatest entertainers ever to play on the Broadway stage.

For the 1919 *Follies,* I was promoted to the group classified as "specialty dancers." There were five of us. We were used in musical numbers requiring brief individual dance routines. For example, the opening act that year was called "A Salad." The male singer, Eddie Dowling, sang short verses identifying certain ingredients of a salad, suggesting that the *Follies* was like a theatrical salad. One of the girls was dressed in an all-green costume, representing lettuce; another dressed in white, representing sugar. The Fairbanks twins were dressed in black and white, suggesting pepper and salt. I was paprika and dressed all in flaming red. We each performed our little routine and lined up with the group and the male singer for our finish.

That was my first appearance as a specialty dancer on Broadway, and I was just fifteen. With the other four specialty dancers, I was also in the finale of the first act, which presented the now famous "Mandy" number. The stage was set like an old-time minstrel show. Van and Schenck sang the song "Mandy," and then Marilyn Miller came down a flight of stairs in the middle of the set and joined Van and Schenck, who stepped aside while she did a lovely soft-shoe routine. Then we five specialty dancers followed with a group soft-shoe and all stood behind Marilyn and Van and Schenck for the closing. The finale received tremendous applause, and the song "Mandy" became Berlin's second big hit of that show. The tune "Mandy" is still well-remembered in theatrical circles.

In showbiz parlance, the chorus dancers were called "ponies" to differentiate them from the taller "showgirls," who were chosen to promenade and be beautiful and never get out of breath—as did the chorus girls chosen to dance in the production numbers. The term "pony" as I understand it came from the Englishman John Tiller, who had trained precision dancing chorus lines, and in one of them had the dancers imitate horses—hence ponies. The showgirls were young, tall, beautiful, and wonderfully costumed and were required only to walk with elegance and grace. Ziegfeld never wanted any obviously projected or emphasized sensuality. He wanted that to flow naturally from the beautiful bodies and the revealing costumes. Often the costumes were scanty enough to be very revealing, but as the nudity increased, the girls' movements decreased.

Each year, Ziegfeld had hundreds of applicants for the showgirl roles, for which he paid several times more than any other producer and certainly more than some of us dancers were making, which averaged about seventy-five dollars per week. Whatever it took, Ziegfeld always hired the youngest and most beautiful girls of any Broadway show, and he was such a perfectionist that he supervised every little detail of costume, color, and movement. His unfailing judgment on such matters and his willingness to spend money to realize his vision set him apart from all other producers. Over the years, it also, inevitably, got him deeper and deeper in debt.

We found the way to Broadway and became *Ziegfeld Follies* girls.

Doris, *Ziegfeld Follies* of 1918–20

Mary, *Ziegfeld Follies* of 1920–22

Pearl, *Ziegfeld Follies* of 1918, 1922–23;
Midnight Frolics of 1919–21

Charlie, *Ziegfeld Follies* of 1921

Three Eatons—Pearl, Mary, and Doris—up on their toes

In the twenty-five years that Ziegfeld did the *Follies* himself, only a few of the beautiful showgirls went on to stardom. (Some of the most notable were Paulette Goddard, Justine Johnson, and Barbara Stanwyck.) Other girls did at times go on to riches, often finding among their admirers wealthy men to buy them jewelry or furs, or offer them marriage—for better or for worse. Some who were too much aware of how quickly youth and beauty fade made impulsive and often bad decisions in their choice of husbands or "protectors." There was often heated rivalry among the girls regarding the quantity and quality of jewelry they wore to the theater. The more abundant and extravagant the jewelry, the more obviously generous was the admirer or admirers. My Broadway education really began in the dressing room with the members of the chorus, listening to their uninhibited and often coarse conversations. I was constantly asking Mama what something meant, and she would respond, "Doris, that is none of your business. Just pay attention to what you are doing."

I think the term "gold digger" originated on Broadway in this era; I recall a play at the Lyceum with Ina Claire called *The Gold Diggers,* and that was the first time I'd heard that term. Finding a wealthy "stage-door Johnny" became a preoccupation—often just to go to exclusive parties with but frequently to marry—and always to receive the extravagant gifts that were the conspicuous love offerings of the twenties. Will Rogers often remarked about the brevity of many of those marriages between Ziegfeld girls and wealthy admirers by saying that a certain girl had found her a millionaire husband, which means she will probably miss shows for the next couple of weeks. As in most of Rogers's jokes, there was a lot of truth to that. Marriages were notoriously brief.

Bernard Sobel, who was the publicist for Ziegfeld, wrote in his book *Broadway Heartbeat,* "The successful [show]girls were usually spoiled, demanding, and philandering; they played millionaires for all they could get, snubbed the lesser members of the ensemble, and achieved a prominence that sometimes obscured the stars of the company. With the passing of the revue [after Ziegfeld's death] these decorative ladies went into obsolescence."

On the other hand, those beautiful girls selected to star as dancers and singers—Lillian Lorraine, Ann Pennington, Marilyn Miller, and soon Mary Eaton—were by definition stars. There was no faster route to the top of Broadway than to be listed among the *Follies'* stars. After appearing in the 1918 edition, Marilyn Miller was clearly established as a top star on Broadway, a position she would hold until the thirties. She had the advantage of Ziegfeld's great attraction to her, but she was also a terrific performer whom audiences loved. Ziegfeld—as he would later do with Mary—insisted early that Marilyn study acting, voice, and dancing almost continuously. Over those early years, she became better and better, and she became one of the biggest stars of the musical theater of the early twenties.

Many of the Broadway sophisticates who had seen several *Follies* would maintain years later that the 1919 *Follies* was the best ever. It was a showcase for Marilyn Miller. Billie Burke (Mrs. Florenz Ziegfeld) in her memoir, *With a Feather on My Nose,* described her this way: "[She appeared] walking down those long, glorious steps in a mock minstrel costume and displaying legs that I believe have never been matched for sheer slim, provocative beauty." Marilyn, who had performed since she was a small child, was stunningly beautiful and a talented performer. She could illuminate the stage. As a comic contrast to Marilyn's elegant appearance on stage, Ziegfeld had placed Fannie Brice in an aisle seat as if she were a member of the audience, and she was free to make whatever zany remarks she wished, commenting outrageously on the action on the stage. Fanny made the most of the opportunity, and the audience exploded with laughter in one of the *Follies'* all-time funniest moments. Every night she did it a little differently, so no one knew what to expect.

Throughout Pearl's association with Ziegfeld and Ned Wayburn, she was a kind of utility hand who did a bit of everything for them. She was often there in the New Amsterdam Theater when "dear old Ziggie," as she always called him (and no one else in the family did), toiled patiently for weeks interviewing hundreds of girls, ultimately sanctioning only a handful to be Ziegfeld girls. Those who were lucky enough to be selected were initially very shy in the presence of Ziegfeld, but they would soon overcome their timidity and discover that their famous boss was friendly and encouraging to all newcomers. Most of the time, Ziegfeld had a kind of softness about him in the way he treated his cast, not like some of the producers we came to know. Later, Pearl wrote in an unpublished draft, "Ziggie frankly admitted that employing a star was simple, but discovering and developing unknown beauty and talent was the exciting challenge. It was really his mania, molding, exploiting, and claiming as his own those rare flawless visions. This was Ziegfeld's true romance with life."

The whole Ziegfeld enterprise was on a scale beyond anything else on Broadway. Of course, there were those huge epics at the Palladium and the Century (where *Ben Hur* was staged using live horses for the chariot race), but for Broadway revues and musicals, Ziegfeld's productions were on a scale without peer: scores of dancers, chorus girls and showgirls, brilliant stars, wonderful music, and the best comic talents in the country. Throughout the

Broadway run, there were replacements being made continuously in the chorus, specialty dancers, and showgirls due to marriages, pregnancies, illnesses, movie contracts, promotions to principal roles, dismissals, and various other reasons. Hiring new girls was an ongoing process. And Pearl was always there, ready to go on if a dancer did not show.

At the same time, there was the road tour to plan and to cast. Everyone in the different groups was asked whether they wanted to go, but some of the girls said no—because they knew that having been a Ziegfeld girl, they could immediately get work on the Great White Way with one of Ziegfeld's imitative competitors, or because for personal reasons they did not want to leave New York. But many of the girls sought the excitement of the road, seeing new parts of the country, having fun in the different cities, where the *Follies* were always greeted with enthusiasm. And believe me, there were plenty of stage-door Johnnies waiting with that well-used line, "So-and-so asked me to look you up and show you our town."

While the hustle and bustle of getting the old show off to the hinterlands was in process, preparations for the next *Follies* were under way, and Ziegfeld was once again on his never-ending search for new and incomparable beauty. At the same time, he had to find composers for the music, find writers for the skits, and renegotiate with his stars—he liked to stay with whatever was working, so he held tenaciously to his favorite comedy stars year after year: Will Rogers, Eddie Cantor, W. C. Fields, Fanny Brice, and Bert Williams.

Pearl and I had both become capable dancers before we were in the *Follies,* and we continued to study dancing whenever we had the chance, including some time at Ned Wayburn's Studios of Stage Dancing. That is where Pearl taught tap dancing part-time a little later on. Ned was the most sought after teacher for Broadway aspirants. His studio attracted the likes of Gilda Gray, Ann Pennington, Fanny Brice, Marilyn Miller, Fred and Adele Astaire, the three Eaton girls, and Charlie too. Ned was simply the best in the business, which is why he spent so many years with Ziegfeld.

Pearl and I worked on specialty dances with a variety of other teachers. It had been easy for me to understudy Ann Pennington because she didn't have any difficult routines and I could do everything I needed to. (If the truth be known, she really wasn't a well-trained dancer, and her routines were simple and cute.) I wanted to learn more about tap dancing with all its variations. And I thought it would be wise to learn some ballet, at least to do some elementary "toe dancing," but I never got much beyond the elementary. I studied with Johnny Boyle, an excellent teacher who taught me a rhythmic tap Charleston routine—which later would stop the show when I danced in the *Hollywood Music Box Revue*. I also studied with Buddy Bradley, who taught me all kinds of rhythmic variations on tap dance, some of which I would later use in a Broadway show that also brought me a rousing standing ovation and, on one occasion, brought me back from my dressing room to take another bow before they could go on with the show.

I really enjoyed versatility in dancing: tap and high kicks and rhythmic body movements, a style of dancing that had come to be known in show business as "eccentric dancing." I suppose it was eccentric because it combined unconventional rhythmic body and foot movements with traditional tap dancing. It became popular among dancing comedians, like Ray Bolger, who incorporated stylized dancing into comic routines. Since the new jazz rhythms had become all the rage, producing a host of high-energy dances, endless adaptations had been made by professional dancers to personalize their performances. Someone called it "dancing with laughing feet." Whatever it was called, that is what I did.

While Pearl and I were dancing in the *Follies*, Mary was asked to audition for George M. Cohan, who was now producing—in a partnership with Sam Harris—rather than performing. Years later, I learned that it was Evelyn who had convinced Harris to arrange the audition for Mary with Cohan. In future years, Evelyn grew bitter because she believed that Mary did not appreciate all the efforts that she had made in her behalf. More pointedly, she felt that Mary, at the height of her stardom, did not extend a helping hand to Evelyn's children, who were just getting into show business.

After her audition with Cohan, Mary told us with much excitement about her experience. As she danced, Cohan watched her intently throughout her routine. Then, without saying a word, he beckoned her with his finger. When she approached him—expecting from his solemn expression to hear words of criticism—he said, "That was beautiful, my dear. How would you like to be in my show?" He hired her on the spot for a show called *The Royal Vagabond*. It turned out to be a popular and successful show, running for over a year in New York and on the road. It was Mary's big break, and while she was not the star, it made her a well-known dancer. Afterward, she was often described as Cohan's discovery. Later, Adolphe Roberts would write in *The Dance Magazine*, "[Mary Eaton was] the dancing hit of the show . . . she caused a sensation by doing two circles of pirouettes around the stage. The stunt has been copied, but she was the first to prove that it could be an exquisitely graceful thing rather than a feat of endurance."

While the *Follies of 1919* was on the road, I had to go on for Marilyn Miller once in Chicago, when she became ill, and later in Philadelphia, after her husband Frank Carter was tragically killed in a car wreck. He was en route to Philadelphia from Maryland, where he was appearing in a play called *See Saw.* It was a devastating blow to Marilyn, and I think she never really got over it. She had tried to convince him on the telephone to wait until he was rested, instead of starting out late at night after a performance, but he had bought her a new Packard and he wanted to give it to her. The rumors were that he was jealous because of Marilyn's great sex appeal and the fact that she was always surrounded by men. Marilyn, who was only twenty-one, was twelve years younger than he, but he had no reason to doubt her fidelity. She was very much in love with him, and they had been married for less than a year. Pearl, Mary, and I remained friends with Marilyn over the next several years— actually, she and Mary were best friends. Although they were often pictured in the press as rivals, they remained very close. Marilyn was Mary's maid of honor at her wedding in 1929.

While Marilyn remained a star throughout the twenties and continued to work hard, she became much more escapist and fun-seeking in her private life. Increasingly, she developed problems with alcohol and appeared to go from one relationship to another. Two years after Frank's death, she married the notorious actor Jack Pickford (Mary Pickford's brother), who had a very bad reputation for drinking and drugs, as well as having syphilis. The marriage was short-lived, and Marilyn was continually involved with other men.

I don't know if the much talked about affair between Flo Ziegfeld and Marilyn ever took place, although it was well known that he hotly pursued her for years. At times, she treated him so rudely and profanely (she could cuss with the best of the "broads") that it appeared at times she had a strange hold on him. In a bitchy way, she made it very clear that she did not find "older men" attractive, and particularly Ziegfeld. Although it is widely known that she had many affairs throughout the rest of her life, I have personally always doubted that Ziegfeld was ever her lover. Of course, there are others who strongly disagree with my opinion on that matter. While agreeing that she found Ziegfeld unappealing, their view is that she had an affair with him to serve her own best interests. Maybe so. Who knows?

Marilyn had a number of announced marriage engagements over the years that never seemed to come to fruition. In 1934, she married a young chorus dancer named Chet O'Brien, with whom she had had a close and affectionate relationship for several years. Sadly, Marilyn died in 1936 while being treated in a hospital for a sinus infection, stemming from a poorly executed sinus operation she had earlier. She was thirty-five years old. The 1949 movie *Look for the Silver Lining,* starring June Haver, was a musical biography of Marilyn Miller. It was a great tribute to her, but like most such movies of that day, it was not a very good biography. Marilyn, herself, starred in three movies. Two movies were based on her hit shows *Sally* (1929) and *Sunny* (1930). The third was *Her Majesty's Love* (1931). We all loved Marilyn, and she spent a lot of time with our family throughout the twenties.

As a rather remarkable coincidence, Mary, Pearl, and I—all three of us—were understudies at different times to Marilyn Miller, and each of us went on for her on more than one occasion. I mentioned going on for her in Chicago and Philadelphia in the 1919 *Follies.* Mary went on for her in *Sally* the following year, also in Philadelphia, when Marilyn became ill. Mary, who was in New York, had to go to Philadelphia by train at the last minute. Ziegfeld would not allow an unknown understudy to go on, so when the show was in rehearsal, he had Mary learn the part. This had led to press speculation that there would be two Broadway companies, with Mary starring in one and Marilyn in the other. A ridiculous idea when you think about it.

At that time, Marilyn was the highest paid performer on Broadway, at $3,000 per week. She was adored by her audiences. *Sally* had been the most successful show of 1920–21, running for 570 performances, and Marilyn was the toast of Broadway because of it. When Mary had to go on in her place, she knew she would face a severely disappointed audience. She arrived in Philadelphia with just enough time for a quick run-through before the curtain. In the play, Sally is a dishwashing waif at the Elm Tree Inn who goes on to become a star of the *Follies,* the typical poor-girl-makes-good "Cinderella" story that seemed to dominate that era in musical comedy.

Mary's performance in Philadelphia captivated the audience. It was one of her great professional triumphs. She was regarded primarily as a dancer, but in that part, she established herself as a singer, with the lovely Jerome Kern song "Look for the Silver Lining," and as an actress, faultlessly creating her own Sally character. A Philadelphia critic wrote that Mary was perfect in the title role, providing "an original and magnetic performance." She received a prolonged standing ovation from the audience, with the members of the company and the musicians joining in the cheering. Mary's dancing was, in fact, superior to Marilyn's, and she had unquestionably made the most of that opportunity. One critic wrote in the *Pittsburgh Leader,* "Mary Eaton, resiliently youthful and incredibly charming and graceful . . . proved that Marilyn Miller has a close rival in her own type of dancing, and a superior in steps requiring a deeper technique and study."

Mary replaced Marilyn for a three-week period, and for the next ten years, she was an established star, never out of work. It was not quite the real-life version of the hackneyed plot—understudy goes on at the last minute and achieves stardom—since Mary had already made a name for herself while starring in the *Follies,* but her triumph did have an almost storybook quality to it, and it became a part of showbiz history. It did seem as though reality was imitating art.

Later on, Pearl understudied Marilyn Miller in *Sunny* (in 1925), which also featured the music of Jerome Kern. The big song hit of the show was "Who," a beautiful song that became a standard ("Who stole my heart away/Who makes me dream all day . . ."). The part required tap dancing—at which Pearl excelled—as well as graceful balletlike pirouettes—at which Pearl was just competent. Neither Pearl nor I was great up on our toes. But when she went on for Marilyn at the New Amsterdam, she came through with flying colors, and she too received favorable notices. Although Marilyn was out for almost two weeks, it was announced only on a day-by-day basis before the curtain that she would not appear. Pearl was never as well known as Mary, and it was tough on her night after night to hear the groans of disappointment when it was announced that Marilyn would be replaced by Pearl Eaton. It was formally reported that Marilyn was having severe sinus problems (which was a chronic affliction), although it was widely rumored that she had had an abortion. Whatever the reason, it allowed Pearl to complete that remarkable coincidence of each of us replacing Marilyn Miller.

The *Ziegfeld Follies of 1919* came along at a historic time in the United States. Women had just been granted the right to vote with the ratification of the Nineteenth Amendment, and prohibition of alcohol had become law with the Eighteenth Amendment and the Volstead Act (which started prohibition on January 1, 1920). Both were the talk of the Ziegfeld crowd, not knowing how each of these momentous changes might affect future shows. Ziegfeld was concerned particularly about his *Midnight Frolics,* on the New Amsterdam Roof, because that was a late-night, racier, cabaret-type production where alcohol flowed. He refused to sell alcohol illegally, and he knew that the days of the *Frolics* were numbered. He did manage to keep the show going for three more years, but the speakeasies had taken over the nightclub crowds, and he finally had to close the doors to the New Amsterdam Roof.

Pearl had been a kind of mainstay at the *Midnight Frolics,* and she loved the late-night crowds and the nightclub environment. Her final association with those shows was when she went on the *Frolics'* only road tour in 1922, and that brought a temporary end to that Ziegfeld late-night tradition. In a few years, he would try it again.

I remember another grand place and another sad closing that prohibition brought about. After I started with the *Follies,* in 1918, we frequently went to the famous Broadway restaurant and nightclub called Rector's. It had long been the nightspot for the theatrical crowd, and in its earlier location, it reportedly had the first revolving door of any building in New York. For the show people of that time, it was the Sardi's before there was a Sardi's—a place to gather after the theater. It was a lobster and champagne house where Diamond Jim Brady and Lillian Russell had dined with their legendary appetites, a place where wealthy playboys took beautiful showgirls, bedecked in diamonds and furs. Of course in those days, a lobster cocktail was a dollar, and a filet mignon was a dollar and a half. Drinks were about forty or fifty cents. It was said by someone that if you were a beautiful showgirl, you might not find a pearl in your oyster, but you might get a diamond necklace with your lobster.

The Rector's I knew was on Forty-eighth Street and Broadway and pro-claimed itself Broadway's first nightclub. They brought in orchestras—at times, four different ones playing in succession—presenting all the new songs from Tin Pan Alley and the Broadway shows. They had a dance floor, with dancing exhibitions by Vernon and Irene Castle, and at one time, young Rudolph Valentino was available to dance with unescorted women. All that for a dollar or so cover charge. It was a huge place that could accommodate well over a thousand people, and for us, it was a wonderful late-night place for supper and dancing. The songs were always played in the nightclubs in an up-tempo style for one-step dancers, adding to the liveliness and high sprit of the place.

I was just fifteen when we first went there, but I didn't look that young, made up and dressed like the other performers. There were always young men from the theater to dance with, although the dance floor was much too small and always terribly crowded. Mama was often there too, not just to chaperone but to have a good time. (She would never let me go out on a date when I was fifteen or sixteen without going along.) Rector's was always festive, gay, and crowded with beautiful people. Whenever I was there, I felt it was a celebration of having arrived in showbiz. After all I was in the *Follies*!

Prohibition was the topic of the time and played a central role in the *Follies of 1919.* Eddie Cantor had a song called "You Don't Need the Wine to Have a Wonderful Time (While They Still Make Beautiful Girls)." No one has ever sung it since, but it does illustrate how the *Follies* always tried to reflect the events of the day. There was another song called "Prohibition," which was played while the beautiful girls paraded about. Another song mocking the hated Volstead Act was "You Cannot Make Your Shimmy Shake on Tea," a high point of the show as sung inimitably by Bert Williams. Another hit song of the show was the suggestive "You'd Be Surprised," written by Irving Berlin, and sung by Cantor while he rolled those big banjo eyes. Cantor also sang "How Ya Gonna Keep 'Em Down on the Farm," which became a personal hit for him. There were much prettier songs, like "Sweet Sixteen," sung by Marilyn Miller, and "Tulip Time," sung by DeLyle Alda. But the 1919 song that would become identified with the *Ziegfeld Follies*, forevermore, was Berlin's "A Pretty Girl Is Like a Melody," beautifully sung by John Steel. Most people think of that scene as beautiful girls descending a white marble staircase, another of those lavish, embellished production numbers—a conception based on the movie version. In fact, no number ever had such a simple, exquisite presentation, the antithesis of flair and ostentation.

The curtain parted on an empty, dark stage. As the music started, the spotlight picked up John Steel walking slowly to center stage from the backdrop. John had a beautiful, clear tenor voice, and he sang the verse and a chorus of the Berlin song. Then as each girl appeared—one at a time—the music switched to refrains of well-known classical compositions, such as Mendelssohn's "Song of Spring" and Offenbach's "Barcarolle." With each "haunting refrain," the spotlight picked up a showgirl, dressed to match the mood of the music. She walked toward John, flirted a bit, and continued past him, fading into the darkness of the stage, while he sang the humorous lyrics of love found and love lost to one of those classic melodies. After all five girls had appeared, John sang a final chorus of "A Pretty Girl Is Like a Melody," as the five beauties surrounded him. To this day, eighty or so years later, I can recall the words that were sung to all five of those well-known melodies. The last one—which was from *The Tales of Hoffmann*—went like this:

At the Opera she said, "My dear,
I love you with all my soul."
While the music filled up our ears,
With Offenbach's "Barcarolle"
When the music died away,
Her love for me grew cold,
And I found she told better tales,
Than old Mr. Hoffmann told.

At the conclusion of that historic scene, the applause was spontaneous and generous, but it always seemed to me that the audience initially seemed somewhat taken aback, still absorbing the loveliness in sound and sight and simplicity that they had just experienced. There was a brief hush in the theater before the explosion of applause. It was a special moment in *Follies* history.

Will Rogers was not a part of that great 1919 *Follies*. As a sign of the times, when the *Follies of 1918* closed in May of 1919, after the road tour, Will left for Hollywood with a lucrative contract with Samuel Goldwyn. A decade before talking pictures came into being, Hollywood was pulling away a good many actors and actresses from New York. It exasperated Ziegfeld, who was a star maker without the power to hold his most famous creations. (When they rebuilt the Ziegfeld Theater on Fifty-fourth Street, it became a movie house, and I am sure that Ziegfeld rolled over in his grave.) In Will Rogers's case, even though he had a successful movie career, he did return in 1922 to do other *Follies*. The road show of the 1918 *Follies* was my only opportunity to appear with Will Rogers, and we never got to know each other beyond a passing greeting. He was a huge star, and I was a fourteen-year-old first-time dancer and understudy, but it was obvious that he was a beloved member of the company and probably Ziegfeld's all-time favorite male performer. Both Mary and Pearl came to know him much better than I.

Several weeks after the 1919 *Follies* opened in June, Eddie Cantor, Ray Dooley, and a number of the other principals walked out to join the Actors' Equity strike against the Producing Managers Association. It caused great friction for a time between Ziegfeld and Cantor, because Ziegfeld was not a member of the Producing Managers Association, and he felt it was an act of personal disloyalty for Cantor to walk out. Also, Ziegfeld and Cantor were almost like father and son, and it was the closeness of that relationship that made it so painful for Ziegfeld. Nonetheless, Cantor was sympathetic to the actors' cause and believed in the necessity for the strike. (Cantor and Ziegfeld soon patched up their differences, and would work together again in great harmony and with great success.)

The actors demands were long overdue and very reasonable. For example, they requested half-pay for rehearsal time and pay for all extra performances. After the Actors' Equity Association was formed in 1913, there had been no vigorous effort to improve the lot of the actor until 1917. It was that year that the two groups—actors and managers—reached agreement about a standard contract and a process of arbitration. But that standard contract left many problems unaddressed. Actors were still not paid for rehearsal time or for special matinees on eleven national holidays. There was no required notice for closing down a company, and actors were required to perform on Sunday evenings without pay whenever the location permitted Sunday performances.

So on August 6, 1919, actors walked out of a dozen different theaters just before curtain time, and a few days later, there was a general strike. Initially, the managers were prepared to wait the actors out, knowing that they would soon be desperate for work. A good number of high-profile performers who opposed the strike organized a group called Actors Fidelity League, and they came to be known as Fidos. They were generally sympathetic to the managers and felt that as artists they were above labor unions, which were for "common laborers." But by far the largest group of successful performers were on the side of the strikers: Ethel Barrymore, Eddie Cantor, Lillian Russell, Al Jolson, Marie Dressler, and Ed Wynn. Public sentiment was also strongly on the side of the actors.

Mary was just beginning to draw rave reviews in the Cohan show *The Royal Vagabond* when the strike came along. She was one of the three stars who walked out. Frederick Santley and Tessa Kosta were the other two. Cohan, who was coproducer along with Sam Harris, was furious at the strikers and his excessive tirades destroyed many friendships with Broadway performers. He took the strike very personally. For a while, he represented the Fido group, speaking out strongly against the strike.

According to John McCabe in *The Man Who Owned Broadway*, it probably did not help Cohan's disposition when Actors' Equity chose the Cohan song "Over There" to create a parody as their anthem:

> Over fair, over fair,
> We have been, we have been over fair,
> But now things are humming,
> And the time is coming,
> When with labor we'll be chumming everywhere,
> So beware, have a care,
> Just be on the fair, on the square everywhere,
> For we are striking, yes we are striking,
> And we won't come back till the managers are fair.

Finally, when hundreds of stagehands walked out of the gigantic Hippodrome, closing down a spectacular production called *Happy Days,* it became obvious that the strength was on the side of the actors. The strike was settled on September 6, 1919. Actors' Equity was a clear winner, and the lot of actors was significantly improved. Cohan swore he would never become a member of Actors' Equity, and as John McCabe wrote, he never did—even though an exception had to be made by Actors' Equity permitting him to perform in 1923 in *The Song and Dance Man,* and later he performed in some other shows without an Equity card.

While the mutual hostility lasted too long between Cohan and Actors' Equity, it was a sad and unwanted situation for a man who was known as the softest touch in show business. He was the kind who sent checks to unemployed actors, stagehands, wardrobe women—anyone he had known in show business who was having a hard time. I heard that years later he looked back on those events of 1919 without anger and could actually joke about them. He never expressed any ill will toward Mary and the other stars for closing his show; indeed, *The Royal Vagabond* resumed after the strike, and Mary stayed with it for a lengthy run, along with Frederick Santley and Tessa Kosta. One critic called Mary "the quintessence of grace, youth, and beauty." When she was on the road with the show in Washington, the critic for the *Washington Times* wrote, "Pretty Mary Eaton made as marked a hit as anyone in the cast. Her dancing so pleased the audience that she temporarily stopped the show." Soon she would be so well known that the rest of us would invariably be introduced or referred to as Mary Eaton's sister or Mary Eaton's brother. No one else in the family achieved the level of stardom and celebrity that Mary did, and she wore it all very well, never flaunted it, and shared generously with the family. Only recently, I heard that some of my contemporary Ziegfeld "girls" described Mary as having been egotistical and arrogant—a bitchy prima donna—but that is so far from what I observed in her that it is as if they are talking of a different person. One of Mary's contemporary Ziegfeld dancers, Dana O'Connell, told me, "Mary was a sweet and lovely girl, who took her ballet dancing very seriously. When she came off stage, if something had not gone right, she could be furious and would not want people around her or to speak to her. But it was because she was so perfectionistic about her dancing. Most of the time she was the friendliest and nicest person you could ever know."

◕ ◕ ◕

Even in those prosperous times, jobs didn't come easily. We had to go looking for them, making the rounds of the theatrical agents, often located on the off-Broadway streets in dingy little offices, usually crowded with performers in the relentless search for work. When we weren't looking for new jobs, we worked on our dancing, tried to improve our singing, and kept abreast of what was going on in musical theater. Our apartment was filled with the sheet music of new songs, which we would sing and learn to play on the piano. New songs were pouring out of Tin Pan Alley in large numbers, and there were some great songs—among the ocean of bad songs that no one now remembers. So many of the songs I recall are a nostalgic and evocative reflection of the mood and the spirit of that time: "I'm Forever Blowing Bubbles," "I'll Remember You," "Someone Like You," "I'll Be with You in Apple Blossom Time," "Whispering," "Let the Rest of the World Go By," and "When My Baby Smiles at Me." A special song for all of the Eatons was "Oh, What a Pal Was Mary."

Our lives were filled with song and dance. We had a passing interest in the success of the "talking plays," the arty productions of playwrights like Somerset Maugham, John Galsworthy, George Bernard Shaw, and Eugene O'Neill, but generally we felt that if you couldn't hum it and dance to it, it was not our kind of show business. Basically, we were hoofers. To us, Broadway was revues and musical comedy.

To perfect our dancing and learn new routines, Mary, Pearl, and I would rent space in the rehearsal halls, of which there were many in New York. They had good wooden floors, a piano if you wanted it, and other dancers around to give you pointers. They were great places to polish your dancing, and we spent endless hours working on new steps. We paid fifty cents an hour for the room, and you could hire an accompanist for a dollar an hour. Six hours work would cost nine dollars. Some of the halls had lockers and showers, which were certainly useful after the rigorous workout we put ourselves through. A very popular rehearsal hall was called Michael's, and it was always a busy place. That is where I worked with Buddy Bradley, an excellent black tap dancer who taught Ann Pennington, Jessie Matthews, Eddie Foy, Ruby Keeler, the Astaires, and the great Eleanor Powell. He may have been the best tap dance teacher in the city, and he certainly helped me develop some of my best dance routines.

I can also remember Jimmy Cagney, years before he became a movie star, coming in to use the room next to ours, where he was teaching tap dancing. As the world would later discover, he was quite a hoofer himself. He got his start as a chorus boy in 1920 in a show called *Pitter Patter,* and he was soon elevated to the role of specialty dancer. He did a lot of work in vaudeville, working with some folks we knew: Van and Schenck, Bill Robinson, and Buster West. Ten years later, Buster teamed up with Charlie for a while in a successful vaudeville act. During his vaudeville years, Cagney taught dancing part-time. He went off to Hollywood in 1930, and—as they say—the rest is history.

With our new successes and greater financial resources, we moved to a large and pleasant apartment at 471 Central Park West, a handsome five-story Roman yellow brick building with limestone trim, built at the turn of the century. It was (and still is) on the corner of 107th Street, and our apartment was on the second floor, looking out on Central Park. Indeed, Central Park was our front yard, green, beautiful, and lush. At last, we had very spacious rooms throughout, with high ceilings and a lot of windows, and it was quite a thrill for us to get out of cramped and stuffy quarters into that wonderful space. And two bathrooms! For the first time ever, we had two bathrooms. Central Park West was—as it remains today—a street of residential hotels, apartment buildings, churches and synagogues, and museums, all facing Central Park, and running from 59th Street to 110th Street. We were just a few blocks from the north end of the park. The entire block was occupied by similar five-story apartment buildings in good condition. In those days, it was the accepted policy to limit apartment buildings that did not have elevators to five stories, and that is why there was such uniformity.

It was a wonderful neighborhood, and we were able to afford help with the cooking and care of the apartment, which made Mama's life easier. Mary even received a new car—a Cunningham—as a gift from one of her admirers, and she immediately pronounced it the family car. I know that receiving a car as a gift sounds basically like an immoral proposition—sexual barter—but it was a twenties-type grand gesture from a very wealthy businessman named Otto Morris, whom I'll say more about later on. When Mary got the new car, no one in our family knew how to drive—although Mary was learning—so we hired a chauffeur, whose name was James. It seems like every chauffeur from that era was named James. "Home, James," became the ubiquitous phrase.

There were Papa, Mama, Mary, Charlie, and I living together—and we knew that Joe would be coming to live with us before too long to go to high school in New York. Many show folks, artists, and writers lived in the area just north of Columbus Circle. While it was certainly an upscale location for us, we were really in the middle-class section of Central Park West, with the ritzier section to the south of us. But for us, we were "uptown" in more ways than one. Mary and I loved to walk in Central Park, although this northwestern end was more naturally rugged, more like a woods than a park, but there were well-developed pathways throughout, lined neatly with rocks. Just to the south were huge, reddish boulders jutting out of the earth. There was the beautiful lake called Harlem Meer and a wide variety of beautiful trees.

In those days, we felt perfectly safe at all hours exploring the area, but it was generally before going to the theaters for the evening performance that Mary and I would walk together in the park. Years later, parts of the Upper West Side would become run-down and dangerous, but in recent years, much of it has been restored, including the area to the south where beautiful Lincoln Center now stands.

Charlie was going to the Professional Children's School, where his fellow students included Milton Berle, Marguerite Churchill, Ruby Keeler, Gene Raymond, Kenny Delmare, Peter Donald Jr., and Helen Mack. He made many friends there, and they shared with each other their individual insights and caveats about show business. They had pretty well seen it all as young children, and they were much more sophisticated than their ages would suggest. The older kids—Milton Berle was two years older than Charlie—were unofficial mentors for the younger. Charlie by age twelve—having gone to school there since he was in the second grade—was about as polished and articulate as any twelve year old in New York. Even with the interruptions of being on the road or in Broadway shows, he was an honors student through the tenth grade, his last year at the Children's Professional School.

Mary left *The Royal Vagabond* during a long road tour in time to become a principal in the cast of the *Ziegfeld Follies of 1920,* opening in June. I was now a principal doing specialty dances, and this would be the only year that Mary and I would be in the *Follies* together. Ziegfeld had seen Mary perform and knew he had found the replacement for Marilyn Miller, who was going into his production of *Sally.* He went to George M. Cohan and bargained to get Mary. Whatever their deal was, Cohan agreed, and Mary left *Vagabond* for the *Follies.* Fanny Brice and W. C. Fields were the *Follies* headliners, again providing the hilarious humor everyone had come to expect. Fanny had three songs that became identified with her: "I'm a Vamp from East Broadway," "Poor Floridora Girl," and "I'm an Indian." But the two big songs were Irving Berlin's "Tell Me, Little Gypsy," and "Girl of My Dreams." Victor Herbert also contributed "The Love Boat," in addition to the music for Mary's ballet. And I had a duet with Bernard Granville, singing "Any Place Would Be Wonderful with You."

The critics praised the extravagance and elegance of the production. A reviewer in the *New York Evening Telegram* wrote, "It attains heights of beauty as never before dazzled the eye of the beholder. . . . It is in a class by itself." The *New York Herald* reported, "There was a blaze of dancing numbers . . . Miss Mary Eaton's toes twinkled like stars of the first magnitude. She stood out above all others in an old fashioned ballet dance with Charles Winninger, as the violin-playing master, floating about with a rosebud grace that made Newton's law of gravitation look foolish. . . . This ingenuous and lovely miss, whose brief moment of glory in *The Royal Vagabond* made a name for her last season, also displayed comedy ability and a pretty little voice."

Mary was in the funniest scene of that year's *Follies,* when she was paired with Fanny Brice, who provided her own matchless humor. The sketch was called "Her First Lesson in the Dancing School." Fanny was playing the part of a ballet student, coming for her first lesson, and Mary was the teacher— pristine, icy, and dignified. It was another of those Ziegfeld incongruities of beauty and grace alongside Fanny's ludicrous clumsiness. Fanny's skinny, out-of-control legs and her patented way of burlesquing ballet never failed to bring the house down. Through it all, Mary retained her beautiful poise and graceful movement and never once broke up. The *New York Telegram* called Mary "the prettiest girl in the *Follies.*" Another critic described her as "a blond and wide-eyed child, [who] looks like a beautiful china doll."

When the *Follies* went on the road, a critic for the *Chicago Evening American* wrote: "The dancer was Mary Eaton, sister of Doris, the two stars, and [Mary] has the most un-Methodist feet. We had Eaton and Eaton . . . but not too much. Just enough to satisfy a hungry audience." I love that quotation because it is the one time that Mary was referred to as the sister of Doris. After that, it was always the other way around.

Charlie, at ten, joined the *Follies* cast in 1921, once again with Mary starring. He played the Dauphin in an act called "The Birthday of the Dauphin," with Raymond Hitchcock playing the King of France and W. C. Fields as a Court Jester. In spite of his reputation for hating child actors, Fields became an idol of Charlie's, and they remained good friends. Backstage he treated Charlie in a kind and protective way that Charlie never forgot. When the *Follies* continued into the summer, and some moviemakers on Long Island wanted Charlie for a movie, brother Joe—home for the summer—took over the part of the Dauphin. As a matter of fact, when the show went on the road, Mary— reverting to the cross-dressing Poli days in Washington—went on herself as the Dauphin. The movie that Charlie made at Famous Players–Lasky Studios (which would become Paramount Studios) was called *Peter Ibbitsen,* with Wallace Reed and Elsie Ferguson. Not long afterward, he made another movie, at the Vitagraph Studios, called *The Prodigal Judge,* with Jean Page, Macklin Arbuckle, and Earl Fox. Brother Robert, who must have been out of work at the time, got a job as an extra in that second movie. It was the only time he was involved in any way in show business.

In the 1921 *Follies*, Mary sang a pretty Rudolf Friml song, "Bring Back My Blushing Rose," and she received great notices, but the memorable song and the showstopping event was Fanny Brice, with tears running down her face, singing the poignant, "My Man." It was one of the great moments in the history of the musical stage. Everyone believed the song to be a genuinely sad reflection of her unhappy marriage to Nick Arnstein, who had serious legal problems at the time and, indeed, was on his way to jail. Brice, the world's funniest woman, having worked her way through burlesque to the summit of show business, had that rare ability to stamp her ownership on every song she sang. She would have you rolling in the aisles or would break your heart. Whichever, she proved in 1920 that she was the best on Broadway at belting out a song. Supposedly, after she sang "My Man," Ziegfeld raised her salary from $1,000 per week to $3,000. At least, that's the story that went around. We were all happy to see Fanny's huge success. She never had the slightest taint of egotism about her. She and Pearl became good friends, and later on in Hollywood, their children became playmates.

Once again, many would say that this was the best-ever *Follies*. The sets of Joseph Urban and the costumes of James Reynolds were the most lavish yet, and it was clearly the most expensive *Follies* to date, costing $250,000. Mary—as had become her habit—received rave notices from the press. One critic said she was "a comely miss whose legs twinkled in and out of ensembles with a speed and grace that was dazzling." And in a column written by Flo Ziegfeld, himself, he had this to say about her: "[She has] a pretty face, a pretty figure, and is graceful. Yet, her audiences are instantly taken with her expression and personal magnetism." It is true. Mary had a stage presence that just seemed to glow. Mary took Ziegfeld's advice and studied voice and dance over several years. Her stardom did not come accidentally to her; she worked very hard for it, and she had the talent to keep developing. From 1918 to 1929, she worked in continuous and uninterrupted successes. And she went from $200 a week to $5,000 a week by the end of the decade. There were few women on Broadway or in Hollywood earning more, and Ziegfeld's well-known generosity ("extravagance" might be the better word) is what made that happen. I don't know whether making that much money in 1929 was good for her career, because she would never again be able to command that level of salary.

Pearl

Mary

Doris

CHAPTER SIX

THE GLORY YEARS

After the 1920 *Follies* had run its course on the road, I made two movies at RKO Studios in Astoria, Long Island. Everyone was talking about movies, and many of the stars had left the *Follies* to begin careers in silent films. So I was excited when I was given the opportunity to find out whether making movies was something for me. The first film was called *At the Stage Door* and starred Billie Dove, who had also been in the 1919 *Follies,* when Billie was sixteen and I was fifteen. She went to Hollywood in 1922 and made over twenty movies before talking pictures began. The second movie was a straight dramatic role for me and starred Pearl White (of *The Perils of Pauline* fame). The movie was called *The Broadway Peacock* and was directed by Theda Bara's husband, Charles Brabin. The movies did not seem to bring me a great deal of attention, but I was intrigued by motion picture acting despite being very uncertain of where I might be heading with my show business career. At the beginning of 1922, Edward Small, an agent that we had often worked with, contacted Mama and me (I was not yet seventeen) and asked us to come to his office.

When we arrived, he introduced us to a Mr. John Glidden, a representative of International Arts in London. He said that he was looking for a leading lady for a movie, then titled *Lark's Gate* (from the novel by Rachel McNamara), which would be made in England and in Egypt. Glidden thought I would be right for the part, and during that first meeting, he offered it to me. Mama quickly said, "When do we sail?" He seemed surprised at her quick response and said that we would need to talk contracts and other details, but he would like for us to sail as soon as possible. As I recall that significant moment, it was Mama who was really in charge. I don't even know if she asked my opinion, but I had total trust in Mama's judgment. Mama never seemed to tire of traveling. She loved it, and no doubt her quick response to Glidden's offer was a reflection of her excitement and joy at the thought of going to England. To my knowledge, she never consulted Papa on her decisions to travel, and of course she was apart from him a great deal.

At that age, I had never made decisions for myself. I don't know that I had the confidence to. While I had gained confidence on the stage, I had little self-reliance off of it. It would be years before I overcame my reticence—and also the troubling feeling that I was not as talented or as beautiful as my two sisters. It was once said—by whom I don't recall, but the words are indelible in my memory—that Pearl had the brains, Mary had the beauty, and Doris had the charm. Well, charm seemed the least of the qualities one admires in performers, and I remained the "little sister" to Pearl and Mary. It took me some years and some bad decisions along the way before I finally felt good about my own abilities and my talent.

So going to England and Egypt was Mama's decision, and what really excited me about the trip was seeing castles and cathedrals, pyramids and the Sphinx. I never gave a thought to what the movie might do for or to my career. It was the thrill of going away with Mama to those storybook places that was my basic teenage reaction. We would be away from the family for a long time. Evelyn would look after Charlie—who was almost eleven—for the several months we would be gone, and of course, Papa would be there to help out.

The movie was to be directed by the English actor-director Donald Crisp, who would later make his career in the United States as a distinguished character actor. He had been introduced to moviemaking by the great David W. Griffith, who made *Birth of a Nation, Way Down East,* and *Intolerance.* Crisp's movie would also star Walter Tennyson (whose full name was Walter Tennyson d'Eyncourt), a true descendant of Alfred, Lord Tennyson. The cast also included Margaret Halstan, Gertrude McCoy, and Warwick Ward. The filming would involve trips to Egypt, Nice, and Paris, and we would be gone five or six months. The movie, which was renamed *Tell Your Children,* would take me away from Broadway at a rather critical time in my career, and in retrospect, it might have been a mistake career-wise. As it turned out, the English movie did not help my career in the United States. Because I had been a principal in the 1920 *Follies,* I probably could have enhanced my career more by staying in New York. But in those days, I don't think Mama gave much attention to career goals, as such. She was focused only on getting the next job.

Mama and I set sail on February 1, 1922, and in five days, we were in London. On two of those days, I was deathly seasick, but by the time we arrived, I was very much alive, excited, and filled with anticipation. We received a great deal of press attention in London, where the Ziegfeld name was well known. I was always described as "a star of the *Ziegfeld Follies,*" and on our first day in London, there was a large press reception for me at the Piccadilly Hotel. The reception was well attended, and it seemed that tons of articles were written about our arrival and the movie we were going to make. We met Walter

Tennyson, whom we immediately liked, and he invited us to go for the weekend to the d'Eyncourt castle out in the English countryside. We did, and it was a lovely castle on vast, manicured grounds, right out of a storybook. Mama was given a very large bedroom, which had a winding stairway to a smaller room above, where I was to sleep. The family had told us with mock seriousness that all castles were haunted, and during the night, when the wind blew through my bedroom windows and lifted the curtains in an eerie, waving motion, I was convinced that the ghost of d'Eyncourt had come to call on me. I didn't sleep the rest of the night.

After a whirlwind ten days in England, during which we did a lot of sightseeing between fittings for my costumes and briefings with the director and cast, we sailed for Egypt, where most of the movie would be filmed. I played a young girl who falls in love with a farmer and gives birth to his child. My character's mother, who dominates the young girl, stops her from eloping with the farmer, has her illegitimate child taken away, and forces the daughter to marry a lord, whom she does not love. The story was made exotic by the beautiful desert setting—camels, pyramids, and the Nile River.

Mama and I had a wonderful time being tourists when I was not needed for filming, including traveling by camel and by donkey. I had quite a time learning how to handle the donkeys. Our Egyptian guides spoke almost no English, so we did not receive much instruction. I discovered that if I pulled on the reins when I wanted to stop, the donkeys would actually go faster. If I stopped pulling on the reins, they would stand still. After a couple of days, I developed a certain rapport with them, and I had a lot of fun. Mama always had a guide walking along leading her donkey, because she had never even ridden a horse, much less a donkey. Mama had gained a lot of weight and was very heavy, so it wasn't easy for her to mount up. But she was game and willing to try anything. She always had a good time. Riding the camels was like sitting in a rocking chair, but we had to hold on tightly to the front of the saddle when they got up or down or we would have been tossed off easily. I have a picture of Mama and me on camels in front of the Sphinx. In retrospect, that exotic experience has such an unreal aura about it, I feel as if I had dreamed the whole thing.

I never saw the finished product of the movie, which was shown in England, and I doubt that many others have. Dawn Costello, who did a research project on my career, learned that the movie never survived the trade shows. It is known that the title was changed twice, first to *Protect Your Daughter* and then to *Reckless Decision*.

What I have recently learned—to my great astonishment—was that *Tell Your Children* was not the only movie made there by that cast and crew. Another film, originally called *His Supreme Sacrifice,* was also apparently made at the same time or perhaps patched together from unused scenes. *The British Film Catalogue* lists the movie, with Doris Eaton, Warwick Ward, and Walter Tennyson (a different order of the same cast from the first movie) playing the roles of an unfaithful wife, her distraught husband, and her clandestine lover. The husband in his anguished state after discovering his wife's infidelity wants to kill his wife or her lover but can't make himself do it, so in despair he goes walking off into the desert to his doom in a sandstorm. International Arts re-released the film in 1927, with the title *The Call of the East.* I suppose the days of silent film making allowed moviemakers to patch together the second film without the actors' knowledge—and without any contractual discussions. Of course, with silent films, if you put new subtitles on the pictures, you get a different story. They got two films for the price of one! That might be the reason that Donald Crisp never listed these two movies among his directorial credits. It appears that International Arts owes me for a picture.

Nevertheless, after we had returned to the United States, I received a very nice letter from Crisp, and he did send along some of the criticism written about *Tell Your Children.* Here is a letter he sent, dated September 14, 1922:

Dear Miss Eaton,

It is just an hour after the Trade Show, and I feel you would be glad to get a note to know how this went off. Everybody loved your performance and I am anxiously waiting the papers coming out tomorrow. I shall send you a few of the cuttings, and I personally want to congratulate you very much indeed. I consider your performance absolutely perfect.

With kind regards to your mother and sister Mary,
Yours sincerely,
Donald Crisp

(He had met Mary on one occasion when he was visiting in New York.) And here's a sampler of the newspaper "cuttings" he sent: "Superbly acted . . . Doris Eaton has an attractive screen presence. . . .The best part of the film is the acting, notably of Doris Eaton. . . . Her acting saves what otherwise might have been a ridiculous situation."

When we returned to the United States, I had an offer waiting to go to Los Angeles to star in a revue called the *Gorham Follies,* at the Cocoanut Grove

Room of the Ambassador Hotel. Mama said that I deserved a starring role and I would not get that if I were accepted back in the *Follies*. And, of course, with Hollywood becoming the West Coast entertainment capital, there might be many other opportunities there for both Charlie and me in films. So Mama, Charlie, and I went to Los Angeles in the fall of 1922.

Joe Gorham was the producer of the show. He asked Arthur Freed—who would become a well-known lyricist and later producer of those great MGM musicals—to write a song that would introduce me as the star of the *Gorham Follies*. Freed wrote a song called "Doris Come Out of the Chorus," which was sung by Jesse Mendelssohn, who beseeched me to come out of the chorus and take the spotlight. I thought that it was a clever way to be introduced in the show. For the first time, I was more than the lead dancer, I was the star of the show, and I received a great deal of attention. It was a very successful revue in Los Angeles, and we also did several weeks in San Francisco. Southern California was a whole new world to me—as different in some ways as England and Egypt. We did not know then how big Hollywood would become, but we knew it was a highly creative and exciting place to be. Everyone seemed to have a keen interest in show business, and the attention given to it in the press was enormous.

In this exciting fairy-tale world, I fell in love with Joe Gorham—at least, I thought I was in love with him. I was only eighteen—and even though I had ten years experience on the stage and around show folks of all description—I was still very naive. (Mama had seen to that.) When he asked me to marry him, I said yes—probably thinking that every day would be as bright and as much fun as dancing in the lights of the *Gorham Follies*. He was thirty-six, and I did not know him all that well. Mama was terribly distraught over my decision and pleaded with me not to marry him, but I would hear none of that. Looking back, I can see that this was an act of rebellion against being dominated by my mother. It was the first major decision I had ever made about my own life, and it still astounds me that I would have defied my mother's wishes so totally. Well, in this instance, Mama really did know best, but nonetheless we were married in a little church with just those from the company as wedding guests. I remember we had Abe Lymon's band there from the Cocoanut Grove, and I think Abe must have known only one strain of the traditional Mendelssohn "Wedding March," which he played repeatedly while we waited for the preacher to arrive. Such debauched music was not a good omen for the marriage.

Mama and Charlie returned to New York, and Joe and I moved into an apartment in a building Joe owned. It did not take long before I began to realize that the marriage was a huge mistake. There was a side to Joe that I had not seen before. He could be very cruel, and he would humiliate me in rehearsals in front of the other performers in ways he never did before we were married. It seemed that he looked for opportunities to belittle me. He was a creative and talented person and often fun to be around, but he was high-strung and became angry quickly. His outbursts were extreme and out of proportion to whatever the irritant was. I had never worked with or for anyone who was so harshly demanding, and he made life almost unbearable for me. The situation was made worse by the fact that we were working together on a daily basis, and almost every day, there was some kind of harsh encounter or conflict.

We were trying to put together an act with the comedian-dancer Ben Blue, but it was taking a long time, and Ben finally took off when he got a better offer. I don't think he liked working with Joe any more than I did. After that, Joe bought a new apartment building, deciding to go into real estate and giving up any involvement in show business. What might have happened in the long run, I have no idea. I was struggling to make the marriage work while fully realizing that the first important decision I had made about my own life (and over Mama's protests) was a very big mistake. Providence took it out of my hands. Several months after our marriage, Joe had a heart attack and died suddenly at the age of thirty-six. He came home one day and lay down on the divan—and he was gone. I was stunned and really lost as to what I should do. The days that followed were days of confusion and loneliness, while I tried to figure out how to get everything taken care of in California in order to get back to my family in New York. I tried to figure out Joe's investment deals and get out of the apartment house whatever Joe had coming, but I was overcome both by my impatience to get to New York and by my overall naïveté about business. I left without realizing any value from Joe's property, turning it all over to his family.

During the time I was in Los Angeles, Mary was starring in the *Ziegfeld Follies of 1922* and was undeniably the big star she had wanted to become. The 1922 edition had a longer run than any of its predecessors, continuing well into 1923. This was the *Follies* that first used that phrase "Glorifying the American Girl," and it became attached to Mary, who would later star in Ziegfeld's movie of that name. Most of the older big-name headliners were gone, except for Will Rogers, who was back from Hollywood. The comedy team of Gallagher and Shean introduced the song that became the hit of the show, "Oh! Mr. Gallagher and Mr. Shean." Mary led a ballet in one of the most spectacular acts, called "Lace-Land," to the music of Victor Herbert, who had written "Weaving My Dreams" for the act. It gave Mary an opportunity to show her wonderful talent as a ballet dancer. Before the opening, Ziegfeld ordered that the costumes be made of real lace and the artificial flowers be removed from the scene and replaced by ten dozen red roses. A standing order was placed to have new roses delivered every day. Ziegfeld was truly a perfectionist—though some would say a foolish spendthrift. It was reported that this one number cost $31,000 to stage. With the use of radium paint and special lighting, a gorgeous effect was created, and Mary's lace gown appeared to change color from white to bronze. Ashton Stevens, in the *Herald Examiner,* described Mary as "the loveliest of the ash blondes, whose hair is platinum, whose eyes are liquid cobalt, and whose smile is coral and pearl. Here is an American girl whose career has been unspotted by scandal and about whom nothing but fine things can ever be said."

It was Mary who taught the ballet steps to the chorus of sixteen dancers, which she obviously had managed to do with great success—transforming hoofers into ballet dancers. Ballet was Ziegfeld's way of adding class to the *Follies,* and Mary was the best classical dancer he ever had. As usual, there were good songs: "Rambler Rose," for one, and "Throw Me a Kiss," which was Mary's big vocal number. Soon the whole family was singing it around the apartment. All of that was going on when I returned to New York. Although I had no idea of what my next step in show business would be, it felt good to be back in the supportive warmth of my family.

Early in the 1920s, Mary had moved to a new high-rise apartment building at 161 West Fifty-fourth Street, just off Seventh Avenue. It was, as it is today, called the Congress. She leased an apartment on the seventh floor, and Papa, Mama, and Charlie joined her there. Soon Harry and Pearl would rent an apartment on the eighth floor. Many show people lived there. George White had the penthouse, and two of the Warner Brothers, Jack and Sam, were on the eleventh floor. Of course, when I returned from California, I moved in with Mary and the others, with Mary and me sharing a bedroom.

It was a beautifully decorated apartment, with two bedrooms, two baths, kitchen, dining room, and living room—not as spacious as the apartment on Central Park West, but wonderfully located in the theater district. In the living room was a lovely Louis XIV piano, which was pale blue with beautiful yellow flowers painted on it. It was explained only as another gift from one of Mary's admirers, and I do not know to this day the identity of that generous person. Ziegfeld might be a good bet because he often gave expensive gifts to his stars, but he never pursued a personal relationship with Mary as he did with Marilyn and, heaven knows, how many others. As I said before, Mary had many wealthy admirers, and as her celebrity grew throughout the twenties, she would have many more.

I must admit that while I received token gifts from admirers—flowers and perfume usually and rarely a piece of jewelry—I was not in Mary's league of receiving cars and pianos and fur coats. I did receive a beautiful diamond ring on one occasion from a well-known gentleman of Broadway, but I'll tell you about that later. I am sure that Pearl got some big tips in the clubs where she danced, but that was expected as part of the work and did not usually have any personal meaning.

In 1923, Mary—following the lead of many other successful performers—rented a summer home at Great Neck, Long Island, for the family, and in the following summers, she leased large houses at Point Pleasant, New Jersey. They served as wonderful retreats for us during the summer months when we could get some time off between shows. We would swim and sun and entertain our friends and relatives. It seems now that there was always a crowd at the summer places. Although most of us worked through the summer months, we had short weekends or a several-day hiatus between jobs, and it was a rare treat for all of us to be together.

At Great Neck, we had a German gentleman named Otto who took care of the house and grounds, and his wife Rosa cooked wonderful meals for us and helped around the house. Mama would always do part of the cooking, but she enjoyed the luxury of having help. Since many entertainers had Great Neck houses, it was really a summer colony of show folk. It was a beautiful area of stately homes and well-manicured lawns, with white wicker furniture on spacious porches, and there were massive backyards sloping down to the blue water of Long Island Sound—a perfect summer retreat.

It was at that summerhouse at Great Neck where we first met Georges Carpentier, the French boxer who lost to Jack Dempsey in 1921. He was staying with friends just a stone's throw away from Mary's house. He was preparing for his fight with Gene Tunney, another heavyweight fight he would lose. He was obviously taken with Mary, and every morning at eleven, he was Johnny-on-the-spot for a morning swim in the sound with Mary. He was a very handsome and beautifully built man, elegant enough to be called Mr. Orchid. Roger Kahn in his memoir of Jack Dempsey quotes a woman admirer of Carpentier as saying, "His profile would make Michelangelo faint." Well, in France, he had a wife and children, but that did not stop rumors from circulating that Mary would marry Georges after he was divorced. In July of 1925, the *New York Times* printed a denial by Mary saying the rumors were "preposterous." "It's the most insane story I have ever heard. . . . I admire him, of course. Any one would admire a sportsman like Carpentier. But marriage—that's another story entirely. . . . Love and marriage are far away from my thoughts now." True enough, but Georges was obviously smitten by Mary, and he would sing to her a new popular song by Isham Jones and Gus Kahn, "It Had to Be You."

I recall one instance when we were all out on the beach when Pearl (who had performed a boxing dance routine in *The Passing Show*) was sparring around with Georges, throwing out her chest, comically flexing her muscles, and being very funny. Georges laughed so hard that he fell down on the sand. For a time, Georges was considered a regular member of our family group. Often, he would be in the company of his friend, Jules Glaezner, vice president of Cartier jewelers and once a suitor of the beautiful Ziegfeld star Lillian Lorraine. He was an interesting and delightful companion. After Georges lost his fight with Gene Tunney in 1924, he returned to France and to his family.

One bright summer day stands out in my mind, when the Prince of Wales (who would later abdicate the throne and become the duke of Windsor) visited Great Neck. On the polo grounds near our house, there was some kind of formal ceremony, with about a thousand uniformed troops and many colorful banners and flags waving in the summer air. The prince was formally welcomed and paid homage by a host of dignitaries, who sat on a platform surrounded by hundreds of tourists and well-wishers. A military band played Sousa marches, and columns of smartly uniformed troops passed in review. Following the ceremony, the prince remained for a long time, greeting the enthusiastic tourists that lined the field. Charlie, who loved military pomp and circumstance, stayed to greet the prince personally, long after the rest of us had retreated to the peaceful quiet of our summer home. Not being one of the invited guests, Charlie—whose gift of gab and sharp-as-a-tack wit always served him well—struck up a conversation with a young man and woman standing in the line. As they talked, he casually inserted himself between them. The young man suggested that Charlie get in line ahead of them both, which he did gratefully, and he was able to meet the prince and shake hands with him.

Point Pleasant, New Jersey, was a much different kind of place. We wore bathing suits almost all day, and didn't dress until time for cocktails at 5:30. Then we would sit out on the porch with whatever guests we had at the time,

In the summer of 1923, the French boxer Georges Carpentier became
a close friend of the Eatons at our summer home on Long Island.

Georges with Mary

Georges with Doris

Georges clowning with Pearl

and it seemed so wonderful, carefree, and luxurious. The first house we had there was a huge, shingle-sided two-story place—maybe fifteen rooms—and it was right on the Manasquan River. We never knew who or how many guests might come along with us for a weekend, but we were always prepared for whatever happened. Mama, who epitomized Southern hospitality, never got excited about another chair or two or three at the table. I recall Frank McHugh visiting there when we were working together in *Excess Baggage,* and he kept everyone laughing. Marilyn Miller was a frequent visitor, sometimes bringing her mother along. Walter Catlett and Paul Gregory and others would come down on the milk train late Saturday night after their performances and remain until noon on Monday. Joe and Charlie fished every day, and often caught wonderful crabs that Mama and Papa could prepare so well for us.

For another summer at Point Pleasant, we had a different big house right on the ocean, and once again, we lived in our bathing suits on the beach. On occasion, relatives from Virginia would come along with friends from New York, and Joe and Charlie loved having others with them on the beach. Evelyn and Bob often brought their children (Edwin, Evelynne, and Warren), and Pearl would bring Dossie, so there were always the delightful sounds of children playing. There was a private pier near the house that we were permitted to use, and we had canoes and rowboats available. Swimming was the perfect way to beat the summer heat in those days, long before air conditioning.

Of course, it was Mary who made it all possible, earning far more money than any of us had dreamed about. It seemed to me that Mary needed the nurturing support of the family around her, and particularly she needed Mama for her unconditional love and unfailing counsel. After age eighteen, I was far more independent, traveling on the road and between the two coasts, but Mary was never far away from Mama. She would always say that it was Mama who made it all happen by getting lessons and training for her early in life, and by encouraging her every step along the way, sacrificing so much of her own life to see that Mary—and all of us—succeeded. Later on, when Mary's life wasn't going well and she was separated from the nurturing support of the family, she gradually fell apart. It was Mama who went to her aid and stayed with her through some painful and confused years.

CHAPTER SEVEN

PEARL, PEARL, THE PARTY GIRL

n 1922, Ziegfeld asked Pearl to evaluate the applicants for dancing roles in the *Follies*, because he simply did not have time to continue doing so himself. So every Tuesday and Friday, Pearl interviewed and auditioned aspiring dancers at the New Amsterdam Roof, where she was still appearing in the *Midnight Frolics*. For some time, Pearl had been rehearsing the specialty dancers in her role as Ned Wayburn's assistant, and this new responsibility was an indication of how highly both Ziegfeld and Wayburn regarded her ability. Pearl was both bright and clever, and she had a good eye for judging talent. While she was a tough taskmaster and took dancing very seriously, it was her rollicking good humor that made it fun to be around her and eased the burden of long hours of work.

She was the only one of us who really was on the inside of the production activity of the Ziegfeld organization. Many years later in writing about the 1922 *Follies*, in which Mary starred, Pearl described the magnitude of the production. By her count, the ensemble consisted of a hundred girls: twenty-four showgirls, twenty-four chorus dancers, sixteen "ponies," sixteen ballet dancers, twelve specialty girls, and eight understudies. Today, of course, a company that size is unthinkable, but even in those days, no one other than Ziegfeld would be so expansive. He never let economy stand in the way of splendor. No wonder he eventually went broke, leaving his wife, Billie Burke, with huge indebtedness when he died in 1932.

It is curious that Pearl never became a principal in the *Follies*, as Mary and I did, although she stayed for five years, working on the production side and as a dancer in the *Midnight Frolics*. She was more an ensemble dancer than a solo performer, and really found her niche in dance direction. Nevertheless, she had her moments in the spotlight, such as in 1922 when the *Frolics* went on the road for the first time and Pearl went along as a featured dancer. In Chicago, she received a poetic tribute in a newspaper column called "This Week in Chicago," signed only "Fleurette." The first line refers to a picture of Pearl's head that appears above the poem:

> It's only her head you see here,
> But wait till she comes on stage,

And then, mon cher, what you notice most there,
Her neat little figure and her mop of blond hair,
Or her legs! Ziggy says they've won prizes,
And Ziggy should know since he—Oh—so wise is,
And she dances—soft shoe stuff—but Dieu glory be,
She dances with brains and it's something to see.
She is sister to Mary, and to Doris she's sister,
She's a dear and a beaut and you'll all want to kiss 'er.

A little later that year, Pearl performed in a play called *The Love Letter,* a musical comedy produced by Charles Dillingham, starring John Charles Thomas. Dillingham, too, was taken with Pearl's dancing and her choreographic ability. He later hired her as a dance director—and later on, as Broadway's first woman stage manager.

But the most significant change in Pearl's life came when she started dancing in nightclubs, going to work around eleven o'clock at night (often after an evening's theater performance) and dancing through the night. I don't know how she managed it, but she seemed to thrive on it. There were times when the last nightclub show was not over until five o'clock in the morning. Remember, it was the roaring twenties, and there was a lot of roaring going on.

What happened after the Volstead Act went into effect on January 1, 1920, was what many had feared. It dealt a terrible blow to the previously legal establishments—the nightclubs and roof gardens and cabarets—many of which went out of business, leading to the proliferation of illegal establishments. The speakeasies became the popular gathering places, where booze flowed not free but copiously for anyone who could afford bootlegger prices. There were thousands of speakeasies in Manhattan by 1922, many of them in the Times Square district. "Nightclubs" became the term applied to speakeasies with floor shows, and they typically featured highly visible hosts or hostesses to give a personal identity to the clubs. They offered dance music and floor shows—which like the booze were of varying quality. Texas Guinan, Helen Morgan, and Harry Richman all hosted popular speakeasies.

Pearl worked in several such clubs in the twenties, but her longest stay at any one club was with Texas Guinan at the famous El Fey Club at 107 West Forty-fifth Street, which opened in June of 1924. It was owned by a shady and notorious character named Larry Fay. (The joke was that the club was called El Fey because Larry couldn't spell his last name. But Larry was not at all dumb or, as they say, he was dumb like a fox.) He had been very successful in the taxicab business—also calling his cab company El Fey—operating 6,000 cabs in New York. Fay would open a number of different speakeasies during the twenties, and finally be shot dead by one of his doormen, a disturbed man who thought Larry was cheating him on his paycheck. Of all of his clubs, El Fey was the most successful and the swankiest. The main dining room on the first floor was decorated with long, hanging rose-colored chandeliers, the walls were covered in red and gold tapestries, and the floors were covered with lush blue velvet carpet. He wanted the club to attract society's best—meaning richest and most famous—and that is what happened. Almost from its beginning, celebrities flocked to it, community leaders loved it, sports figures and mobsters made it a favorite rendezvous, and it became ritual for high society to end each evening's activities by dropping by El Fey. Larry actually asked me out to dinner on one occasion, but I declined as politely as I could while making it clear that Mama didn't allow me to go out with "older men."

When El Fey opened, *Zit's Weekly Newspaper* printed a review that included the following reference to Pearl: "The names of persons who attended the opening of the club might well be taken from the Blue Book of Society. Most every well-known star of the Theater and Motion Picture World present in New York . . . were to be seen in the club. . . . Pearl Eaton, sister of Mary Eaton, last seen in the *Midnight Frolic,* scored a decisive hit and was welcomed back into the limelight by her many friends."

Texas Guinan's "Hello, Suckers" greeting to her customers became her trademark. (Later on, when customers began to discover they really were suckers to pay the high prices, she dropped the greeting, but it always stuck as her signature salutation.) She was approaching the age of fifty, with obviously dyed blond hair and heavy makeup, but she was still a striking and attractive woman, although not conventionally pretty. Years later, in 1945, a movie would be made about Texas Guinan, which starred the very pretty Betty Hutton and was called *Incendiary Blonde.* The movie wasn't an altogether truthful portrait, but the title certainly fit.

Texas always treated her "little girls"—the dancers—as if indeed they were her little girls and she was looking out for their best interests. The girls were picked for their ability to perform individual acts—some specializing in tap, others in high kicks, and some as singers of popular songs. Of course, they all had to be young and pretty. Together they formed a highly talented chorus, and the show was considered by many to be the best nightclub act in New York, as well as "the most beautiful and artistic club." It was clearly the place to see and be seen. It was also the most expensive. Those who chose to eat dinner there could pay astronomical prices for food. Dinner for four could run as high as $1,000, with drinks and wine. In the beginning, the cover charge was low, ranging from two to eight dollars, depending on the night of the week, but that increased substantially with the growing popularity of the club and the affluence of its clientele, eventually rising to twenty dollars. You could buy a bottle of "champagne"—which often meant sparkling cider with alcohol added—for thirty-five dollars a bottle. A bottle of club soda or ginger ale sold for as much as a bottle of bourbon before prohibition, so even if you brought your own flask, you weren't off the hook. Texas "innocently" claimed in public that the club sold only setups and "ignored" the fact that a lot of illegal liquor was sold every night. The booze was all stored in a house next door and passed through a hole in the wall. And consistent with all images of speakeasies, there was a door with a peephole for you to be seen before being admitted.

According to a recent book by Louise Berliner, *Texas Guinan—Queen of the Nightclubs,* Texas's real name was Mary Louise Cecilia Guinan from Waco, Texas. She never drank liquor and never ate meat. She ate oranges in large quantities, drank black coffee, and chain-smoked cigarettes throughout the long nights. She had been in silent pictures, having made several Westerns, enough to be called the "female William S. Hart." She was also called the "queen of whoopie," which seems a well-deserved title. The legend has it that she loved to go horseback riding in Central Park, sometimes in the wee hours of the morning. She never tried to appear to be someone she was not, and she never kept it a secret that she had been around the block a few times. If she didn't know a man's name, she would say, "Hello, Fred!" It was also said that she originated the phrase "the big butter-and-egg man," which was the occupation of one wealthy out-of-towner and she generalized it to all such customers. That is where George S. Kaufman got the title for his play.

She had the reputation of being the quickest wisecracker on Broadway, as well as being one tough lady. But she always kept it clean in her club. Clean enough "not to offend nuns," someone said. It's hard to believe, however, that in the wee hours—with all-night drinking—the place didn't get a bit raucous. Of course, it was a time of sexual revolution and New York was the avant-garde of that movement. As the twenties progressed and Pearl went on to different clubs, there was more near nudity in the shows and the clubs became a little wilder.

At El Fey, Pearl was a featured dancer with a chorus ranging from six to ten. (Barbara Stanwyck—whose real name was Ruby Stevens—and Ruby Keeler danced there for a while, and several other Ziegfeld girls were in the chorus at different times. George Raft also appeared there as a dancer.) Initially, the shows were produced by Nils T. Granlund, a colorful Broadway character I worked for later on. There was a show every two hours throughout the night, and as each featured dancer did her own specialty routine, she drew from Texas Guinan her stock response, "Give this little girl a great big hand." Because the audiences at El Fey included some of the biggest names in New York, members of the press would hang out there—Walter Winchell, Damon Runyon, Ed Sullivan, Mark Hellinger—and Winchell said that El Fey is where the gossip column was born.

Sometime in the mid-1920s, El Fey was closed. Texas Guinan went on trial as a "public nuisance" for violating the Volstead Act, but she was acquitted. Soon she was in another club called Intime and others called the 300 Club and Argonaut. Pearl had a warm relationship with Texas and felt that she was always fair and maternally protective. They seemed similar in their comedic and wisecracking abilities. Once in discussing the great generosity that Texas showed to people in need, Pearl remembered another of Texas's wisecracks: "I'm a sucker for succor."

Afterward, Pearl danced at another famous speakeasy called Dover, which was also opened by Larry Fay. Its claim to fame was the appearance of Clayton, Jackson, and Durante, one of the most popular and comical song and dance acts of the time. They appeared in many different clubs in Times Square, after the federal agents had closed Club Durant in 1923. Club Durant had been a rather sleazy club, but it was a launching pad for Jimmy Durante, whose over-sized nose, fractured grammar, and self-deprecating humor made him a huge hit. His signature song, "Inka-Dinka-Do," came out of that early period. Of course, before too long, Durante would be out in Hollywood making movies and would later become a star on the Broadway stage, but it was in the speak-easies that he became a well-known and beloved performer.

Mama enjoyed going to the clubs with a small group of us to see the shows, and the crowds there were always interesting to watch—including, now and then, the appearance of one or more mobsters. Sometimes, they came to the clubs to be in the company of the higher society and showbiz celebrities; sometimes, they came because they had a "sweetie" dancing in the chorus. Chorus girls often got involved with some of these prohibition-era mobster types because they had power and wealth and maybe even the excitement of danger. All of that—but especially the wealth—had a magnetic appeal to the ambitious and the careless. Too often, the girls' poor judgment led to misery and pain. One former Ziegfeld showgirl named Kiki Roberts—whom Charlie was sweet on when he was about sixteen (and so was she)—married Jack "Legs" Diamond, who later was gunned down by rival mobsters.

It is amazing to me that in those wild days of prohibition, outlaws were often treated like heroes, particularly when they were rubbing shoulders with the social elite. So many were repelled by the Volstead Act that there was little respect for the law, and consequently the lawless gained a certain appeal. That is what made the speakeasies socially acceptable institutions to a far greater extent than the legal saloons had ever been. Ziegfeld's publicist, Louis Sobol, wrote in *The Longest Street:* "[Prohibition] brought decent women up to the bars for the first time." The pillars of society—distinguished men and women, clergy, and civic dignitaries—gathered in these places and thumbed their noses at the law. In my own experience, the behavior in the clubs was typically proper, drinking (by most) was moderate, and the atmosphere gay and festive. Of course, on occasion, the joints—which Walter Winchell called "Sin Dens"—could get pretty raucous, particularly in the wee small hours of the morning. But by that time, Mama and I weren't around.

Mama never raised any objection to Pearl working in such places, although the hours were very long and the lifestyle troublesome. Mama knew that Pearl was her own person, a strong individualist who was going to lead her own life in the way she chose. So whatever objections Mama might have had, she kept to herself. She was like that, able to accept reality for what it was and go on. It was Evelyn who often criticized the way Pearl was living her life, and perhaps she was far more aware of what was going on than the rest of us. For years, Evelyn tried to change the course of Pearl's life, at times with turbulent confrontations that did no good. She once described Pearl as living a "loose life," but I don't know what facts she based that judgment on. Pearl's marriage was over, and she loved to party. What relationships she had with other men she kept to herself, and I never really knew much about her private life in the twenties. I did know that Pearl was always more adventurous than Mary and I and that she found excitement and pleasure in the hedonistic atmosphere of the clubs. She enjoyed the intimacy of the shows, and the light-hearted bantering with the customers. She always had a host of off-color jokes that she loved to tell, and she could do comical impersonations of all the characters in that world of the night. Her language could get pretty salty at times, and someone once told me she could talk like "a longshoreman." She probably cleaned it up a little around the family, but she never feigned a prim and proper manner. Whatever else she may have been, she was a tirelessly hard worker and must have had great stamina to work so hard night after night.

Pearl was the only one of us who seemed made for the twenties, and I don't know if she was ever happier than she was during that wildly pleasure-seeking era. She became very popular in the clubs, and I'm sure she was well rewarded for her terrific, energetic dancing. The patrons spent huge amounts of money in the high-dollar clubs. Pearl, along with the other dancers, was generously tipped by their well-heeled (and well-lubricated) fans.

After Pearl's work with Ziegfeld ended in 1923, the nightclubs presented the best available opportunity for her to keep dancing on a regular basis—even though she continued to appear as a dancer in Broadway shows when the opportunity arose. Since she never commanded the high salaries that Mary did, the additional income from the clubs permitted her and Dossie to have a higher standard of living and to live near Mary and the rest of us in the upscale neighborhoods. Pearl had a close-knit group of other dancers that she enjoyed being with—they were like a sorority, and among them, they knew everything that was going on in the Times Square district.

The Chantee Club, which featured the very popular George Olsen's band, was a great place to dance and also featured Pearl for a time as their lead dancer. Of all the nightclubs of that day, the Chantee was known for the best dance music in New York. Pearl appreciated the fact that when Texas Guinan left New York to open an El Fey club in Miami, she publicly endorsed the Chantee Club as the best place to go in the city—still looking out for her "little girls."

By 1924, the character of the twenties was well established. That year, Cecil Mack and Jimmy Johnson wrote a song named "Charleston" for a show called *Runnin' Wild,* and a seventeen-year-old black dancer named Mae Barnes introduced to Broadway the dance that really started the Charleston craze. Later, Mae Barnes would be known as a cabaret singer, but in the twenties, she was called by Bill ("Bojangles") Robinson "the greatest living female tap dancer." Soon this energy-charged dance could be seen everywhere, and when such songs as "Five Feet Two, Eyes of Blue" and "Yes Sir, That's My Baby" came along a year or so later, the twenties had the signature songs of the era. Those songs, particularly, out of a host of wonderful songs that decade, truly evoke the spirit and the energy of the twenties.

I loved to dance the Charleston, and I had an admirer, George Bessler, who was in his senior year at Princeton and who shared my enthusiasm for the dance. He would come to New York on Saturday nights, along with his buddy and his buddy's girlfriend. The four of us would cover one or two nightclubs, dancing the Charleston on postage-stamp-size dance floors. The nightclubs were no longer those huge, elegant places—like Rector's—that they had been before prohibition. Typically, the dance floors were just large enough for six or so chorus girls. So when the show was over and the dance music started, the dance floor was packed in no time. If you didn't get kicked while doing the Charleston, you weren't really dancing. Of course, we were young and full of energy, and we moved through the patterns of the Charleston with the freedom of the wild.

Looking back now on that period of my life, in spite of those fun-filled Saturday nights, I feel like I was more of a spectator than a participant in the revelry of the twenties. Of course, it was a time, especially among the young, when there was an unspoken credo to live for the moment, and the pursuit of pleasure—even the glorification of pleasure—was the dominant force in the lives of many young people. But my life was centered around work, and while I loved having a good time, I always seemed to be thinking of tomorrow's performance. Most often, when we did go out, Mama and I were the first to go home. Because of my unhappy and short-lived marriage to Joe Gorham, I was not anxious to develop other relationships with men, so I was quite happy with my spectator role.

I do think that we were aware that it was an exciting time of change. The decade had given new energy to the drive toward equality for females, and many young women had started doing the things that men did: smoking, drinking, pursuing sexual relationships, and generally living freely. In show business, these tendencies were perhaps more exaggerated than in the hinterland, the pleasure-seeking more frenetic and the attitudes more permissive. In Peoria, life may have been different, not so far out and unconventional. But in the showbiz circles of New York, the changes were revolutionary—not unlike the conspicuous social changes that came about among young people in the sixties.

In show business of the twenties, the emphasis on youth and beauty was so overwhelming that many girls looked upon thirty as the end of the road (as it so very often was!). I saw many women performers—girls really—caught up in the sybaritic life of the clubs, their lives in shambles by their mid-twenties. A lot of the sexual promiscuity, I think, can be attributed to the desperation experienced by young women—particularly those in show business—to make the most of their charms before it was too late.

While most of us Eatons were a part of that world, certainly touched by it, and maybe influenced by it in ways we never understood, we were not carried away by it. We always kept one foot in a saner, firmer world. And Mama was largely responsible for that. She kept things balanced and within tolerable limits. We all liked to go out and party, and we too thumbed our noses at the Volstead Act, but for the most part, we always seemed to have enough sense to avoid going over the edge. Pearl was probably the biggest rebel among us, the only one who regularly smoked, drank more than the rest of us, ran with a fast group, and made the clubs her natural habitat.

Pearl's last appearance in the *Follies* came when she went on the road with the *Ziegfeld Follies of 1923*. Although she had not been in the cast of the Broadway production, she was a specialty dancer on the road tour, and she did one of her own dance routines to "Alexander's Ragtime Band." Of course, Berlin's great song had been written many years before (1911) and was borrowed for the road show. Pearl was a big hit, and all the reviews along the way praised her spectacular dance number. That road tour, I believe, was the only time that Pearl was ever listed in the program as a principal, and as it turned out, that tour brought to an end her five-year association with Ziegfeld. I am sure she treasured the great reviews she received for that show.

This was also the year that her daughter Dossie reached school age. During her first six years, Mama often kept Dossie while Pearl worked, but when Pearl started working the nightclubs, she had hired a maid/governess to look after her. Harry was gone most of the time, and—as I've said—he and Pearl were essentially separated and heading for a divorce. The marriage was over years before they actually divorced. With Dossie almost six, Pearl decided it would be in Dossie's best interest for her to go to a boarding school, which would provide good care as well as a good education for her. She found a first-rate boarding school in Manhattan, and Dossie spent all her school years there, although Pearl had her every weekend. Indeed, we all saw her frequently, and Mama always enjoyed having her to care for.

The producer Charles Dillingham saw Pearl when she went on for Marilyn Miller in *Sunny* in 1925, and he was once again taken with her. He hired her for several subsequent roles. One was in a musical called *The City Chap,* with music by Jerome Kern, for which Pearl directed some of the ensemble numbers. The young George Raft, whom she had met at El Fey, was also in that show and actually danced the Charleston. Later, in 1926, Pearl had an important role in *Criss Cross,* in which she understudied Dorothy Stone.

It was after that that Dillingham hired her as New York's first woman stage manager, for his production of *Lucky* at the New Amsterdam, which starred Mary and in which Charlie, now fifteen, also had a role. Dillingham thought a woman stage manager could maintain better decorum backstage and in

Pearl with her daughter, Doris Levant, whom
the family called Dossie. Dossie never followed
us into show business, but she did become an
instructor in a West Coast Arthur Murray studio.

the dressing rooms, and he believed that Pearl was tough enough and skilled enough to stay in control. While the show did not last long, from March 22 to the end of May, Mary received terrific reviews for her performance, and the show received great publicity. It was the first time that Mary's name was alone in lights above the title.

The *New York Times* called it "an opulent musical comedy . . . and [Mary Eaton] surrounded as she was with talent on every side, still managed to stand out from the throng. [It was] Miss Eaton's induction into the sisterhood of musical comedy luminaries." The *Times* reviewer thought it would run as long as *Sally*. In the *Evening World,* E. W. Osborne wrote, "Local astronomers, a merry host of them, scrutinized the new luminary carefully, listed it as a star of the first magnitude, and accepted it as the Mary Eaton." And Stephen Rathbun, in the *New York Sun,* wrote, "It is beautiful, charming, and beguiling . . . Mary Eaton bloomed as a full-fledged star." However, Rathbun thought—except for the dancing—the show was slow paced and the humor below par. Unfortunately, a good many theatergoers agreed with that evaluation of the show.

With book and lyrics by Otto Harback, Bert Kalmar, and Harry Ruby and score by Jerome Kern, and with supporting performances from Walter Catlett, Skeet Gallagher, and Ruby Keeler, it seemed to have everything going for it. Paul Whiteman's orchestra also played in the second act of *Lucky,* including a version of Gershwin's "Rhapsody in Blue." And even though that was a very popular attraction, it was not enough to keep the show going very long. (It seems clear, looking back, that any musical comedy that pauses for "Rhapsody in Blue" in its second act is bound to have problems.) Each evening, the show ran until a quarter to midnight, and even those who liked the show thought that was simply too long. And there was not a compelling story to hold it all together or memorable songs ("Dancing the Devil Away," "When the Bo-Tree Blossoms Again," and "The Same Old Moon"). That same year, Kern was doubtless pouring his genius into *Show Boat,* not into *Lucky.* While it had a lot going for it, the show's tragic flaw was its extravagance. Dillingham tried to outdo Ziegfeld in extravagance and splendor and it proved very costly. The reports were that Dillingham ended up losing $133,000.

During the run, Charlie got acquainted with Bing Crosby, who was one of the three Rhythm Boys with the Whiteman orchestra, and they would visit each other in Hollywood in the years to come. It was Charlie who introduced Dixie Lee to Bing on a movie set in Hollywood in 1929, when Charlie was filming *Harmony at Home.*

While it was Mary whose name was in lights in 1926, Pearl received a great deal of publicity that year. One highly visible appearance involved her singing a song to the Mayor, Jimmy Walker, at the annual "Old-Timers Night" sponsored by the Newspapers' Club. The song was called "The Newspaper Blues," and of course, every newspaper in New York gave it good coverage. The selection of Pearl to do that routine may have resulted from the frequency with which she was seen by members of the press who visited the nightclubs. They knew that Pearl could do the song with the appropriate comical touches and the burlesque-style teasing that the situation called for. Pearl loved being a clown and putting someone on—even the mayor of New York. It was definitely her time.

I've always found it interesting that while Mary was the star, it was Pearl's caricature that was hung on the wall of Sardi's in that famous gallery of Broadway luminaries—a caricature that now resides in the Library of the Performing Arts at Lincoln Center.

Beautiful Mary

CHAPTER EIGHT

"OUR MARY"

Having starred in three *Follies,* Mary had achieved real celebrity status by 1923, and the press had an item about her almost every day—or so it seemed. Those supermarket tabloids of today may be more irresponsible than the New York papers in the twenties, but some still refer to that earlier time as the heyday of yellow journalism. Even in those days, reporters were constantly pursuing celebrities and speculating about their private lives, and writing stories that very often had little regard for reality.

The press started speculating that Mary was about to marry a wealthy businessman named Otto Morris. Mary had been dating Otto for some time, and they were often seen together in the fashionable clubs and restaurants. Then one night, she made headlines by getting a speeding ticket while driving Otto's car—a Cunningham, which he later gave to Mary—across the Queensboro Bridge at the outrageous speed of forty miles per hour. For months, the press presented a picture of Mary as a kind of Zelda Fitzgerald character, the fun-loving, liberated, uninhibited star who loved cars, high speed, and wealthy suitors. And while she did little to dispel this view, we Eatons all knew that behind those glamorous and adventurous public images was really a very innocent, ingenuous girl. She trusted almost everyone—including the press—to the point of naiveté.

The Mary I knew was quite traditional in her attitudes and very much "ladylike" in her behavior. She was incredibly hard working, continuing her ballet and voice studies, and taking very good care of herself. She rarely had a drink, although she might nurse a cocktail throughout the evening. On occasion, she would accept a cigarette offered her, but she didn't really smoke (even though she did advertisements for Lucky Strike). To the distress of many of her suitors, she avoided sexual involvements to the point of being called "icy." Many years later and after my sister's death, a review in the *Detroit News* of the play *Lend Me Your Ear* described one of the characters as "Mary Eatonish, incredibly pure." I thought at the time that yes, that was the Mary I knew and remembered so well—not from the characters she played, but just from the way she was.

In that fabulous time, there were those around who could not spend or throw away their money fast enough, especially when it was in praise of beautiful stars. Mary's *Follies* costar Raymond Hitchcock gave her a Marmon sports car—the second car given to her. Other than the two cars and the beautiful piano, she received a mink coat, a Persian lamb coat, about three dozen pairs of satin-and-gold slippers, paintings, etchings, Chinese lamps and vases, orchids by the truckload, a pinkie ring with sapphires and diamonds, a diamond bracelet, and Lord knows what else. Mary's attitude about all that was peculiar. It never moved her a great deal, she simply thought that was all something that went with her position as a Ziegfeld star. And if men wanted to anoint her in that way, she felt in no way obligated to make an emotional response. The generosity of her benefactors never earned them a significant role in her life. What some may have perceived as egotistical in her reactions was more accurately innocence—the innocence of a little Alice in a Broadway wonderland.

As Pearl once observed about Mary's response to her ardent admirers, "Mary never vested passion into anything other than the stage." Even several years later, Mary was quoted in the *New York American* as saying, "I don't know what [romantic] love is like. I've never been in love. I hope . . . that love never catches up on me." Well, in time, of course, it did, but that's another story.

Mary left the *Follies* after the road show of 1922 because Ziegfeld had delayed signing a new contract with her. That delay was presumably because he was having problems with Marilyn Miller, who wanted to cancel her Ziegfeld contract to move on (or to get away from his ardent pursuit). The press reported that this was out of Marilyn's jealousy about Mary's stardom, something which both Mary and Marilyn denied. They also joked about it and remained good friends. Ziegfeld had promised to put Mary in a new musical comedy, after she had successfully replaced Marilyn Miller in *Sally*, but he had some misgivings about a show that Eddie Cantor was pushing him to produce. When he reluctantly relented and agreed to produce the show, he signed Mary to be featured in *Kid Boots*, with Eddie Cantor as the star.

It was Papa who negotiated her contract. While Papa was never very involved in the show business affairs of the family, he took a keen interest in Mary's career. The rest of us always talked about Mary being Papa's favorite, and that was probably true. Beyond their father-daughter closeness, they were kindred spirits in ways difficult for me to express in words. They were both very inward and private people, and they rarely shared with others their innermost thoughts and feelings. They also shared a kind of babes-in-the-woods vulnerability that would become more evident in the years to come.

Largely at Evelyn's insistence—and she could be very insistent—Papa had negotiated Mary's previous contracts with Ziegfeld, and he did the same with the three-year contract for *Kid Boots*. As Mary's stardom grew, Papa had become increasingly fearful of her being exploited by the producers, and he was determined to protect her interests. Mama was quite willing for him to look after Mary's affairs, particularly when it had become obvious that Mary was going to be a very big star and things were getting more complicated. When she was offered the role in *Kid Boots*, Papa insisted that Mary be listed as a costar with Cantor, but as Herbert G. Goldman points out in *Banjo Eyes*, his recently published biography of Eddie Cantor, Cantor "categorically refused [to give Mary star status] but finally consented to Eaton's being featured." They all agreed to the wording: Eddie Cantor in *Kid Boots* with Mary Eaton. But then Papa insisted that Mary's name be put in lights the same size as Eddie Cantor's, and Ziegfeld agreed. That was written into her contract, and Papa (to the delight of the press) even climbed a stepladder to measure the size of the letters on the marquee of the new Earl Carroll Theater to make sure that the contract was honored. When the show opened on December 31, 1923, a critic for *Time Magazine* wrote, "Mary Eaton's name is prominently displayed in the electric illumination above the playhouse." Papa was very proud of himself.

Ziegfeld had tried to get a provision in the contract that Mary would not get married while under contract to him. Mary initially refused to sign, and she became public in her opposition to such a restraint. It was a matter of principle with Mary. The press was full of stories about her disagreement with Ziegfeld on that issue. Nevertheless, the contract was signed with or without such a marriage clause. I do not recall which. Mary was advised that the clause was not legally binding anyway, so it became an insignificant matter. The contract was a terrific deal for Mary. She received $2,000 a week, far more than she expected and clearly a top star's salary at that time.

For both Cantor and Mary, *Kid Boots* became a long-running success—success that rewarded Cantor for his singular persistence in getting Ziegfeld's support. The story has often been told that Ziegfeld, after watching an early rehearsal of *Kid Boots*, decided not to go ahead with the show. Eddie Cantor, who along with an associate, William Anthony McGuire, had come up with the idea for the show—pleaded with Ziegfeld to give it a chance. Cantor believed that his own strength and incredible energy level as a performer could carry the show. Grudgingly, Ziegfeld let the show open in Detroit, where the audience response was so positive and the box office so strong that he not only brought it to New York, he added $20,000 in sets and new costumes to dress up the opening act. To make up for that, the best tickets to *Kid Boots* on Broadway cost $16.50—a new high for Broadway. *Kid Boots* ran on Broadway for fourteen months before going on the road, and altogether had a total of over one thousand performances.

I don't think Cantor ever got over sharing the marquee with Mary, and while he was publicly kind to her, he never showed any personal warmth or friendliness to her or any of the Eatons. Years later when he wrote about *Kid Boots* in his memoirs, he never even mentioned Mary's name. Gratuitously, in his curtain speeches, he would often say, "*Kid Boots* is a sweet and simple show. Mary Eaton is sweet and I am simple." That was his only public acknowledgment of Mary's contribution. Cantor's biographer says that Cantor referred to Mary as "lighthearted"—but there were no words about her talent and no compliments about her performance.

Cantor—now commanding his own show—began to manifest a huge ego and became a backstage tyrant. He never treated Mary as an equal or even a professional colleague, and although they were together for many months on the road, he never socialized with her. Nevertheless, the show did a great deal for Mary's career, keeping her near the top of Broadway and enhancing her celebrity. When the show ran over into the next season, it was moved from the Earl Carroll Theater to the Selwyn, where it ran until the spring of 1925. After that, it was on the road for almost a year. It was reported that for Flo Ziegfeld, it made more money than any of his *Follies*.

Kid Boots had Cantor in the role of a canny golf pro who was also a bootlegger, and as the plot developed, he became a matchmaker. It was Cantor's first musical comedy (so-called book musical), and he dominated the action throughout with his inimitable style of song and dance and his great physicality and mobility, prancing around the stage with incredible energy. Initially, Cantor did not have great songs to sing. Over the course of the run, some of the unremarkable songs were dropped and new ones were tried. As it turned out, the best song for Cantor was not added until late in the road tour; that was "Dinah." Then sometime later, after Jolson rejected a song called "If You Knew Suzy," Cantor tried it and liked it, and it became his signature song.

While the play is remembered as Cantor's play, Mary clearly received star treatment. She had two pretty songs, "If Your Heart's in the Game" and "Someone Loves You After All," which she sang with Harry Fender. The critics were generous in their praise of her. One unidentified review in Mary's

Mary, 1926

scrapbook reported, "She danced with airy grace . . . as delicate as a Dresden doll . . . as sweet and pretty a ballerina as ever tiptoed her way into the heart of Broadway audiences." *Time* called it "the best musical of a five year period. . . . Cantor is inordinately funny, [and Mary Eaton's] fine flavor of respectability made an excellent foil for Cantor's semi-Rabelaisian style of turbulence. . . . The only objection that can be raised is the practical impossibility of getting tickets." Most of the critics remarked about Mary's stunning beauty, set off by the gorgeous costuming of the show. In one scene, she wore a pink tutu and an Empress Eugenie hat, with a long green plume that swirled when she did her distinctive pirouettes. It was a picture of her in that costume that appeared in the local papers of cities all over the country where the road show appeared. One critic said that she had "limbs so perfectly pretty" that only two others he had seen could match her—Marilyn Miller and Anna Pavlova. Mary loved being put in that company. Walter Winchell, writing in the *Vaudeville News*, paid Mary his compliment in this way:

> [*Kid Boots* is] a delicious musical comedy. . . . F. Ziegfeld produced it. We liked it and Eddie Cantor, Mary Eaton, Jobyna Howland, Ethlyn Terry, Harry Fender, Mary Eaton, Olsen's Orchestra, Mary Eaton, Beth Beri, Mary Eaton, Marie Callahan, Harland Dixon, Mary Eaton, Mary Eaton, and not forgetting Mary Eaton.

According to an article in her scrapbook, Mary was later quoted as saying, after her long run of successful shows, "I began to believe I'd been born in a bed of four-leaf clovers with a necklace of horse shoes around my throat and a cushion of rabbits' feet." I don't know whether Mary said that or if it was dreamed up by some press agent, but it is true that Mary was elated with her good fortune and the bright prospects for the future.

Very few performers of that day could boast of the uninterrupted successes that Mary had enjoyed as dancer, singer, and actress. But it was hardly luck. No one worked harder than Mary to improve continually. Even after she was well established as a star, she was taking three dance lessons a week with Ivan Tarasoff and three singing lessons with a Mr. Jeanette, and practicing both between her eight performances a week.

Mary's greatly enhanced celebrity brought her added opportunities and obligations. Mary had been appearing in newspaper and magazine ads for several products—Life Savers, Lucky Strike cigarettes, Maybelline, and the Fiat Sedan Deluxe, just to name a few. It was common to pick up a magazine and see a full-page picture of her endorsing something. Her picture seemed to be everywhere in the United States, and she was recognized wherever she went. She was the one Eaton who fulfilled our mother's ambition to have famous children.

When *Kid Boots* finally closed on Broadway, it moved to Boston for several weeks. Then the cast had a six-week hiatus before moving the show to Chicago. Mary was at the point of exhaustion and wanted very much to get away for a restful vacation. So she suggested to me that we go on a European vacation. We had all been leading pretty hectic lives. I had been on the road with *The Sap,* and I was certainly ready to get away for a while. Mary and I agreed that we would take Mama and go to Europe for six weeks, sharing Mama's expenses.

In July of 1925, we sailed cabin class on the *Aquitania* and thoroughly enjoyed the luxurious treatment accorded us. We met a fellow voyager, Edna Ferber, who had a play on Broadway called *Minnick,* which she had written with George S. Kaufman. While not many remember that show, she was just getting started. Her next play with Kaufman, *Dinner at Eight,* would be a big hit of the 1931 season. Of course, she wrote the novel on which the great Jerome Kern–Oscar Hammerstein musical *Show Boat* was based in 1927. That show, produced by Florenz Ziegfeld, changed forever the Broadway musical.

We developed a delightful onboard friendship with Edna Ferber, and with her charm and good humor, she added a lot to that fun-filled, restful crossing. For five memorable days, we enjoyed the luxury of our shipboard idleness. We were all carefree and relaxed, never tiring of each other's company. Mama would say in the midst of some pleasurable moment that we had surely come a long way from Rhode Island Avenue in Washington, D.C. Indeed, we had.

When we arrived in Paris, we were entertained by our handsome boxer-friend, Georges Carpentier. He went to great lengths to be a wonderful host, showing us Paris nightlife. We went to elegant restaurants, theaters, and night-clubs. I recall that at one posh nightclub, both Mary and I danced the tango with Georges, causing quite a stir in the crowd. It was all very rich, gay, and truly memorable. During the day, we went to all the museums and well-known tourist attractions. After an unforgettable week, we continued on our grand tour of Europe, first to Rome, then to Venice (which we loved, particularly at night, with the twinkling lanterns on the gondolas and all the light reflections in the canals), then to Toledo and Como, and to Interlaken in the Swiss Alps, and to beautiful flower-bedecked Geneva, and back to Paris, where we shopped for clothes. It was an unforgettable vacation. We did it all in grand style—the best of everything. That was the way we wanted it for once in our lives. As we sailed home on the S.S. *Paris,* standing on the deck and gazing out over the indigo blue water, we reflected on our good fortune and our great success. We really did feel blessed.

Mary returned for the road tour of *Kid Boots,* several months of which were to be in Chicago. After three months in the Windy City, she became ill with pneumonia and had to be replaced for several weeks. Ziegfeld, who had always taken a paternal interest in Mary, insisted that she go to Palm Beach to recuperate, which she did. In those days, Palm Beach was the choice resting place for celebrities, so while there Mary spent time with Rudolf Friml, who had written the music for *The Royal Vagabond;* Will Rogers, whom she knew well; and Al Jolson, who had left *Big Boy* because of illness. A rested and recuperated Mary rejoined *Kid Boots* in Milwaukee for the remainder of the tour.

Mary was forever grateful to Ziegfeld for his kindness toward her. He had always been generous to Mary, not only in her contracts but also in the public praise he accorded her. During the run of *Kid Boots,* he wrote the following for the *Times:*

> [Mary Eaton] came to me after a very brief experience as a child actress and started to work in the "Follies." . . . She had already been trained as a dancer, so that when I created a special opportunity for her she acquitted herself with such extraordinary brilliance that her future great success was assured. . . . But I looked further ahead and higher for her even than she did for herself. I outlined a course of study for her, to which she applied herself diligently. It included dancing, voice, culture, diction, art, literature, and languages. She went from one position to another with me, rising steadily until she became the principal feature dancer and one of the "Follies" stars. Success did not go to her head, but seemed only to make her more persistent and tireless in her efforts. Today she is the feature supporting artist with Eddie Cantor in "Kid Boots" and is recognized as one of the greatest artists of her type in the world.

It would not be long before the New York critics began to use the phrase "Our Mary" to describe my sister. She was often compared with Mary Pickford, who was "Hollywood's Mary," so the phrase "Our Mary" just grew out of the comparison and we Eatons found it an endearing expression of the esteem and affection in which Mary was held. The adjective most often used in the hundreds of articles and reviews written about her in city papers all over the country—many of which I still have packed into boxes—was "lovely." "Lovely Mary Eaton" was a phrase so often used that it was almost like a name.

During the New York run of *Kid Boots*, Mary made a movie directed by Sam Wood at Astoria, Long Island. The movie, *His Children's Children,* was warmly received, and Mary, in her role of "baby vamp," drew the usual favorable comments. One critic wrote, "When her beautiful face appeared on the screen, there was a gasp in the audience." Another said that Mary proved she was more than a dancer: "She can act." Mary was enthusiastic about making the movie. She was quoted as saying, "I was more thrilled when I went before the camera than I was on my first appearance on stage."

When Cantor was asked to make a movie version (silent, of course) of *Kid Boots* for Paramount, he agreed to do so, but Mary, so far as I know, was not asked to join him. The script was entirely rewritten, and the final movie version was only vaguely related to the stage version.

In 1926, Mary replaced Marilyn Miller in *Sunny* for the road tour. Marilyn was ill and did not want to continue in the role. So once again, Mary took over for her, and she received the customary plaudits for her spectacular dancing and her lovely stage presence. *Sunny* marked the end of Mary's stage association with Ziegfeld; she would go on to star in shows for other producers. First, there was *Lucky,* which involved Pearl and Charlie, and then her biggest hit, *The Five O'Clock Girl,* which I'll tell about later. She would return to Ziegfeld in 1929 to star in his first movie, *Glorifying the American Girl,* which fortunately has preserved on film—now videotape—Mary's dancing and singing.

FOUR ON BROADWAY

Brother Joe returned from Washington in 1924 to live with the family while completing high school at DeWitt Clinton High in New York. With Joe's return, there were six of us living in that wonderful (but not spacious) apartment at the Congress. It was not really large enough for all of us. Joe and Charlie slept in one bedroom, Mary and I in the other, and Mama slept on the couch in the living room. Papa, who at that time was working part-time as a proofreader for the *New York Times,* would come home in the early morning and sleep in the bed that Joe and Charlie had slept in during the night. This went on for some time, but there was growing dissatisfaction not only with this inconvenient arrangement, but in the strained relationship between Papa and Mama. While there were few conspicuous displays of hostility between them, it was pretty obvious that their love and affection had cooled. So Papa moved into a room at the York Hotel, and while we still saw him often and he was frequently there for family meals, he essentially lived his own life away from home. He was only fifty then, and while none of us could ever imagine it, we never knew whether he ever sought the company of another woman.

Charlie was becoming a seasoned actor. At ten, he had appeared in a Shubert production called *Spices of 1921,* and when he was twelve, he went into *Peter Pan* with Marilyn Miller, who had temporarily left Ziegfeld to work with Dillingham. During that time, Charlie remembers being asked by the wonderful actor Pat Rooney Jr. how old he was. Charlie said, "Twelve." Rooney said, "I thought I heard you say backstage the other day that you were fourteen." Charlie replied, "That was just for the benefit of the women in the cast." That was typical behavior for Charlie. He was a veteran at twelve, and he could hold his own with older and more experienced performers. His wit and sophistication—along with his acting ability—helped to make him a very busy young actor.

During this same year, he was teamed with a ten-year-old actress named Miriam Batista to do the balcony scene from *Romeo and Juliet* for the vaudeville circuit. We were all jubilant when their act was accepted on the bill for a week at the Palace Theater—the one and only Palace, with the best entertainers and the most discriminating audiences in New York. How Mama got them onto the bill at the Palace I don't really know, but it was quite an achievement. To appear at the Palace meant a great deal to one's career—a make-or-break affair—or in Joe Laurie Jr.'s rather extravagant words from his book, *Vaudeville:* "When an actor made good at the Palace, he was knighted with the golden sword and admitted to the inner court circles of the aristocrats and blue bloods of the kingdom. . . ." That is the way we felt, so naturally we were all very excited about Charlie's opportunity.

The vaudeville acts at the Palace in today's language would be called "G-rated"; no profanity, vulgarity, or any hint of immorality was permitted. It was a family show. It was often said that vaudeville was wholesome, the revue was titillating, and burlesque was dirty. According to Laurie, a sign that appeared backstage at the Palace at that time read: "Remember this theater caters to ladies and gentlemen and children. Vulgarity will not be tolerated. Check with manager before using any material you have any doubt about. Don't use words: hell, damn, devil, cockroach, spit, etc." That would all change by the end of the twenties, as the ban on vulgarity was more and more relaxed, but for a long time, the management took it very seriously.

Charlie and Miriam Batista "opened cold"—no out-of-town trial run—and they were a big hit. Both received rave notices for their acting. The critics were particularly taken with the quality of Charlie's voice, which they found remarkable for a twelve-year-old boy. And Miriam was faultless in her delivery. On Tuesday—after a Monday opening—they were moved from third to fifth position on the bill. That was regarded as a prize spot—next to the last act before intermission. After their week at the Palace, they were held over for a second week, which was followed by a successful road tour of vaudeville theaters for several weeks. Many decades later, Charlie still remembers those famous lines and will break into a sonorous recitation at the slightest cue:

But, soft! What light through yonder window breaks?
It is the east, and Juliet is the sun!
Arise, fair sun, and kill the envious moon,
Who is already sick and pale with grief,
That thou her maid are far more fair than she . . .

After the vaudeville tour, Charlie went on the road, in a play called *The Naked Man,* with Henry Hull and Anne Morrison. He was now being billed as "the leading boy actor in the country." Of course, Mama always went along with her "baby boy."

Charlie goes dramatic.

The Awakening, Broadway play,
1918—age seven

Silent movie Peter Ibbetsen,
1921—age nine

Romeo and Juliet, Palace Theatre,
1923—age twelve—with ten-year-
old Miriam Batista

Created role of "Andy Hardy"
in play *Skidding* on Broadway,
1928—age seventeen

It was about this time that we met William S. Hart, whom everyone called Bill. He often came to our apartment for social gatherings or just dropped by when he was in New York. He looked amazingly like our father, and we often joked about that. He was the number one Western star in silent films and probably the highest paid actor working in Hollywood. He started writing, directing, and producing his own movies, making his masterpiece *Tumbleweeds* in 1925, when he must have been in his mid-fifties. He had a wonderful voice, having started in show business on the stage as a serious actor playing Romeo, Macbeth, Iago, and Messala in *Ben Hur.* He first did *The Squaw Man* on the stage, before Cecil B. DeMille made a movie of it. And the same is true for *The Virginian.* In 1912, he had starred on Broadway in *The Trail of the Lonesome Pine,* which was his last New York play before starting silent movies. He certainly could have made it in talking pictures, but by that time, he was tired of movies and never did any sound pictures. My guess is that he didn't like the idea of "older men" roles.

He took Mary out to dinner on a number of occasions, but as usual, Mary did not give him much encouragement, and there was never a romance between them. He was old enough to be her father, but it was very obvious that he was enamored of her. Even when he knew he would never have a romantic relationship with Mary, he continued to visit us on occasion, and I can recall wonderful conversations with him. Mama was very fond of him and thought him the perfect gentleman, and Charlie sort of idolized him as the great American hero. He was a bright and thoughtful man who was a great storyteller. He gave me inscribed copies of the two books of poetry he had written, which I still have in my library as treasured possessions.

During the 1924–25 season, we were all busy on Broadway, and Mary, Pearl, and I were appearing in different productions in three adjoining theaters. Mary was at the Selwyn in *Kid Boots,* Pearl was at the Times Square in *Annie Dear* with Billie Burke (the wife of Ziegfeld), and I was at the Apollo in *The Sap* with Raymond Hitchcock. Charlie was just down the street in the revival of *Peter Pan* with Marilyn Miller. I don't know if that is a record—four family members in four different plays on Broadway at the same time—but it does seem to be a very rare occurrence. Although not in adjoining theaters, it all happened again in the 1927–28 season, with Mary in *The Five O'Clock Girl* with Oscar Shaw, Pearl in *She's My Baby* with Bea Lillie, and me in *Excess Baggage,* where I met and became a friend of lovable Frank McHugh. Charlie was in his biggest Broadway hit *Skidding,* in the role of Andy Hardy.

During those years, we would always have midnight dinners at home with Mama, Mary, Joe, Charlie, and me. Papa was never there at that hour, and we only rarely brought a guest with us. Mama would cook for us, and she always included some especially delicious dish that was a family favorite. That is what we looked forward to after we finished at the theater, eating Mama's great food and visiting about the events of the day. None of us went out often after the theater, except perhaps on weekends, and none of us wanted to miss Mama's cooking and the chance to reflect on the day's activities.

When Pearl left her show, Dillingham hired her for *City Chap,* both to dance and to work as production assistant to David Bennet in staging the ensemble dance numbers. Irene Dunne and Betty Compton were getting started on Broadway, and they were in the show. The star was Richard (Skeet) Gallagher, and the music was by Jerome Kern. By this time, Pearl was well known for her work on the production side, choreographing, teaching, and dance directing.

In 1925, Mary and I went on the road with our shows following the Broadway run. I loved touring with Raymond Hitchcock, whom everyone called Hitchy. He was a great friend of us all and had made a name for himself with many Broadway performances, including several appearances as a principal in the *Follies.* Earlier, he had been a producer as well as an actor, and he hired Cole Porter to write the music for a show called *Hitchy Koo of 1919,* for which Porter wrote his first hit song, "Old Fashioned Garden." Hitchy had been very attracted to Mary—as apparently all men were—and, indeed, he had given her a car (a sporty Marmon) when they were working together in the *Follies.* For me, he was a wonderfully entertaining companion on the road. He was always the gentleman, and our relationship was about as platonic as a brother-sister relationship (like Hart, he was about the age of my father), but we had great times together. He was a well-seasoned showbiz veteran, and he was so relaxed—what today we would call laid-back—that nothing seemed to bother him. We drove in his car from town to town and often on roads that were far less than adequate. It was at times quite an adventure, motoring through the night in all kinds of weather, hoping more than knowing we were heading in the right direction. I remember late one night—it was well after midnight and as usual the roads weren't that good—we almost hit a cow lumbering along in the middle of the road. Hitchy, as he frantically swerved to miss the cow, said, "There she is! Street walking again!"

Later that year, Pearl took a dancing role in the *Earl Carroll Vanities,* in a year in which Carroll tried something new. He built a supper club atmosphere in the theater, putting tables into the orchestra section, and had the performers greet and usher people to their tables. It was a natural for Pearl, who had done so much nightclub work, interacting with the audience. With her gift of gab and instinctive sense of humor, she could work the crowd very well. The show received mixed reviews, but Pearl received great notices for her dancing and probably the greatest visibility she ever had as a performer. She was quoted in the papers as saying, "Maybe one day they will refer to Mary as Pearl Eaton's sister. You know it has always been quite the other way around." With regard to that 1925 edition of the *Vanities,* the *New York Evening Journal* said, "It seems that no musical comedy or revue is produced nowadays without an Eaton girl in the company. The distaff side of the famous theatrical family is represented by three beautiful and talented members, Mary, Pearl, and Doris."

The fact that Pearl never achieved stardom must have disappointed her, because she worked very hard and had great talent, but her disappointment was never expressed as envy or hostility toward Mary. The two really remained very close, and Pearl often worked with Mary throughout the twenties on dance ideas and techniques. Mary often said that Pearl would have become a star had she not taken time out at a crucial moment in her career to have her baby. I don't think that is true, but what seems very clear to me is that Mary was closer to Pearl than to her other sisters and brothers, and that closeness would continue until Mary's death in 1948.

After we finished the road tour of *The Sap,* I went into a show on Broadway called *No Other Girl.* Bert Kalmar and Harry Ruby did the music, and I had primarily a dancing role. My dance partner was William Sully, who was a well-known eccentric dancer. We had a number of dances together that turned out to be real showpieces. One critic called me "an educated exponent of syncopation." That experience was further evidence for me that I was born to be a dancer—not an actress or a singer, but a dancer. The critic Courtney Terrett wrote, "Doris Eaton is swell when she is allowed to dance her own style." Another critic wrote, "Doris Eaton is dancing her way to stardom." (I wish.)

It was probably my success in *No Other Girl* that led to what would be my biggest role on Broadway, with Al Jolson in *Big Boy,* which was a popular show primarily because of the superstar status of Al Jolson. I was not in the original cast, but I replaced the leading lady a few months after the show opened.

The show had started at the Winter Garden, but Jolson became ill and took a hiatus for several weeks, before reopening the show at the Forty-fourth Street Theater. When he first appeared on stage at the reopening, he received a nine-minute standing ovation. He was probably the only performer in New York who could have done that. The *Times* said, "He is more vibrant and magnetic than ever." Alexander Woolcott had written extravagantly about the earlier Winter Garden opening: "Jolson was magnificent . . . capable of rocking the Winter Garden with an ancient laughter and flooding it with the rue and the tenderness of an ancient art."

Jolson totally dominated every show he was in. Whatever the plot, it was simply an excuse to get him on stage. In this flimsy story, he was a jockey and stable boy, and he played, as always, in blackface. His big song was "How I Love You," by Lew Brown and Cliff Friend. Later, they added "Nobody but Fannie," which was a nice song, and they kept moving songs in and out, which does not happen with today's musicals after they open. While I received some favorable mention for my dancing, it was hard for anyone other than Jolson to be noticed.

From our earliest days in New York, Jolson knew my whole family, and he could not have been nicer to me. He had a well-earned reputation for being a highly egotistical person. He knew he was great and never kept that a secret. But in my experience, he was a good team player—maybe I should say team captain—and he got along well most of the time with the company, although he rarely spent time with any of us between shows. He did have a furious temper, and I saw him on occasion tear into a performer mercilessly for not doing something right. There was never any doubt that he was the star and clearly in charge, and he was a demanding taskmaster. If he thought the cast was getting sloppy, he would call a rehearsal to get things back to the high standard he demanded. He was the king, and the king could do no wrong.

When we took the show to Chicago's Apollo Theater, Mary and Eddie Cantor were in town at the Woods Theater in *Kid Boots*. Mary and I shared a suite in a hotel, and we enjoyed being with each other between shows. Jolson and Cantor had their rooms in another apartment hotel, and very often they would get together for a late dinner and to talk—they were great friends and also jealous rivals. Cantor idolized Joley—as he called him—and as someone said, the two got along so well because they both idolized the same person. After three months in Chicago, Mary became ill and left the show for a time. And coincidentally, in time both Cantor and Jolson had to leave their roles because of illness. They both expended so much energy during each night's performance, it's a wonder they lasted as long as they did.

Of course, Jolson went on to become a showbiz legend. In 1946, Jolson's career was reborn with *The Jolson Story*. It was a wonderful movie, with Larry Parks playing Jolson and Jolson himself on the soundtrack singing his memorable songs: "California Here I Come," "April Showers," "Swanee," and so many more. Jolson, for a whole new generation, became once more a major star. And in the mid-1990s, the biggest hit of the season in London was a musical play called *Jolson,* and another generation discovered those same wonderful songs.

CHAPTER TEN

COAST TO COAST

Following the road show of *Big Boy,* I returned to the West Coast to explore new opportunities there. I was a little bored with the quality of roles being offered to me in New York, and maybe I still had some of my youthful ambition to become a dramatic actress. I thought that I might be able to get more interesting work in the movies.

In those days, everyone going from New York to California did so on the train. You took the Twentieth Century to Chicago and changed to the Santa Fe Chief for the trip to Los Angeles. Over the years, I made that three-night trip several times, and I always had books to read along the way.

On the first day after I arrived in Hollywood, I was walking down Sunset Boulevard and I ran into Larry Ceballos, the well-known dancer and choreographer, who had directed the dances in one of my shows in New York. He said, "Doris, what in the world are you doing here?" I told him that I had come to Hollywood looking for work, and he said, "You are just the one I need." He explained that he was putting together a new show for the *Hollywood Music Box Revue,* produced by Carter DeHaven and called *Fancies.* The Irish tenor Morton Downey was starring, and they needed a lead dancer.

Well, that turned out to be one of the pivotal experiences of my life. Nacio Herb Brown, who would soon become one of the top movies songwriters (usually teamed with lyricist Arthur Freed), wrote a special dance number for me, the "Doll Dance," and it became a favorite of audiences. I continued to do the dance for years, and my picture appeared on the cover of the sheet music for the next two decades. As a matter of fact, I actually wrote the lyrics for "Doll Dance," which was originally just an instrumental. While my lyrics were published with the sheet music, I never received credit for my work. Herb Brown got the credit, a slight that I never protested.

I also had a dance number called "The Evolution of the Charleston," which traced the development of the Charleston down through the ages and involved the dance known as the black bottom, which always brought audiences to their feet. The dancing in the show involved everything I had learned, from tap, to buck and wing, to soft-shoe, to the shimmy and the Charleston.

And it was for me an important success. The critic for the *Los Angeles Examiner* wrote about me, "She was a wow!"

Nacio Herb Brown was thirty years old and I was 22, and once again, I was swept off my feet. Maybe it had something to do with the air in California. This time, however, the love affair did not lead to marriage—through no fault of my own, I must confess. We had an ongoing relationship for several years, and I felt certain we would get married. Without really declaring his intentions, Herb certainly implied that we would. But it didn't happen. I was crazy about him, and I guess a little foolish. The only time I ever lied to get out of a performance was when I claimed to have a sprained ankle and could not dance so that I could spend an uninterrupted weekend with Herb at a hotel in San Francisco. Isn't that ridiculous?

Herb was a very attractive, clever man, who was fun and interesting to be with. He was a natty dresser and always immaculately groomed, with a thin little mustache and dark, glowing eyes. He was quite a guy. He had started out running a popular menswear store in Los Angeles and investing his money wisely in real estate. He made a great deal of money in the land boom in and around Beverly Hills and was composing because he loved doing it rather than needing it as a way of making a living. Herb and Arthur Freed wrote such great songs as "Singin' in the Rain," "Temptation," "You Were Meant for Me," "Pagan Love Song," "You Are My Lucky Star," "All I Do Is Dream of You," and many others.

At the time I met him, he was in the process of getting a divorce from his first wife, and he often had with him his small son, who was called Sonny. The three of us often went to Herb's beach house at Malibu, and Sonny and I became quite close. I recall that after the divorce, Sonny's mother took him with her to Florida, and Herb broke down and cried inconsolably, hating to see Sonny being taken so far away. He saw Sonny as often as he could, and I think they continued a good and loving relationship.

After our relationship ended, Herb would go on to marry three other women—maybe altogether five marriages—before his death in 1964. I did not see him during the last twenty-five or so years of his life. Sonny told me later that he had once complained to his father, "Dad, you always marry the wrong woman." He also told me that he wished I were his mother. Sonny and I continued to visit by phone over the years until his recent death in California.

Well, to confess all, there have been only two great loves in my life: my husband of fifty years, Paul Travis (who died in June of 2000, at age 99), and—for a time long ago—Nacio Herb Brown. Although he did not write much music after 1950, the great Hollywood classic *Singin' in the Rain* (1952), which starred the late Gene Kelly and was produced by Arthur Freed, featured the early music of Brown and Freed. *Singin' in the Rain* had only one new song, "Make 'em Laugh," which made a bigger star of Donald O'Conner, who did one of the most engaging and novel dance acts ever filmed. According to Michael Feinstein, in *Nice Work if You Can Get It,* Herb Brown was widely criticized for writing a song that was too much a copy of Cole Porter's "Be a Clown" (written in 1949), even though Porter never made an issue of it.

Curiously enough, another song had been written twenty-five years earlier for Fanny Brice by Blanche Merrill and Edwin Weber, with the identical title, "Make 'em Laugh." Here the "borrowing" seems even more direct:

> If you want to knock 'em dead
> Make 'em laugh, Fanny, make 'em laugh . . .
> Everybody in the town knows in your heart
> You're just a clown,
> So make 'em laugh, Fanny, make 'em laugh.
> (See Barbara W. Grossman's *Funny Woman:*
> *The Life and Times of Fanny Brice*).

I don't know who borrowed what from whom, but anyway, the Brown and Freed song with Donald O'Conner's dancing made for one of the great moments of slapstick dancing ever put on film.

As long as we are on the subject of "Singin' in the Rain," I might as well tell you that—believe it or not—I was the singer who introduced that song in the *Hollywood Music Box Revue* in 1929, and I have the program and the newspaper clippings to prove it. Herb Brown wrote that song for me to do in a special dance production number before its inclusion in a motion picture later that year called *Hollywood Revue,* in which the song was sung by Cliff Edwards. "Ukulele Ike" Edwards is listed in music archives as having introduced the song, obviously because of the movie. The truth is, I sang it every night for seventeen weeks in the 1929 *Hollywood Music Box Revue.*

Actually, the song did not attract much attention at the time of the movie, even though the movie itself was nominated for an Academy Award as best picture. The *Times* movie critic wrote simply that the song was "pleasingly delivered and charmingly staged." That same year, Herb and Arthur Freed did the music for the film *The Broadway Melody,* which went on to win the Academy Award as best picture of the year (1929) in the second year of the

Academy Awards. Herb actually appeared in that movie's opening scene as a piano player. He played the title song, which was sung by the star of the movie, Charles King. It was MGM's first talking picture, and they advertised it intensively: "ALL TALKING, ALL SINGING, ALL DANCING!" It was a huge success. *The Broadway Melody* was remade in 1936, 1938, and 1940, each time featuring the dancing of Eleanor Powell. In the 1940 version, the original music was discarded for the music of Cole Porter (including "I Concentrate on You" and "Begin the Beguine"—neither of which was written specifically for the movie). Still, the 1929 version is the one most readily available on video.

A less well-known movie that Brown and Freed also did that year was *The Pagan,* for which they wrote a song that became one of the most popular of the year, "The Pagan Love Song." It was the biggest year of Herb Brown's music-writing career, and he became quite a celebrity in the moviemaking business. Of course, his partner, Arthur Freed, went on to greatness as the producer of those extraordinary MGM musicals.

I had met Arthur Freed in 1923, when he was just getting started and he wrote that cute introductory song, "Doris Come Out of the Chorus," and we had continued a friendly relationship. He and Herb did the music for several other movies: *Lord Byron of Hollywood, Good News, Going Hollywood,* and *Babes in Arms.* In 1939, Arthur started producing Hollywood's greatest musicals: *Lady Be Good, Strike Up the Band, Good News, Going Hollywood, Panama Hattie, For Me and My Gal, Best Foot Forward, Meet Me in St. Louis, The Harvey Girls, Till the Clouds Roll By, Show Boat, An American in Paris,* and of course, *Singin' in the Rain.* Years later, Pearl, when she was no longer active in show business but desperate to get back in, tried to get Arthur interested in some of the scripts she had written. He showed some interest in them—perhaps simply out of courtesy—but nothing ever came of it.

Getting back to that earlier *Hollywood Music Box Revue* in 1927, when the show closed, I went into a Franchon and Marco production called *The Serpentine Idea,* as the lead dancer with a chorus of twenty-four dancers, referred to as the Zulu Dancers, and we danced what was called "the African." The dances were created by Larry Ceballus, and they delighted audiences throughout California. Later, the name was changed to *The Follies Idea,* and the chorus was expanded to thirty dancers. We played in Los Angeles, San Diego, Sacramento, and San Francisco, as well as in Portland, Salem, Tacoma, and Seattle. The tour was seventeen weeks and four shows a day! What was a new experience for me—not an altogether pleasant one—was that our show alternated with the feature picture in movie houses. In Los Angeles, for example, the movie was

The Demi-Bride with Norma Shearer. The live show and the film had no relation to each other, except that we shared a theater. It was the threshold of a new era for vaudeville and for the motion picture business as well.

I returned to New York in 1927, at a time when Mary was having the biggest personal hit of her career in Philip Goodman's production of *The Five O'Clock Girl,* at the Forty-fourth Street Theater, with Oscar Shaw as her leading man. The show also featured the bright comedy team of Al Shaw and Sam Lee, who were hilariously funny. Bert Kalmar and Harry Ruby wrote the songs, the most memorable one being "Thinking of You," which was sung by Mary and Oscar. There was another catchy song that Mary sang called "Up in the Clouds." The show was billed as "a fairy tale in modern clothes"—one of those stage confections of "poor girl finds love and wealth" that audiences loved: the Cinderella story of a poor girl who after a day of work in a dry cleaners would call on the telephone a handsome, rich young man every day at five, leading him to believe that she was a wealthy socialite. She eventually meets him and wins him, even when he learns the truth. The show ran for 280 performances on Broadway and then had a long successful road tour.

It was a personal triumph for Mary and, along with *Lucky,* is the show in which she is singularly regarded as the star. For her, it was the culmination of the Broadway years. Robert Benchley called it "a great show," and Walter Winchell called it "the town's current 'flash.'" The well-known critic Bide Dudley wrote, "She is just about the neatest blond vision anybody ever saw. If any girl can be prettier, dance more gracefully, and sing—well, 'more good enough' than Mary, I'd like to see her . . . and she is just as delightful and real off the stage as she is on." The *Times* said of Mary, "She is a picture of blond loveliness . . . the show serves to reveal the talent of Mary Eaton more auspiciously than in recent productions. She has lost her icy passivity and acquired a decidedly becoming animation." I pondered that phrase "icy passivity" for a good while. There was an inherent truth in those words about Mary's reaction to the world around her and particularly to the passionate pursuits of so many of her admirers. Perhaps in life as well as on stage she was developing more of a "decidedly becoming animation." Also, in the *Times* review, there was a phrase that had been used more often to describe her singing than any other. The review said, "She dances well and sings acceptably"—what Bide Dudley had called "good enough." Mary hated those minimal words like "acceptably" and "good enough." As I've stated before, she had a melodic and pretty voice, but not a strong voice, and in some houses, it didn't carry well. With a microphone, she would have been terrific. Later, she would be passed over for a movie role that required a lot of singing, losing out to a stronger singer named Jeanette McDonald.

Even at the height of her stardom, she remained so loyal and caring to Mama and Papa and the other Eatons that there was no hint in her behavior of her superior achievements. While she certainly enjoyed her success and the applause it brought her, she remained always sweet and generous as a daughter and a sister. There was nothing moody or morose in her personality, and she was—as Cantor had called her—lighthearted and nice. When we were growing up, Mama never allowed much narcissistic behavior, from the time we were with the Poli stock companies, when there was so much adulation and people always making a fuss over us. Mama's constant admonition was, "Just don't get a big head. Remember that someone else can always take your place. So be polite and don't get too big for your britches." We always thought of ourselves as working people, thankful to have a job. We never expected to get special treatment. We knew so many talented people out there who had not been nearly as lucky as we.

It was not long after *The Five O'Clock Girl* opened that the rumors started that Mary was having an affair with her handsome leading man, Oscar Shaw. Pearl was the first to hear it, because she was so well connected to the chorus girl rumor mill, a real communications network. Oscar Shaw had established himself as a first-rate actor and singer on the musical stage, having had featured or starring roles in many successful shows. His last featured role before *The Five O'Clock Girl* was in the Gershwin musical *Oh, Kay,* with Gertrude Lawrence. He was a journeyman actor/singer, and very well liked by the producers, who kept him busy throughout the twenties on the musical stage.

There was only one problem: Oscar was married. Mary, who had been so reserved and uninvolved with her admirers over the years, truly fell in love with Oscar and, I think, he with her. The backstage word was that his wife would never give him a divorce without creating a public scandal that could ruin both of their careers. Well, my feeling is that the affair continued through the run of their show on Broadway and on tour, a period of over two years. Immediately afterward, they both went into the Marx Brothers' movie *Cocoanuts,* which they followed with the Ziegfeld movie *Glorifying the American Girl.* Somewhere along the way, the affair ended. I do believe it was the first time Mary had really been in love, and perhaps that relationship was more responsible for her losing her "icy passivity" than her continued study of acting and voice. We never had a heart-to-heart talk about the affair—that was hard for Eatons to do, and it was particularly hard for Mary to share her intimate thoughts.

Mary's star billing for
Lucky, 1926, at the New
Amsterdam Theater

Costars Oscar Shaw
and Mary in *The Five
O'Clock Girl*

My feeling is that the breakup with Oscar Shaw was one of the factors in her rushing into a marriage with another man in 1929.

During the 1927–28 season, Charlie appeared with Ethel Barrymore in a play called *The Royal Fandango,* which featured a young actor named Edward G. Robinson in one of his early Broadway appearances. He had made his debut a little earlier in *The Adding Machine,* and he was just beginning to get established. Also in the play, in the role of a photographer who had only a single line (which was something like "O.K., that's it. Thank you.") was a young actor named Spencer Tracy, who was then twenty-three and making his first appearance on the Broadway stage. The story is told that Ethel Barrymore noticed backstage that Tracy was extremely nervous before going on, and she said to him, "Just relax. In a hundred years, no one will remember this anyway." She was right about *The Royal Fandango.* Larry Swindell writes in *Spencer Tracy . . . A Biography,* that after the terrible reviews the play received on opening night, the "actors arrived at the theater in despair, and a child actor named Charles Eaton was crying. Miss Barrymore called the company together. She told them all to smile, relax, and get ready to do their best." It closed after twenty-four performances. *Time* called the play "an assemblage of junk," but praised Ethel Barrymore for her comedic acting, mentioning no one else in the cast. For Charlie, it was a memorable experience to be on stage with one of the great ladies of the American theater, and in years to come, he could always say that he worked on Broadway with Spencer Tracy and Edward G. Robinson.

That same season, Pearl appeared in a dancing role at the Globe Theater with Beatrice Lillie in Dillingham's production of *She's My Baby,* which also starred Clifton Webb and Irene Dunn, with the songs of Rodgers and Hart. Even with all that talent, the show ran only nine weeks, one of Rodgers and Hart's few failures at that time in their career, with none of the songs surviving the run. Both Bea Lillie—that wonderful clown—and Clifton Webb were friends of Pearl and soon became friends of the whole family.

At the University of Pennsylvania, where he was a sophomore majoring in English, Joe appeared in an all-male production of the Mask and Wig Club, in which he was dressed as a woman with his blond wig modeled after Mary's hair. The family went to Philadelphia to catch Joe's hilarious portrayal. He would continue to perform in the Mask and Wig Club annual show throughout his student days, and each play would go on a short road trip. In his senior year, he actually performed in New York at the Metropolitan Opera House, and that ended his short happy life on the stage and as a leading lady. Had he taken it

Brother Joe never pursued showbiz but was a "leading
lady" for four years in Mask and Wig productions
during college years at University of Pennsylvania.

seriously and studied for it, I think Joe could have been a very successful performer, but he had no desire to do that.

I had one of my best roles in the 1927–28 season in a play called *Excess Baggage,* with Miriam Hopkins, Eric Dressler, and Frank McHugh. For me, it was a dramatic role, but my character was a vaudeville dancer, and in one scene, I was asked to develop a dance for my character. I borrowed the "Doll Dance" for that scene, and it was very well received. The play had a long run, over two hundred performances, and the best part of all was getting to know Frank McHugh, who was such a sweet man. He later had a successful movie career as a character actor, appropriately playing good-guy roles. Some of his movies were *Gold Diggers of 1935, Ever Since Eve* (1935), *Stage Struck* (1936), *Going My Way* (1944)—one of the many times he was a priest—and *State Fair* (1945). He continued to work in movies through the sixties. Over the years, we visited with him from time to time, and during the Broadway years, he visited us at the Point Pleasant summerhouse on the New Jersey coast.

John McGowan was the author of *Excess Baggage,* and during rehearsals, he and I became very friendly. He invited me out to dinner a few times, and we always had fun being together. He was a redheaded Irishman with big blue eyes, and we all called him Jack. I never regarded our relationship as a romantic one, but after he received an offer from MGM to go to Hollywood as a screenwriter, he asked me to marry him and go with him. I was stunned and declined his proposal. Later, Pearl told me I was awfully naive because "it was obvious that he was crazy about you." It is true that I never got myself in trouble for being overly sophisticated.

Charlie, who was staying very busy for a sixteen year old, went on the road with Mary Boland in *Don't Count Your Chickens.* They were going to return for a Broadway run, but after a long, successful road tour, Mary Boland, a very talented and popular actress, dropped out of the cast, and the show never opened in New York. I think this was probably Mama's last road trip looking after one of her kids. Charlie went back to Broadway, and afterward, when he went to Hollywood, we all moved there. Lord knows how many miles Mama logged over the years, but she never complained. It was her special role that started in 1911 and continued until 1928, traveling with me or Charlie or both of us.

When I returned from California at the beginning of the 1927 season, there had developed a Sunday afternoon custom of having friends and fellow performers to our Congress apartment—which was typically called "Mary's apartment"—for relaxing talk and drinks and snacks. Show folks like to be with show folks, and there was always a pretty good crowd there. I remember that once Mary brought in a large carton of caviar and placed a sign beside it on the table that read "I paid $25 for this. Eat it all!" That was really a celebration of our affluence, which was so different from the early years. We were living well—as if there were no tomorrow—enjoying the fruits of our hard work.

Broadway was dark on Sundays, so it was a day off for show folks. Although the group's composition changed from week to week, the regulars there were Marilyn Miller, Beatrice Lillie, George Gershwin, Oscar Levant, William S. Hart, Al Clark, Ramon Navarro, Clifton Webb, Peggy Wood, Frank McHugh, and Oscar Shaw. Two of the Warner brothers, Jack and Sam (we never met the other two, Harry and Albert), who lived above us in an apartment on the eleventh floor, actually came to the door one day and asked if they could join the party. The Warner brothers had already established their Hollywood studio, but they continued to keep apartments in New York, where much of the advertising and promotion was handled. They were about to revolutionize the business with the first commercial talking picture. Jack particularly wanted to meet Marilyn Miller, and he and his brother became Sunday regulars after that. Sam befriended Charlie and gave him his very first radio. Jack and Marilyn Miller reportedly had an affair years later in Hollywood.

Pearl also lived in the Congress, and sometimes she would host the Sunday afternoon group in her eighth-floor apartment. Oscar Levant, when he was a teenager, spent some time with Pearl and Harry. She often referred to him as "the brat," and Harry was always after him to practice the piano. Now almost ten years later, he and Pearl got along just fine. They were, in fact, very close. Oscar's biographers, Sam Kashner and Nancy Schoenberger, suggest that Oscar had a real love for Pearl and greatly admired her intelligence and wit. Oscar was two years younger than I, and I liked him very much. I recall he was really into Tchaikovsky at the time I was studying piano, and he would extract beautiful melodies from various compositions, while trying to explain to me what Tchaikovsky was all about.

Oscar was a genius, I thought, even when he was nineteen or twenty years of age. Although his first love was classical music, at that time he was struggling to become a successful songwriter. He had written a couple of songs I knew. One was "If You Want the Rainbow, You Must Have the Rain," which he wrote with Billy Rose and Mort Dixon. And the other was "Lady, Play Your Mandolin," which had become quite popular. He was clever and very sharp in those days, long before he became so obviously neurotic and depressed in middle age. Twenty years after the Eatons were out of show business, Oscar was making a profession of being hostile, obsessive, and anxiety-ridden, even though he had a successful career as a concert pianist, a radio wit on "Information Please," and an actor in several movies. In the fifties, he would be the resident nervous wreck on the Jack Paar show. He once remarked that his favorite exercise was "groveling, brooding, and mulling." That was a different person from the one I knew.

On occasion, the Sunday group would go to Marilyn Miller's apartment—she lived not far away with her mother—but more often than not the gathering would take place at Mary's apartment. Charlie named it Chez 161 (for 161 West Fifty-fourth Street), and there was rarely a Sunday without a party.

When Herb Brown was on the East Coast, I would have him come by, and he got to know the whole family. Charlie remembers sitting at the piano with Herb and singing, "Laughing at the blues . . . I'm laughing at the blues." It was a new song that Herb was developing at that time, two years before the final version appeared as "Singin' in the Rain," when Arthur Freed wrote the better-known lyrics.

Once in awhile, someone would bring other celebrities in—including on one occasion the very famous Charles Lindbergh and the aviatrix, Ruth Elder, although sadly I was not there at that time. It was about a year after Lindbergh's historic flight across the Atlantic in May of 1927, and he was the Great American Hero. Mary had met them one evening on Fifth Avenue as they were leaving a reception and going out to eat. She brought them home with her "to have cold cuts out of the refrigerator." The *New York Daily News* reported it this way: "[Lindbergh and Elder] proceeded, at Miss Eaton's command to her home, and there was a grand old theatrical folk party, with Broadway's best entertainers making things cheery for the popular young man who likes his fun without cameras, blaring of trumpets and such. . . ."

On a few occasions, Fred Astaire—who was a youthful twenty-seven or so—dropped by, and Charlie remembers teaching him how to sing scat. Charlie had learned scat singing from the Rhythm Boys during the run of *Lucky,* and he would often break into an energetic display of this jazzy way of singing. Astaire was taken with it and liked to join in "to get the hang of it."

Most often, the special visitors were attracted there because they wanted to meet or to be with Mary, who was now as vivacious and fun-loving as she was beautiful. She was at the peak of her career, with *The Five O'Clock Girl* being one of the season's smash hits. Of course, Mary was making so much more money than the rest of us that she paid the lion's share of the expenses. But never did she make a point of this, or use it in any way to claim rights that the rest of us did not have. To her it was all "ours"—although to others outside the family everything was Mary's—Mary Eaton's sister Pearl, Mary Eaton's brother Charles, Mary's apartment, Mary's summerhouse, Mary's car, and so on. We all got used to that; it is what stardom does—like the sun, everything orbits around it.

At those social gatherings, someone would always bring in bootleg liquor, and Mama, who had a black woman named Gertrude helping her, would cook up wonderful food for the group. Not a sit-down dinner, just good things to munch on, mostly Southern-style food. Everyone talked about Mamie's biscuits and her fabulous Virginia baked ham. And she could roast or fry chicken that was out of this world. There were always cold cuts and cheeses and relishes from the delicatessen and breads and desserts from the bakery, and sometimes guests would bring boxes of chocolates or other delicacies. I remember that at that time, Mary had a green parrot that had been given to her by Ivan Tarasoff and his wife. The parrot would stand at the end of the table, carefully selecting whatever morsels he wanted—he loved biscuits. He had a one-word vocabulary, welcoming people with "Hello." Pearl tried to teach him to say "Hello, Sucker," but she didn't succeed.

In those days, I don't think anyone in the family drank very much, except for Robert, who had developed a serious drinking problem (and never came to the Sunday parties). Papa would sometimes get happy, and it never took much alcohol to make him tipsy. As far as I know, he never drank a lot or often, but much of his life is obscured by his nightly visits to newspaper plants. We did not know much about his nocturnal life, but the occasions were few and far between when he arrived home a bit tipsy. Years later, others in the family—Pearl, Mary, Charlie—would develop drinking problems that would become severe, but that was not the case during the twenties.

Often the Sunday parties would go long into the night. They were always fun and relaxing. George Gershwin, who was not yet thirty, was becoming the biggest name in American music. In 1918, George—at twenty—was the *Follies* rehearsal-pianist for Marilyn Miller, and they had known each other over the years since then. I suspect that she was the compelling reason for George to come to those Sunday gatherings. He had written his first song, "Swanee," with Irving Caesar when he was twenty, and Al Jolson recorded it in 1920. From 1920 to 1924, he wrote music for the *George White's Scandals*. His great composition "Rhapsody in Blue" debuted in 1924, with George, himself, playing the piano solo with the Paul Whiteman Orchestra.

Oscar Levant started playing "Rhapsody in Blue" when he was just a teenager and before he ever met George Gershwin. He really loved the composition and played it at concerts whenever he had the opportunity. After he finally met George Gershwin, probably in 1925, he became not only an ardent fan and an expert performer of his music but also a close friend. They were quite a pair. Some say that the relationship was one-sided, and Oscar frequently was very trying for George.

In 1924, *Lady Be Good* (with Fred and Adele Astaire) was George's first musical with Ira Gershwin, and it turned out to be their first big hit, with "Somebody Loves Me" and "The Man I Love" being the biggest songs. (I can't remember Ira Gershwin ever coming to the apartment, but George was a frequent visitor. Both of them had penthouse apartments on Riverside Drive and were known for their own fabulous parties, but I was never there.) For the 1926–27 season, they had written the beautiful "Someone to Watch Over Me" for *Oh, Kay*, which was sung by Gertrude Lawrence—who also came to Chez 161 on at least one occasion.

Gershwin had a childlike enthusiasm for playing his own music, and he was more often than not the one at the piano on those wonderful Sunday afternoons. He and Oscar would always come together and leave together. They both were very fond of Mama, and she treated them like members of the family. She was so comfortable with everyone, no matter how great or notorious they were. And she always had as much fun as anyone. I often thought that what went on there at those grand gatherings was much better entertainment than what was taking place during the week in many of the theaters surrounding us.

Those years in the latter part of the twenties were truly a special time for Broadway music, and our Sunday get-togethers often involved hearing new songs or just enjoying playing and singing the current hits. There has never been a better collection of songwriters at one time in New York. Cole Porter was just beginning to have some success. Rodgers and Hart were turning out the best music of their partnership (with "My Heart Stood Still" being the big song from 1927's *Connecticut Yankee*). Jerome Kern, the busiest composer on Broadway, had teamed with Oscar Hammerstein to do *Show Boat*, which set a new standard for the Broadway musical and was filled with great songs. And Irving Berlin, whom we knew from the *Follies*, was still in his prime, with much of his best work still ahead of him. What a great era for Broadway music!

Often a small group of us would go out to eat at Sardi's, Delmonico's, Dinty Moore's, or Luchow's. It seemed theatrical people were always at those places, and tended to be there later than the usual patrons, typically after the theater. These were all interesting and colorful places that were very much a part of that time. In the early 1980s, Luchow's closed the wonderful old Four-teenth Street restaurant—with the vast mahogany bar, the high ceilings, the mounted stags' heads, the German steins, and all the Old World charm. It was the end of an era that had started a hundred years before, when Fourteenth Street was the theatrical center of the city in the old gaslight days. Luchow's was the last surviving monument to those golden years, and it was a sad day when it at last closed its doors in a neighborhood that had gone to ruin. Of course, Sardi's, in the theater district, continues today as a favorite gathering place for Broadway folks.

We also enjoyed going to the Hollywood, a restaurant and club that had beautiful showgirls. Nils T. Granlund was the master of ceremonies, and we became well acquainted with him. The Hollywood was one of the popular places of that era, and later on, Charlie fell in love with one of the beautiful showgirls, Marian Martin, so it became his favorite place to go in New York. That relationship did not endure, but Charlie was certainly moonstruck for a time. Charlie, who never married, could often be found in the company of beautiful women, even when he was a teenager.

While we lived at the Congress, we were only a short distance from the new Ziegfeld Theater, which was on the corner of Fifty-fourth Street and Sixth Avenue. When *Rio Rita* opened there, in 1927, Charlie would eat his dinner early and take off in order to be at the theater when the beautiful chorus girls arrived. One of them was Kiki Roberts—the same one who later married Jack "Legs" Diamond—and Charlie struck up a conversation with her. Her real name was Marian Strasmick, and she was a beautiful brunette and a lovable person. Although she was only sixteen, she had already been in the Ziegfeld chorus, and she was now dancing in the premier show in Ziegfeld's own theater.

There was a very popular drugstore near the Ziegfeld Theater, where showgirls liked to hang out with wealthy playboys and other admirers. Char-lie and Kiki met there for a while for lunch or soft drinks (Charlie was only about sixteen himself), and then they went their own ways. Charlie was often permitted backstage by Ziegfeld's stage manager, Billy Schroeder, and he never tired of being there. He loved the give and take with show folks, and the excitement of a theatrical production. Once during *Rio Rita,* he encountered Flo Ziegfeld while he was hanging out backstage. Everyone knew that Ziegfeld had a hard-and-fast rule that there would be no visitors backstage, and Charlie was frightened at what Ziegfeld might do. Ziegfeld immediately recognized Charlie and greeted him with his loud, nasal twang, in an openly friendly way, "Hello, Charlie, it's good to see you." Charlie had expected something like,

"What the hell are you doing back here?" He was greatly relieved by Ziegfeld's friendliness.

On occasion, the whole family would go to the Mayfair Club's special events. The Mayfair Club was a social club for the aristocracy of show business (meaning whoever could pay the high membership dues), and it had gatherings every other Saturday at the Ritz Carlton Hotel. Mary had a table booked for the season at these events, as did many other celebrity friends: Marilyn Miller, Bea Lillie, Clifton Webb, Charlie Winninger, and many others—including celebrity visitors from Hollywood. In addition, there were many of the social elite who were not in show business. With all the furs and diamonds on parade there—as Pearl observed years later—you could have paid all of the delinquent bills of Russia. Charlie remembers meeting Mayor Jimmy Walker at one of the gala gatherings. The power brokers and the deal makers generally made it to Mayfair functions. Of course, Jimmy Walker was well known for his enjoyment of New York nightlife and his unspoken repudiation of prohibition.

I remember dancing with my brother Joe at a Mayfair New Year's Eve party, and it was so crowded on the dance floor that it was virtually impossible to move. An angry dancer—a large, older man who we were wedged against—shouted at Joe, "Will you get out of my way!" Joe, looking around helplessly and shrugging his shoulders, replied, "Sir, there's just no place to go." And we all started laughing. Funny how we remember those silly little moments so clearly.

Even though we may have danced professionally all week, we still loved to go out dancing when we had the chance. While Mary was acting, singing, and dancing, Pearl and I more often than not were hired simply to dance—we may have acted and sung a little too, but basically we were hoofers and that is what got us hired. The twenties of course was a great decade for dancers, and many of the images that represent that era involve dancing. The dances that grew out of ragtime and jazz were high spirited and uninhibited—first the hootchy-kootchy, then the shimmy, and on to the Charleston and the black bottom. In the 1919 *Follies,* there was a number called "The World Is Shimmy Mad," and in the same show was the prohibition spoof, sung by the great Bert Williams, "You Cannot Make Your Shimmy Shake on Tea." In 1922, Gilda Gray stopped the show every night with her frenetic shimmy to "It's Getting Dark on Old Broadway." The song had a racist meaning, referring to the existing fears that blacks were moving from Harlem closer to Times Square, but it was the medium and not the message that got the ovation. Few could dance with such frenetic abandon as Gilda Gray.

A few years into the twenties, the Charleston replaced the shimmy as the dance of the decade, and even today the "flapper" doing the Charleston is one of the most enduring images of "the roaring twenties." Then, as an extension of the Charleston, Alberta Hunter introduced the black bottom, so named because the sluggish footsteps were like trying to trudge through the black bottom of the Swanee River. (There are others who give an alternative origin of the name that is less poetic.) Buddy Bradley, a very talented black dancer-teacher, was one of the great popularizers of the black bottom through his teaching of the dance to white performers. As I said before, Ann Pennington, who had left the *Follies* and had gone on to the *George White's Scandals,* was also regarded as a popularizer of the black bottom. Both the Charleston and the black bottom had been great crowd pleasers in my act in Los Angeles, and I would be asked over the years to do them again and again.

But most social dancing in the clubs and cabarets still centered around the one-step or the fox-trot. In the early twenties, small dance bands started appearing in clubs, dance halls, theaters, and hotels, which encouraged social dancing. Also, radio and records were becoming popular and brought social dancing even into people's homes. It became the heyday of social dancing—which had actually become popular in the teens—and in New York, a young man by the name of Arthur Murray was getting started on his way to becoming America's number one social dance teacher. In a decade, he would play an important role in a whole new career for me.

In 1929, the Warners made *The Jazz Singer,* with Al Jolson, and motion pictures started talking. It would have a profound effect on our lives in show business. Already, motion picture theaters were springing up in neighborhoods all over the country, and in 1927 alone, hundreds of silent films were produced. Some of the best were: *Beau Geste, The Big Parade, What Price Glory, The King of Kings, The Way of All Flesh,* and *Seventh Heaven.* The new movie houses opening around Broadway were larger, more opulent, and more elegant than the legitimate theaters, and the cost of entertainment was far less. The Roxy and the Rivoli led the way to a new era.

At the same time, radio was becoming increasingly popular, and many of the stars from vaudeville would soon be heading for national fame on radio: Eddie Cantor, Jack Benny, George Burns, Fred Allen, Fanny Brice, Bob Hope, and so on. We didn't realize how ominous these changes really were at the time, but we would soon know.

In 1928, I had a featured dancing role in a musical called *Cross My Heart,* which had a moderately successful run. My best number was an innovative syncopated tap dance, which drew from the jazz rhythms that had become so popular. It was a variation of the Sugar Foot Strut that I had worked out with the great Buddy Bradley. It turned out to be a showstopper. I received standing ovations almost every performance, and I was repeatedly called back for bows. One critic wrote in *Billboard:* "[Doris Eaton's] dancing is among the brightest lights of the show, and her next-to-closing specialty almost stops the proceedings."

About this time, my nephew Edwin Mills (Evelyn's son) was drawing favorable notices for his performance in *Courage,* which had a successful run on Broadway and then went on the road. Evelyn was now in the role that Mama had played for so many years, traveling with her offspring, which also included her daughter, Evelynne (whose name she pronounced Ee-va-len), and later Warren, both talented child actors. As I said earlier, each of them would go on to moderately successful careers in show business, although never achieving star status. Edwin had roles in fourteen Broadway hits. In addition to *Courage,* there were *Once in a Lifetime, Merrily We Roll Along, Lean Harvest,* and *Boys from Syracuse,* among others. He also had parts in twenty-five movies, one of which was with Raymond Massey in *Abe Lincoln in Illinois.* And he did some radio work, appearing with Helen Hayes in *Mayor of the Town.* His career extended over five decades, until a brain tumor incapacitated him. He died at age sixty-three in 1981.

Evelynne started out as a baby in *I'd Rather Be Right,* with George M. Cohan, and she did *The Man Who Reclaimed His Head,* starring Claude Raines. She was with Frederick March in *The American Way* and with Bea Lillie and Bert Lahr in *The Show Is On,* as well as appearing in the 1931 revival of *Show Boat* with Dennis King. She starred on the road in *Junior Miss.* But she decided to give up show business when she married the well-known radio announcer Eddie King and began to raise a family. She became estranged from her mother sometime after the birth of her daughter Julie, when their being together always ended in disagreement, arguments, and hurt feelings. In 1964, Evelynne would die young, at age thirty-nine, of a viral infection of some kind.

Warren was in *Lady in the Dark,* with Gertrude Lawrence, and also in the cast of *As Thousands Cheer* and *The Great Waltz.* He did a good deal of radio acting, appearing on shows with Fred Allen and Rudy Vallee and on "Dr. Christian." Warren and Charlie got along well, and Warren spent some time working with Charlie during the fifties in Cuba on the vacation-dance programs. Evelyn's children were somehow marked for tragedy, and Warren, who left show business to write a novel that he rhapsodically believed would catapult him to the ranks of Wolfe, Hemingway, and Faulkner, died at his own hand in his brownstone home in New York in the early seventies. Evelyn would never talk about his death, so I never learned the circumstances. I think it was such a devastating blow to Evelyn to lose two of her children—Evelynne and Warren—so tragically that she never got over the trauma. Edwin's brain tumor incapacitated him for years, although he did not precede Evelyn in death. Such incredible tragedies added greatly to the growing bitterness and disillusionment that dominated Evelyn's later years.

In 1929, I returned to Hollywood to do the new *Hollywood Music Box Revue*, and it was in this show that I sang "Singin' in the Rain." Once again, Herb Brown and I resumed our relationship, and we actually began to talk about marriage. Somewhere along the way, we had some pretty serious conversations, and I recall telling him that if we got married, I would continue to have some of the responsibility for my mother and father, that I would need to help my sisters provide for them, probably $300 a month. I think that scared him off, fearing that he might get saddled with more than he bargained for. It was not just the money, but the complications of what he must have perceived as taking on a whole family. I don't think he really took into account my talent and my ability to succeed independently as a performer and even as a lyricist—I really wanted to try writing. (He liked the lyrics I wrote for "Doll Dance," although he never publicly gave me credit for writing them.) Well, that was the beginning of the end of our relationship.

During that year, 1929, all of the performing Eatons would find their way to Hollywood. Charlie was in his most important role on Broadway, in a play called *Skidding*, in which he created the role of Andy Hardy, and starring Walter Abel. The Andy Hardy role would be taken by Mickey Rooney in the famous series of Andy Hardy motion pictures. Charlie received very good reviews for his work. The *Billboard* review stated, "Charles Eaton, as a wisecracking go-getting youth with an interest in girls that is just blooming, shows to excellent advantage and carries the bulk of the comedy on his young shoulders. Eaton is a flowering comedian and his current part will do much in setting him in a definite spot." That same issue of *Billboard* reported that *Excess Baggage* (my show) had completed 176 performances and was still running and that *The Five O'Clock Girl* (Mary's show) had completed 274 performances and was still going strong. So the three of us were working in successful productions throughout the 1928–29 season.

In the spring of 1929, before she left for Hollywood, Pearl created some musical numbers at the Hoboken Lyric Theater for a benefit performance of the Jersey City Junior Service League. What was important for her is that she worked beside Agnes DeMille, who was creating and directing a ballet number. The play was the historically important *The Black Crook,* which was first produced in 1866 at Neblo's Garden in New York and was considered the forerunner to the American musical comedy. In its first production, the play revealed the legs of beautiful girls dancing on stage, which had two immediate consequences: it made the show a big hit, and it provoked a virulent protest against its immorality. In spite of the strong opposition, the show survived and ran for 475 performances in New York, with many revivals over the years.

The Black Crook had little plot—a black crook makes a pact with the devil to deliver one soul a year—just a thread to tie together a succession of musical acts that went on for over five hours. There were lavish scenes, ballet numbers, huge production numbers, and stunning stage effects. It was the first time chorus girls were used throughout in musical numbers. Pearl's participation in reviving this all-but-forgotten relic gave her the opportunity to create scenes and dance routines and sparked a strong interest in her to write—music, lyrics, plays—and it was good preparation for her work as a dance director for RKO.

While *Skidding* was still running strong, Charlie received a call from the well-known agent Mike Connelly. At the time, Charlie was enjoying a Sunday off at our leased summer home at Point Pleasant, New Jersey, with a lot of relatives and friends. Connelly insisted that Charlie return immediately to New York, because Fox Studios wanted a young actor for their first talking picture and they were interested in Charlie. So, at seventeen, Charlie, along with Mama, packed up and headed for Hollywood. Charlie did a screen test for the starring role in a movie to be called *The Ghost Talks*. They did not give him a script for the test. They simply told him to start talking in front of the cameras, saying whatever he wanted. Not really knowing what to do, Charlie just launched into one of his routines, with comic movements and exaggerated facial expressions, and everyone on the set started laughing. He got the part and a contract with Fox. Other cast members for that first sound picture at Fox (who were well-known at that time) were Carmel Meyers, Earl Fox, and Elizabeth Patterson. The movie was successful and attracted a great deal of attention as Fox's first full-length talking movie. Charlie, whose budding-detective character referred to himself as Camera Eye Franklin, received very good notices. One critic wrote that he "aroused gales of laughter from a host of spectators at the Roxy Theater." In the role, Charlie was "an enthusiastic budding Sherlock Holmes, even with a calabash pipe and a double-peaked cap." Sadly, from everything we can learn, no copies of this film remain, so Fox's first talking film and Charlie's starring performance are lost to film history.

Almost immediately, Charlie went into a second movie, called *Harmony at Home,* during which he got to know a fellow performer named Dixie Lee and became very fond of her. One day, Bing Crosby came by the set. He and Charlie had become acquainted in New York during the short run of the play *Lucky*. The show's second act had an appearance by Paul Whiteman's band with the Rhythm Boys, one of whom was Bing Crosby. Charlie introduced Bing to his new girlfriend, Dixie Lee. Some months later, Bing and Dixie were married.

Another friendship that came out of that show was with the great trumpet player Henry Busse. His famous rendition of "When Day Is Done" was a high point in *Lucky* and remained his theme song throughout his career. He and Charlie shared a dressing room, and Charlie invited him to the apartment to meet the rest of the Eatons. Henry fell in love with Mama or her biscuits—it's hard to know which was paramount in his feelings—and he rarely missed an opportunity to come by for biscuits and coffee with her.

Mary decided to move from the Congress, since we all had decided to try Hollywood, and while winding things up in New York, we moved together into a suite in the Park Central Hotel. Soon Mary was in Hollywood with Papa, Mama, and Charlie; Pearl and I followed shortly thereafter. So with all of us on the West Coast, we bought a lovely house for the family at 712 Camden Drive in Beverly Hills, and Pearl had her own house nearby. We were all prepared to make it in the movies. Pearl had developed a close relationship with Fanny Brice, who had also moved to Hollywood and into a home near us in Beverly Hills. Dossie and Fanny's children (a girl about ten and a boy of seven) spent a lot of time together. (Fanny didn't stay too long in Hollywood at that time. She was later quoted as saying, "I was out there eight months. I worked five weeks and got three years' pay.")

Soon Joe came out after graduating from the University of Pennsylvania in 1930. With Pearl's help, he had been given a job at RKO as a reader in their story department. He would read scripts that had been submitted and write summaries of them for the producers.

I made two movies for RKO-Radio, *Street Girl* and *The Very Idea*. *Street Girl* was a musical, with music written by Oscar Levant and with one hundred dancers directed by Pearl. It was the first talking picture made by the newly combined RKO and Radio Studios. I was listed in the ads as "Doris Eaton and the Radio Pictures Beauty Chorus." I sang a song called "Broken Up" and had several dance numbers, but the stars were Betty Compson, John Herron, Ned

Sparks, and Jack Oakie. The studio didn't really have a music department at that time, so they hired Gus Arnheim's band to provide the music because they happened to be playing at that time at the Cocoanut Grove. It was the story of a Hungarian violinist (Betty Compson) who takes over a down-and-out four-piece band and leads them to great success. They played a Levant song called "Lovable and Sweet," which was the theme throughout the sound track. RKO remade the picture with a different cast in 1937 and called it *That Girl from Paris;* it was remade again in 1942 as *Four Jills and a Jack. Street Girl* had a spectacular premiere, at which the movie was accompanied by a stage show with Jack Benny as the master of ceremonies, and featured Ann Pennington and "Pearl Eaton's Radio Picture's Dancing Chorus." The *Hollywood News* called the picture "one of the most entertaining and tuneful talkies of the year." *The Very Idea,* which starred Frank Craven, in which I had a straight comedic acting role—no singing or dancing—was a poorly produced and poorly conceived comedy. Probably the first time ever for public consumption, it was the story of a childless couple selecting surrogate parents to have a child for them. It was not very successful and would, in fact, end my short, happy movie career. Pearl continued her work for RKO as a dance director, making several movies, the best of which were *Rio Rita* and *Hit the Deck.* She attracted a great deal of show-biz attention for her inventive and spectacular approach to dance sequences, using a chorus of a hundred dancers in *Hit the Deck.* While the $500-per-week salary she was earning was the highest of her career, her work was now entirely off stage or behind the cameras. She would not again appear as a performer.

There is another one of these great coincidences involving the Eaton family and movie history. Charlie, Pearl, Mary, and I were all involved in firsts where sound movies are concerned. Charlie did the first feature-length sound movie at Fox *(The Ghost Talks)*. Pearl did the dance direction for *Rio Rita,* the first sound movie for RKO, and *Street Girl* was the first musical under the name of RKO-Radio. Mary did Ziegfeld's first sound movie for Paramount *(Glorifying the American Girl)*. The love of my life at that time, Herb Brown, did the music for the first sound picture at MGM *(The Broadway Melody)*. With the exception of Herb, none of us went on to careers in movies, but where "talking pictures" are concerned, we were certainly there at the beginning.

After he made *The Ghost Talks* and *Harmony at Home,* along with a couple of short features, Charlie was idle for a couple of months. He too was drawing $500 a week on his contract with Fox, but they weren't offering him any parts. Mama went to the executives of Fox to tell them that Charlie did not just want to draw money, he wanted to act. And she suggested that Fox buy the rights to the play *Skidding* and make a movie about Andy Hardy and his family. Mama was told that the studio was very pleased with Charlie and that other parts would come along, but that the American audience was not interested in family pictures and they had no interest in doing an Andy Hardy movie. Well, a little later, MGM was interested and bought the rights to the Andy Hardy character. Of course, Mickey Rooney was selected to play the role, and the series made movie history.

While still in New York, Mary made the film version of the Broadway show, *The Cocoanuts,* with the Marx Brothers. It was the first movie for the Marx Brothers, and it is clear, viewing that movie today, that the personalities of the three—Groucho, Chico, and Harpo—were indelibly established. George S. Kaufman wrote the book, and it was basically a collection of wisecracks and slapstick. Mary was dissatisfied with her undistinguished role in the movie. Actually, the nonstop antics of the Marx Brothers almost shut out the love interest of the story. The *New York Times* movie critic wrote, "Groucho Marx monopolizes things allowing scant time for fair Mary Eaton and her partner, Oscar Shaw, to rhapsodize on love in the music composed by Irving Berlin." Mary and Oscar did have one pretty good song, "When My Dreams Come True," and Mary was given a rather gratuitous dance number in which she performed her distinctive pirouettes to an unlikely song called "Monkey Doodle Doo." The music was not considered up to Irving Berlin's usual standard, and it was not remembered beyond the movie's run. The story is told that Berlin had offered a new song to the film's producer Sam Harris but that he turned it down. The song was "Always," and wouldn't it have been something if Mary had introduced that wonderful song? Just the other evening, I saw *Cocoanuts* on a classic movie channel, and I realized that seventy years later, people can still see and listen to my sister. Ironically, it was the success of the Marx Brothers for so many years that led to the movie being preserved and so readily available today on video. Many of those today who remember Mary, remember her because of that movie. Nonetheless, I am pleased that Mary's two films, *The Cocoanuts* and *Glorifying the American Girl,* have had a continuing existence. Although in many ways, she is the forgotten star of the twenties, something of her beauty and talent is lastingly preserved.

In watching *Cocoanuts,* I was greatly surprised and amused to see a scene in which twelve chorus girls seated on three steps did a hand-to-body slapping routine very similar to that recent and popular scene in *Will Rogers Follies* to the song "Hooray for Our Favorite Son." Obviously, Tommy Tune did not create that delightful number out of whole cloth. Interesting how these ideas live on in show business to be adapted sixty or seventy years later in such an effective and entertaining way. To us old hoofers, there is satisfaction in knowing that such creative ideas do not always leap newborn from the mind of choreographers!

Mary was much happier with *Glorifying the American Girl,* which was produced by Flo Ziegfeld and was essentially the *Ziegfeld Follies* brought to the screen: the small town girl who dreams she is in the *Follies* and becomes a big star. The movie was actually made at the Paramount Studios in Astoria. Ziegfeld wanted to have the first talking picture, but his slowness in getting the picture completed kept that distinction from him, and the technical facilities of the studio in New York could not match the quality in Hollywood, so the quality of the sound suffered. Nonetheless, Mary was the first to do ballet dancing in a sound movie, and her work in the film was widely praised even though the film fell far short of Ziegfeld's vision.

In typical Ziegfeld casting, *Glorifying* had many walk-on cameo appearances by celebrities: Eddie Cantor, Rudy Vallee, Mayor and Mrs. Jimmy Walker, Ring Lardner, Texas Guinan, Irving Berlin, and even Flo and Billie Ziegfeld. There were also some good songs: "Blue Skies," "Vagabond Lover," "Baby Face," and "At Sundown."

The director of the movie was Millard Webb, whose claim to fame was *The Sea Beast,* with John Barrymore and Dolores Costello, a silent movie based on Herman Melville's *Moby Dick* that was made in 1927. Millard started dating Mary and soon proposed marriage. As I said earlier, Mary was coming off her affair with Oscar Shaw and may have rushed into that relationship a little blindly. Nevertheless, Mary was very happy, and so was Mama. Together they spent huge amounts of time planning a wedding the way one plans a theatrical production.

The wedding was a Hollywood wedding if there ever was one. Mary was stunningly beautiful in her white chiffon and satin gown with pearls, a Dutch cap of lace and tulle, outlined by orange blossoms, forming a very long veil. Marilyn Miller—making a movie *(Sally)* in Hollywood at the time—was Mary's maid of honor, and Evelyn, Pearl, and I were the bridesmaids, along with a friend from Chicago named Katharine Robbins. Charlie and Joe were ushers. Evelyn's two older children, Edwin and Evelynne, were ring bearer and flower girl. The invitation list read like a who's who of Hollywood in 1929. Among the guests were: the John Barrymores, Oscar Levant, Beatrice Lillie, Hoot Gibson, Billie Dove, Louella Parsons, Louis Milestone, Constance Bennet, the Buster Keatons, Helen Hayes, and Richard Barthelmess.

It was a happy occasion in every way, with all the family involved, and with the splendor and extravagance of a Ziegfeld production. The wedding was at the All Souls Congregational Church at 4:30 in the afternoon on a very hot August day. The guests were slow in coming—so many egos waiting to make an entrance and, above all, trying to avoid the stigma of an early arrival—and some were just reluctant to enter the hot-as-an-oven church. The ceremony finally got under way by 5:00. As quickly as possible, they said their "I do"s, and the wedding party almost ran down the aisle and departed for the much more comfortable Beverly Wilshire Hotel for the reception, which went far into the night.

Their marriage would be tragically brief. Millard lived only until 1935, when he died of a heart attack. At the time of their marriage, Mary had enjoyed a much more successful career over a longer period of time than Millard, and she was in better shape financially. Following their marriage, neither of them worked to any extent again in movies. I do know that Mary auditioned for the starring role in a movie opposite Nelson Eddy, but they did not think her voice was strong enough for the part. Instead, they hired Jeanette MacDonald for the role, and as they say, the rest is history. Pearl always blamed Millard for destroying Mary's career. She said that Mary was offered a contract by one of the studios at something well under $5,000 a week, but Millard insisted that she hold out for at least $5,000, a sum larger than studios were then paying their top stars but the amount Ziegfeld had paid Mary for filming *Glorifying the American Girl*. Soon the studio grew tired of waiting and dropped the idea altogether, and no other offers came. With proper management, Mary might very well have been as big a star in films as she had been on Broadway, but that was not to be.

Millard had a history of drinking heavily and had been on the wagon for a time before he and Mary met. Soon he was back drinking heavily again, and this time, Mary joined him. They went to Hollywood parties and entertained others, and I am sure Mary remained optimistic that "something would come along" for both of them. They lived on Mary's money, and they lived very well, even by Hollywood standards, while Millard tried in vain to find pictures to direct.

What none of us had realized on that joyous day when Mary and Millard were married was that the glory days of show business for all of us were about to come to an abrupt end. The stock market crash in October of 1929 and the depression that followed would have a drastic effect on all of our lives.

Doris introduced the "Doll Dance" in the *Hollywood Music Box Revue* in 1926. Later she wrote the lyrics for the music by Nacio Herb Brown, but received no credit.

Doris—success in Hollywood

The Doll Dance, 1926,
Hollywood Music Box Revue

Evolution of the Charleston, 1929,
Hollywood Music Box Revue

Babe Ruth and Doris
in publicity stunt, 1926

Doris introduced "Singin' in the Rain" in the 1929 *Hollywood Music Box Revue*.

Pearl was enticed from Broadway to choreograph the first movie musicals for RKO Studios.

Charlie was persuaded to leave his success in the Broadway show *Skidding* to star in the first talking movie for Fox Company in Hollywood. Charlie with Helen Twelvetrees, 1929.

All of us in Hollywood

Clockwise from top left: Charlie,
Mary, Pearl, Mama, and Doris, 1929

Papa joins us with grandson Warren,
Evelyn's youngest son, 1929

Mary's wedding, the climax of our glory years in show business

Top row: Joe, Mama, Papa, Evelyn, and
Charlie; seated: Pearl, Mary, and Doris, 1929

CHAPTER ELEVEN

HARD TIMES

At first, the thirties weren't so bad. We were all together in California, having finished a decade of great successes. We were experienced, well-known, and confident performers at the threshold of new careers in Hollywood. It seemed there was every reason to be optimistic about our futures. Evelyn came with her family to California to make a new start, and to get her three talented children into the movies. Bob, her long-suffering husband, once again faced the task of starting up anew in the insurance business, and he knew that was going to be a formidable task. Charlie, who was still only eighteen or nineteen, was prosperous from his Fox Studio contract and was working on his third movie, called *Joy Street*. He bought a new car for Bob to help him get started, and Bob was so happy, he could do nothing but cry. He was coming off some rough years in New York, where it had been very difficult to get established, and he knew he could not make it in California without a car. He was forever grateful to Charlie for his generosity.

Pearl's final film at RKO was *Cuckoos,* starring Bert Wheeler. Although she had become a very popular Hollywood figure and her work was widely praised, the studio let her go in 1930. It was one of those cruel rejections so common in show business, coming after superb work. But an important change was under way. Soon the RKO musicals were all Fred Astaire's, and he wanted his own choreographer, Hermes Pan. He did *Flying Down to Rio* and later *Follow the Fleet,* which was a remake of *Hit the Deck*—both films teaming Fred Astaire with Ginger Rogers, and the latter movie featuring new songs by Irving Berlin ("Let's Face the Music and Dance" and "I'm Putting All My Eggs in One Basket"). In *Rio,* they introduced the Carioca (they would later introduce the Continental and the Piccolino) that became so popular with theatergoers. Well, Pearl missed these great dancing years at RKO, and she never again worked in show business. She did open a small dance studio in Encino and began to teach children, but I don't think that lasted very long.

About this time, she met and became engaged to an executive with the Richfield Oil Company named Richard Enderly, and they were married in 1931. Her wedding was not the extravagant affair that Mary's had been. It was a simple ceremony in a small church in Hollywood. We all liked Dick Enderly, an obviously successful and highly capable man. Pearl seemed very happy, and Dossie, now a teenager, was extremely fond of him. He treated her like his own daughter from the very beginning. Their lives were shaped to a great extent by the social obligations that Dick had as a corporate executive and a recognized leader in the petroleum field.

In the early years of the thirties, with the sudden change of lifestyles and the absence of the rigorous schedules of show business, both Mary and Pearl began to develop drinking habits that would eventually create very serious problems. Mary and Millard often got together with Pearl and Dick to play bridge (which had become a popular social pastime among the Hollywood set), but inevitably the occasions turned into drinking bouts. Both Millard and Dick were heavy drinkers, but Dick could manage his drinking far better than Millard, who was a serious alcoholic. Sadly, those days started a downward spiral of too much alcohol and too many pills, which in time would have tragic consequences for my two sisters.

Years later, when Pearl was trying to stay sober and attending Alcoholics Anonymous meetings, she wrote about how seductive the lifestyle was of going to dinner parties at seven, with dinner planned for eight, but with stragglers coming in until eight-thirty or so, and finally dinner at nine. "So a bunch of drunks were around the table, with no appetite left, and too much alcohol fueling their egos and their anger. I have witnessed so many ugly verbal battles between husband and wife—who were otherwise very nice and gentle people—that you would not believe it." Well, I am afraid that became Mary and Pearl's lifestyle for much of the rest of their lives.

In 1930, Joe was also working at RKO, and Mama and Papa were living in a new flat on Olympic Boulevard, since Mary and Millard took over the house on Camden Drive. I was the only one on the road, working the West Coast vaudeville movie houses in various dancing shows, with names like *Thanksgiving Gaieties* and *Merrymakers' Revue,* alternating with such movies as *The Cuban Love Song,* with Laurence Tibbett, Lupe Velez, and "Schnozzle" Durante (that was the way he was billed). That kind of vaudeville circuit was really not my cup of tea, but the old Eaton ethic of a job's a job was in my bloodstream, and it kept me going. It was not, however, the kind of show business that I was accustomed to, and I didn't enjoy it. I survived it largely because of books—filling my idle moments in lonely hotels with reading.

This joining of vaudeville entertainment with motion pictures would spread across the country, and in New York, grand movie theaters such as the Roxy, the Rivoli, and Radio City Music Hall were virtually the only kinds of places left for vaudeville. Even the great Palace Theater would start showing movies within a few years. Of course, there was burlesque, if you wanted that. The burlesque houses, particularly in New York, struggled to stay open by becoming more risqué, more naked, and more vulgar in their humor. Times Square was being transformed into a trashy amusement district. A fifth of the theaters in the district were standing empty, and some were converted to burlesque houses, most to the cheap bump-and-grind type. As early as 1931, *Variety* had reported that Times Square was "going to seed." It was not too long before the great Apollo Theater on Broadway became a four-shows-a-day bump-and-grind burlesque house.

Finally, by the mid-thirties, the city cracked down on the raunchier burlesque houses, and many were closed down. Most of us drew the line and stayed away from burlesque, but I knew many out-of-work performers who felt they had no choice. I certainly couldn't blame them. Georgia Southern, Ann Corio, and Gypsy Rose Lee, three talented actresses, would probably not have found their way into burlesque except for the depression. As it happened, they brought to the burlesque stage a large measure of talent and beauty—and in Lee's case, more tease than strip.

In the summer of 1930, before the disillusionment and while our optimism was still high, Mary and Millard, Mama, Charlie, and I returned on the train to New York. Mary had an engagement to dance in a show in London, so she and Millard were making it a delayed honeymoon trip. Mary was a featured dancer in a revue at London's Piccadilly Theater called *Folly to Be Wise,* which ran for a respectable thirty-one weeks. Mary was once again the principal ballet dancer and enjoyed great celebrity in London. While she was not the star, she received "guest star" treatment from the beginning, in an otherwise all-British cast. A London critic wrote, "Mary Eaton, a very pretty American blonde, dances attractively and is fortunate in having the solo part in the prettiest scene in the show, namely a ballet number which derives from *Les Sylphides,* and is full of grace and beauty." It would be Mary's last big moment in the spotlight.

At age nineteen, Charlie was on his way to Peekskill Military Academy in upstate New York to finish high school. Charlie's movie career had slowed to a standstill, and he was excited about the opportunity to complete his high school education. Of course, we did not know then that his acting career was essentially over, and while he would do a few things in vaudeville in the thirties, he would never again achieve the celebrity status he enjoyed as a teenage actor. As with so many child stars, there are few bridges to adult success.

Doris at Nils T. Granlund's Hollywood Club in New York, 1932

At the time, there was no place for Mama to go, because none of us was in New York, so she went to stay with Robert and Jean and be closer to where Charlie was going to school. Papa decided to stay for the time being on the West Coast with Joe. It was another of those separation-by-convenience actions that I never really understood. It seems obvious now that they preferred being apart—like being divorced within the marriage. Mama was away from Papa very often during her years on the road with one or more of us; then later in the twenties, Papa moved out of the Congress to the York Hotel; and then in the thirties, they lived on opposite coasts. I wish I had talked more with Evelyn about their relationship. She would have understood more about it than the rest of us, but I missed that opportunity.

My return to New York was short-lived. I had wanted to explore what possibilities might exist for me in the theater, since movie offers had not been coming my way. I also thought it was time to put some distance between me and Herb Brown, since I had become convinced that our relationship was going nowhere. Unfortunately, Broadway didn't have much to offer me either, and it was not long before I returned to Hollywood and lived for several months with Pearl. The only part I was able to get was dancing in the chorus of the Eddie Cantor movie *Whoopee!,* which had been a big hit on Broadway in the 1928–29 season, produced by Flo Ziegfeld. The movie and the title song, "Makin' Whoopee," were very big for Cantor, but the part did nothing for me. I was a chorus dancer not even listed in the cast. Gus Kahn and Walter Donaldson, who did most of the music, wrote another good song for Cantor that became a big hit, "My Baby Just Cares for Me."

By the way, Herb Brown contributed a song he did with Edward Eliscu, "I'll Still Belong to You." But as I said, by that time, Herb Brown did not belong to me, and I was determined not to see him while I was back in California. One day, while I was still staying with Pearl, Herb sent a beautiful gift to the house—perfume or something—suggesting that we get together. I asked Joe to return the gift to Herb, and that was that. While ending that affair caused me a great deal of pain, I knew it was the right thing to do. Herb had never asked me to marry him, even though he was about to embark on more of his serial marriages.

By 1932, I was beginning to be filled with apprehension about my future in show business. The idea of a career had just become the agony of looking for another job. However, Nils T. Granlund, who ran the Hollywood restaurant and club in New York, reached me in California to offer me a job as a lead dancer in his *Hollywood Revue of 1932.* I immediately returned to New York, and for several months, my spirits were lifted.

Nils did not like the presence of mobsters in the clubs, and even though early on he worked in places owned by the mob, he insisted on a free hand in running the clubs and putting on the shows. When he started the Hollywood, he led the way to a different type of establishment, away from the more raucous, high-dollar, liquor-dominated clubs to a more sober, moderate clientele. He attracted larger numbers of customers, abandoning the high cover charge and refusing to sell liquor. He felt the best way to stay away from mob involvement was to stay away from the bootlegging business. Of course, people could bring their flasks and he sold setups, but he never sold liquor during prohibition. He hired beautiful girls for his shows, and the word was that the Hollywood restaurant and club had the most beautiful girls in New York. Nils even worked as a talent scout for Ziegfeld, as well as a press agent. He was really Broadway's jack-of-all-trades. He had a highly regarded reputation—even with Ziegfeld—for finding beautiful girls. He discovered Harriet Hilliard (who married Ozzie Nelson), Alice Faye, Joan Crawford, and I don't know how many others who eventually became stars.

Nils described his place as "the family man's club," and he avoided the excesses that characterized so many clubs of that time. He also opened another huge club called Paradise, located in the upstairs space that once was Rector's dance hall, where Ted Lewis and his orchestra had played. Later Nils went to Las Vegas, where he produced girlie shows at the Flamingo. In 1957, he wrote a book about his experiences in the twenties titled *Blondes, Brunettes, and Bullets.* That same year, he was killed in a car wreck in Las Vegas, while riding in a taxi.

Nils always treated me in a warm and engaging way, and several times invited me to have lunch with him. He loved to talk about the Broadway scene and the goings-on of the day. He was very tall, thin, and highly animated. He had been born in Lapland and came to America with his family at nine years of age. Like most Broadway characters, he was a nonstop talker, full of colorful expressions and fascinating stories. One day, he invited me to join him for lunch at the Astor Hotel, and in the midst of lunch he gave me a beautiful diamond ring and said, "This is yours. I want you to wear it." Well, I was dumbfounded. I didn't know what to think. I never thought there was any romantic interest in our relationship, and even on that day, there was no such indication. Of course, in the prohibition era, men gave extravagant gifts to women, particularly to women in show business, but none like that had come my way. So thanking him through my obvious embarrassment, I reluctantly decided to keep the ring, which I still have to this day.

He never made any romantic overtures toward me (except whatever's implicit in the gift of a dazzling diamond ring); however, others told me that he had a crush on me and was looking for a more intimate relationship. Well, all performers are not sophisticated, and I just may have been too naive to know what was going on. Pearl always thought of me as a babe in the woods and often told me so.

After completing several months in the show at the Hollywood, I started looking for the next job. That is the never-ending cycle of show business— working, looking, working, looking. It was what I hated most about the show-biz way of life. There was always that haunting fear that maybe the next job would not be there. Of course, in the thirties, that fear was reality bound. Nonetheless, I managed to get a role in a play called *Page Pygmalion* at the Bijou Theater. It was a terrible flop. One critic accurately called it "an incredibly silly play." Another, choosing understatement, said, "It was a slight embarrassment." Of course, its run was blessedly brief, and back I went to making the rounds to find new jobs. Fortunately, Millard and Mary had leased an apartment on the East Side, on Fifty-seventh Street, which they permitted me to use, so at least I had a roof over my head.

The depression was upon us in earnest, and I could not find any work as a performer. With so many neighborhood movie theaters and the incredible popularity of radio, it was hard to get people to come out to the theaters. You could stay at home and listen to the great vaudeville comedians who had gone on to star in radio programs or listen to the music of the day on the radio without it costing you a cent. There were songs like these big hits of 1932: "I Told Every Little Star," "April in Paris," "How Deep Is the Ocean," "Night and Day," and that unforgettable song of hard times, "Brother Can You Spare a Dime." You could have heard a complete opera (for the first time) on your home radio from the Metropolitan Opera House, on Christmas Day, 1932, when NBC broadcast Humperdinck's *Hansel and Gretel*. The world of show business had changed.

That would have been a terribly lonely Christmas for me, except that Evelyn and her children had come back east, where Evelynne at seven was appearing in the role of Kim in the revival of *Show Boat*. She played the granddaughter of Cap'n Andy. Most memorable was the poignant scene between

Kim and her father, Gaylord Ravenal (played by Dennis King). It was beautifully acted, and made a name for Evelynne as a gifted child actress. Evelynne's first appearance on Broadway had been when she was eleven months old, a baby in a high chair. Evelyn appeared on stage with her in a nonspeaking role in a play called *Mismates,* in which her son Edwin also had a role.

Evelyn's decision to return to the East Coast, just as Bob was trying to get established on the West Coast added a good deal of strain to a marriage that had already suffered a lot of stress, and the marriage would end in a few years. Evelyn's obsession to see that her children succeeded in show business had taken precedence over the marriage as well as over Bob's own professional interests. As a matter of fact, the income that was earned by Edwin, Evelynne, and Warren was what the family was living on. Bob had the patience of Job, but his limits were about to be exceeded.

Tired of pounding the pavements in New York, I started working for the Thatcher Stock Companies in New England. I worked as the ingenue in a number of different plays—*Stepping Sisters* and *June Moon* were two of them— in Hartford, New Haven, Worcester, and other such places. In the year that followed, I worked for several months in a stock company in Hempstead, Long Island, where I did a succession of unremarkable plays, but it was a way of making a living. I wonder now who has ever heard of *Her Unborn Child, As Husbands Go, The Late Christopher Bean,* and *Polly with a Past*—if anyone has produced those in the last fifty years, I don't know who it would have been.

Meanwhile, Charlie was having a very successful experience at Peekskill Military Academy. He was a very good student, and in his second year there (1931–32), he played football. He was something of a campus character at Peekskill, where as he describes it, "There was nothing theatrical there except me." He was older than his classmates, and much more sophisticated. The bull sessions in Charlie's room were about Hollywood and Broadway, and God knows what tales Charlie might have told. His fellow students did not know what to make of Charlie, and many were skeptical about his name-dropping. On one occasion, with a long weekend off, Charlie and a small group of his eighteen-year-old friends took the train to New York to go the Cotton Club, where Cab Calloway was appearing. His song "Minnie the Moocher" had made him well known, and the club was packed. While Charlie's group was sitting at their table, Flo Ziegfeld and another man entered with three beautiful girls—"stunning broads" according to Charlie—and they sat at a table not far from Charlie's. Charlie told his friends he knew Ziegfeld, and their response was a typical, "Yeah, Charlie, we know. You know everyone." So Charlie got up and walked to Ziegfeld's table. He said, "Excuse me, Mr. Ziegfeld. You may not remember me but . . ."

Ziegfeld looked up at him and with a big smile on his face he said, "Ahhh, the Dauphin," referring to Charlie's 1921 role in the *Follies*. Ziegfeld asked about all of the Eatons and then asked Charlie if he would like to dance with one of the beautiful girls, which, of course, he did. When he returned to his table with a prideful grin on his face, he said, "OK, you bastards, I told you." They nodded and in chorus said, "We believe, we believe!" Charlie finished school with a renewed credibility and an enlarged number of pals crowding into his room for the bull sessions.

Because of Charlie's penchant for name-dropping, a similar incident took place years later, when Charlie was serving as a captain in the Army Air Corps in Foggia, Italy, near the end of World War II. He was dining with a few of his fellow officers in the headquarters hotel when Irving Berlin came in with two general officers and sat at a nearby table. After receiving looks of incredulity when he said he knew Irving Berlin, Charlie got up and walked to Berlin's table and—while Charlie was receiving get-out-of-here looks from the generals—Berlin jumped to his feet shouting, "Charlie, how the hell are you?" Then Berlin asked, "How's Doris? How's Mary? How's Pearl?" The fellow officers who never knew what to make of Charlie's oft-mentioned claims about being in show business finally began to believe he wasn't making it all up.

When Charlie finished school in 1932, he returned to Hollywood to try to get back into pictures. While Charlie knew quite a few people who were doing well in motion pictures, he was at an awkward age: there were not many parts available for a twenty-one year old. The comedic actor Arthur Lake (remembered for an almost endless series of Blondie movies) was a good friend of Charlie's, and he mentioned to Marion Davies that Charlie—the brother of Pearl Eaton—was in Hollywood looking for work. Marion, who had been in the *Ziegfeld Follies of 1917*, was a famous film star by that time, and she knew Pearl quite well. She had her secretary call Charlie and invite him to a showbiz gathering at the Santa Monica beach house owned by her lover, William Randolph Hearst. Although they lived together for more than thirty years, they never married because Hearst's Catholic wife would not give him a divorce. As I recall, that beach house was called Wyntoon, and it had 110 rooms. Charlie ended up staying there for two weeks. He met the high and mighty and felt that he was often in the role of court jester, but ultimately—in spite of Marion's heroic efforts on his behalf—no work came of it, and Charlie returned to New York. At twenty-one, he was too old for juvenile roles and not old enough for leading roles. So he gave up on a movie career and thought he might try whatever had survived of vaudeville.

After returning from England, Mary had no luck with any of the Hollywood studios and neither did Millard. In those days, actors were contract-bound to certain studios, and Mary had missed her chance to sign a contract when she was at the top of her career. That chance did not come again. Millard tried writing movie scripts and was given one directorial job for what Pearl called a "C" picture. By 1932, Mary had taken a starring role in a "tabloid version" (condensed version) of *Sally*. She was playing that same West Coast circuit of movie theaters that I had played earlier—Seattle, Portland, San Francisco, and so on. The show had a cast of sixty, which probably means that no one was being paid much, but a lot of actors had no work at all. The show ran for an hour and fifteen minutes between the screening of whatever film was showing, and there were four shows daily with a total twenty-eight costume changes for Mary.

The *Seattle Daily Times* asked the question, Why would a big star like Mary be doing a four-a-day? Her answer was that she didn't "fancy the idea of sitting in a Beverly Hills chimney corner this winter curled around a good book or knitting on a long woolen muffler." She went on to say that "Broadway this season has sunk to new depths [and] the big vaudeville time is all gone. I wouldn't do plain vaudeville, but *Sally* is a good story and I like the show." We all knew that Mary did *Sally* because she couldn't face a life without dancing. It was her great passion in life, and I know there must have been a lot of desperation in her accepting that miserable four-a-day routine. It was a terrible comedown for Mary, who was the toast of Broadway a few years before. Even more poignant, it would bring to an end her dancing and acting career, and she was only thirty-one.

Back in New York, Charlie and I took an apartment at the Whitby Apartments at 325 West Forty-fifth Street. Evelyn had once lived there, and it was a great location for Charlie, who got parts in a few short running plays, during the 1932–33 season: *Incubator, Tommy,* and *Growing Pains.* In the summer of 1933, Charlie got a role in a show called *Lady Luck,* which ran for two weeks. Ed Sullivan reported in his *Daily News* column of July 26, 1933, that when the show closed, the cast "divided up the money in the till and Charlie Eaton's share was eighty-five cents."

Living at the Whitby was not so convenient for me, since I had to take the train each day to Hempstead, Long Island, for my work in the stock company, and back again late at night. I would arrive home after midnight and leave again at seven in the morning to be at ten o'clock rehearsals. I spent most of my time on the train learning the next week's show.

Meanwhile, a friend from the glory days named Buster West, a successful second-generation vaudevillian, gave Charlie a part in his new vaudeville act. Buster was a successful performer in the twenties, and even much later had a great success in *Follow the Girls,* a musical hit of 1944. But in the early thirties, he had been in a popular vaudeville act called Wells, Virginia, and West—who were really father, mother, and son. They had been a huge success in the *George White's Scandals,* and afterward they toured with a skit called "Two Sailors and a Girl," always as the top act in the best vaudeville houses. When Buster's father died and his mother no longer wanted to perform, Buster took his father's role, had Charlie take his old role, and hired Lucille Page to replace his mother. They toured successfully for some months, appearing in short runs in various cities from New York to Chicago.

When Charlie's tour ended, he and I took a flat on 106th Street, to reduce the amount of rent I was paying. Mama had stayed for a while with Robert and Jean, but they were having serious problems, so Mama came to stay with Charlie and me. We had little furniture, and my bed during the time we stayed in that hovel was an army cot, the regular folding model.

Charlie and I decided to team up to do a vaudeville act with the help of a young writer named Tom Ahern. Evelyn—who God knows could not afford it—loaned us a hundred dollars to have money to pay Tom and to get started on the vaudeville circuit. This was another one of the loving gestures that she made throughout the years to help any member of the family in any way she could.

Well, the act turned out to be dreadful, but we took it to Philadelphia anyway to test it out. Sure enough, it was as bad as we had feared. After our first performance, the theater manager asked us to cut ten minutes out of our twelve-minute act, so we got the message and packed our bags for home. Charlie still remembers a song that Ahern had written for that act. It was called "Upside Down." I am sure that I didn't understand the song then and I don't now, but the title sounds like a comment on our lives at that time—which had certainly been turned upside down. Charlie's memory produced these lyrics—maybe you can figure them out:

Upside down,
That's the way our pictures are,
If we only had some stardust,
We could paint the falling star,
But the movies wouldn't let us,
All the stars were contract bound,
So we did a starless star part,
Starring upside down.

It is easy to see why I lost all memory of that song. In fact, I can't remember anything about that whole misbegotten vaudeville act. There is something pathetic, even heartbreaking, about that frantic effort to stay alive in show business. It was really our dying gasp. Our careers were really over, and we had not yet been able to accept that harsh reality. Letting go of the only life we had known wasn't easy to do. In the modern idiom, you would say we were "in denial," and—because some never learn—that would not be the last time in my life that I would try to stick to a lost cause.

I recall that while we were there on 106th Street, Robert came to the apartment one night. Jean had told him that she wanted a divorce, and he was very drunk and deeply depressed. As always, Mama took him in and tried to get him to sleep there until he could sober up, but he became very agitated and tried to jump out the window. We restrained him enough to keep that from happening, and he eventually did go to sleep. Poor Robert, he looked terrible, so dissipated and worn. His good looks had been used up by alcohol and drugs. It broke my heart just to look at him. It was my first glimpse of his inevitable self-destruction.

In 1934, when my engagement with the stock company ended, I got a minor role in the Kaufman and Hart play *Merrily We Roll Along*, at the Music Box Theater. The play starred Walter Able and Mary Philips, and Evelyn's son, Edwin, had a juvenile role. Only twenty-three shows that season had more than a hundred performances, and we were one of them, with 155. But in five months, it was all over except for a road tour. It was my last appearance in a Broadway play, and while I didn't have a featured role, it kept nickels in my purse to eat baked beans at the Automat, and it kept hope alive.

When I had to go on the road, Mama decided to go to Norfolk to stay for a while with her brother, Joseph Saunders. At a former time, Uncle Joe had seen the instability of Mama's life, with our ups and downs in show business, and had told her that if she ever needed it, she had a home with him and his family. At this point in our collective lives, there seemed to be no place for Mama either on the East Coast or the West Coast. So she ended up staying with Uncle Joe for several months.

I went on the road with *Merrily We Roll Along*, which rolled along only for four weeks, and then I was back in New York, jobless. Evelyn, knowing my predicament, invited me to live with her family in their apartment in Astoria. Evelyn was working hard to keep her three children in Broadway shows, and while they were having some success, there weren't many long-running shows. Evelyn was always uptight about lining up the next job. They had only a small apartment, and with the growing tensions between Evelyn and Bob, the situation was increasingly uncomfortable for all of us. Evelyn was just plain cranky and quick to anger, and though I loved her dearly, it was increasingly painful to be around her. Sadly, her ill humor and bitchiness became chronic, alienating almost everyone close to her, and she would experience great loneliness in her later years.

In the meantime, Charlie had moved into a single room in a brownstone on Eighty-fifth Street, with Papa, who had come back from the West Coast, where he had been lost and lonely living by himself. Now in New York, Papa would make the rounds of the papers every night looking for something to do, but he wasn't able to earn any money, so he would just hang out. Charlie had very little saved up, and he was out every day looking for some kind of employment. I wanted desperately to escape from the unpleasant situation in Astoria, so I moved into that single room with Charlie and Papa.

There were only two cots in that small shabby room we had on Eighty-fifth Street, so at night, I pushed together two upholstered chairs, with magazines stacked between them, and pulled a blanket over me, and that was my bed. That miserable room was a long, long way from the Congress apartment on Fifty-fourth Street and the summerhouses at Great Neck and Point Pleasant. These were the darkest days of our lives. Charlie would even go around to the theaters trying to get work as a stagehand to pick up a little change, and Papa continued his efforts to get menial part-time work at the newspaper plants. I recall one time when Mary had sent him a little money—which she did from time to time—he came home after a night at the newspaper plant where he had been playing poker, and he proudly announced, "I won thirty-five dollars!" He threw fifteen dollars in my lap, and said, "Here, you can have fifteen!" To us, any extra money meant food—more beans and bread—and fifteen dollars seemed like a huge largesse.

Joe joined the new Civilian Conservation Corps in California, part of Franklin D. Roosevelt's New Deal, and he was doing well, with the rank of sergeant—the CCC being organized like the military—and soon was making thirty dollars a month. Since he was provided his room and board, he began to send us twenty-five dollars a month. That was the only way we made it through those dark days of the depression. Joe had received help, now he was helping. That is the way the family had been through the years: whoever was up helped whoever was down. We all looked out for each other, yet it was hard to realize that after more than a decade of rather impressive prosperity, we had saved so little.

In 1935, Mary and Millard were having it rough. Mary particularly was having a difficult time coping with her lost stardom and showbiz appeal. They both had started drinking quite heavily; Millard began to encounter health problems, and his heart finally gave out. He may not have been good for Mary—as Pearl always insisted—but she did love him very much. His death was such an emotional blow to her that her grief was severe and almost unending. She asked Mama to come to live with her, and they sold the house on Camden Way, moving into a bungalow on Olympic Boulevard. In another of those geographic "divorces," Papa stayed on the East Coast with Charlie and me.

In a year or so, Joe, whose work was in northern California, wrote Mary telling her that he was leaving the CCC and asking if he could live with them. As always, Mary said he was welcome. So Joe left the CCC after serving for two years, and with the help of Pearl's husband, Dick Enderly, he was given a job running a gasoline station for the Richfield Oil Company.

Over time, Mary went back to drinking heavily, trying to drown her sorrow in liquor. She could not pull herself together well enough to resume her career—even if an offer had come along. Her grief, I have always felt, was twofold: the grief from losing Millard so suddenly and the grief for her lost career. She loved everything about performing, and she loved the theater in ways that the rest of us did not. Her dancing was the expression of her deepest self and was so much a part of her identity that she was truly lost without it. I believe that was the grief that lasted the remainder of Mary's life.

While Mary improved enough over time to resume a social life, she remained a very fragile person. She did, however, make one heroic effort to recover and return to show business. She went to the Ernest Belcher Studios and resumed the study of ballet. She practiced diligently for seven or eight months. She danced in a Belcher production (not allowing her name to be used in the program). And while she danced well, the old magic wasn't there, and she realized—at thirty-four—that she would not regain her previous form. She later said to me, "Nobody ever tried any harder than I did."

In a few years, she married a wealthy rancher named Charles Emory, and for several years, she had a better life. Charles was called Chuck by all of us, and early on, we liked him a great deal. They moved into Chuck Emory's ranch house, and Papa joined Mama and Joe in the house on Olympic Boulevard. Eventually, Charlie moved there also, wanting to make one more try at getting back into the movies. Mary and Chuck traveled often, spending much of each summer in a home Chuck owned in upstate New York. However, they both drank too much, and soon Mary's alcoholism grew worse. She did not have a high tolerance for alcohol, as Chuck apparently did, so their lifestyle was increasingly debilitating for Mary. Chuck would get terribly angry at Mary because she got "sloppy drunk." By the end of the decade, Emory divorced her, and Mary went to a rehabilitation center. The Los Angeles papers all covered the settlement. Emory was to provide $500 a month so that Mary "could continue to live in the manner to which she had become accustomed."

But Mary would never again be the lighthearted, confident person she once was. It has always seemed to me that show people have a very difficult time standing on their legs when they are no longer a part of show business. They work so hard to get there and to succeed, and then when something happens and they no longer have the adulation and attention—indeed when no one even notices them at all—it is a terrible blow. Ziegfeld filled his choruses with sixteen- and seventeen-year-old beauties, and most of them were out of show business by twenty. Many tried to marry quickly to anyone of great means and make life an endless party. But life is not that way, and the party often ended in sadness.

I have seen so many tragedies occur when the makeup is gone and the stage lights go out. As someone said, show business has more tragedies than comedies on life's real stage. And if there is an occupational hazard in show business, it is alcohol. Show folks drink to celebrate success, drink to pass the time in strange towns, drink to unwind after an evening's performance, drink to drown sorrows and disappointments, drink as part of the camaraderie of showbiz. It is a problem that I've never had, but I lived within a circle of family and friends where it seemed endemic. With the exception of Robert, excessive drinking was never a problem with the Eatons in the glory years, but after 1930, it hit the family like a plague.

In 1935, Charlie and I were called to a veterans' hospital in New York, where our brother Robert had been hospitalized. He had pneumonia and was terribly undernourished, suffering the debilitating effects of chronic drug and alcohol use. He looked so frail and emaciated, and his breathing was shallow and heavy. The last thing he said to me was, "Doris, please give me a cigarette." But I had been told he could not smoke, and so I had to refuse him. The doctor said he had to have a blood transfusion, and Charlie and I were tested to see whether our blood type matched. Charlie's did, and so he gave blood for Robert. But it was too late. Robert did not have any resiliency left. He had battered his body into such a weakened condition that he just couldn't make it. He died that day while Charlie and I were at the hospital. He was just thirty-nine.

We buried Robert in a veterans' cemetery in Brooklyn. None of my sisters was there, just Mama, Papa, Charlie, and me. Mama had come back from Uncle Joe's for the funeral. She was the only one who had stayed very close to Robert, as he had become increasingly alienated from the rest of the family. His death was a tragedy of self-destruction, and for many years, I asked myself the nagging question, What could we have done differently?

With the family's tragic turn of events and the terrible consequences being produced by the depression, I knew that we could not go on doing what we had done in the past. Something had to change. One day when I had finished dressing and "fixing up" to go out and once more pound the pavement looking for work, I simply collapsed in tears. Shaking my head from side to side, I said to Charlie, "I can't go out there again. I can't spend another day having people tell me there is nothing—just nothing." That day, I made a fundamental decision to leave show business and get some kind of a salaried position doing something—anything—in another field. I was going to know where my next meal was coming from. What I did not realize then was that with the first job I ever had outside of show business, my life really was going to be changed forever.

CHAPTER TWELVE

THE MAGIC STEP

I n *Of Human Bondage,* Somerset Maugham wrote, "There is nothing so degrading as the constant anxiety about one's means of livelihood." How right he was. And that terrible and constant anxiety is even worse when it follows twenty years of productive and creative work. We had been very fortunate. Although Mary was the only one of us to achieve real stardom and become famous, the rest of us had fared pretty well, and at least we had become well known within the show business world. We had stayed busy doing what we loved doing, and for the most part, we had lived in the upper echelon of the entertainment business. We had enjoyed the esteem of producers and fellow performers and had reveled in our success. Nothing had prepared us for the degrading poverty of the depression—and particularly for the painful rejection by the entertainment world that had once been so receptive to us. There is an inherent cruelty in show business that leads so often to the casting off of seasoned and talented performers because they have reached a certain age or tastes have changed or producers seek new directions or new faces. And that rejection profoundly affects the lives of many show people—just as it did the Eatons.

Our situation in the mid-thirties was desperate. Neither Charlie nor Papa had found work, and we couldn't even pay our rent. Fortunately, our friendly German landlord, who was very fond of Charlie, was permitting us to stay in the tacky room on Eighty-fifth Street, saying in his thick accent, "Oh, something vill come along, and you vill be able to pay me one day." When something did come along, it always proved to be short-lived. Not many people would shell out the price of a ticket unless a play was very big. Theaters all over the Times Square district were standing empty. With our landlord's beneficent patience and the money Joe was sending us, we were able to stay alive, but that was about it.

I had been searching the want ads and came across an ad for dance partners at a particular club where customers paid to have you as a dance partner. I did not fully realize the nature of such clubs and the kind of life represented there, so I decided to apply for a job. Those places became known as ten-cents-a-dance clubs and were made notorious in Rodgers and Hart's plaintive song, "Ten Cents a Dance," which Ruth Etting sang in *Simple Simon.*

When I think that those words might have become my anthem, I shudder at how close I came to that life. But a good friend named George Besler, whom I had known since he was a student at Princeton, intervened at the right moment. He and I had spent some time together during the heyday of the twenties. He loved to do the Charleston, and we often went out dancing. A few times, he invited me down to Princeton for parties and dinners, and that was my only taste of college life in the twenties. Of course, it was about Princeton that F. Scott Fitzgerald wrote *This Side of Paradise,* with the jazz age images of fun-loving, flask-carrying, raccoon-coat-wearing boys sowing wild oats. I can't remember the raccoon coats, but everything else seemed to fit. It seems now as though I saw them only in a perpetual party, and that was how I viewed college life.

George also had taken me to his palatial home, where I met his parents and his sister, Helen. His father was an important stockholder with New Jersey Railroad, and they were obviously well-to-do. Helen and I became friendly, and she told me that she wished I would marry George, but I never loved him in that way, and he knew it. I might have been very cautious too after my tragic experience with Joe Gorham, and I wasn't ready for an intimate relationship. I wanted to have fun, go out dancing, and have good companionship, none of which included marriage. And putting modesty aside, George got a kick out of going out with someone who was successful on the musical stage, and his greatest pleasure was in showing me off. In time, however, he did become serious about me, and when his folks were about to take him to Germany for an extended vacation, he told me that he hoped I would marry him when he returned. But I told him no, that would not happen. I may have loved him, as one loves a friend, but I was not in love with him.

When we met fortuitously in 1936, just as I was at my wit's end, he asked me to go with him to visit Helen in New Rochelle. I agreed with pleasure, looking forward to spending time with both George and Helen. He knew I was out of work and having a rough time. When he saw the place we were living in, he shook his head and said, "Doris, this place is a dump." So, naturally, when we were at Helen's home, our conversation got around to my present predicament and my desperate need for a job. Helen told me she had been taking her oldest son to the Arthur Murray Dance Studios for tap dancing lessons, and she thought I might be able to get a job there. She thought they had only one tap dancing teacher and needed another.

The next day, instead of going to the dime-a-dance joint, I went to the Murray studio, on Forty-third Street. There must have been five floors of studios in that building. It was obvious that it was a very large operation. I went to the reception desk and asked if I could speak to Mr. Arthur Murray. Then I heard this voice behind me saying, "I am Arthur Murray, and I'd be glad to speak with you." I turned to introduce myself, feeling lucky that he was just right there. I told him who I was and that I had danced in the *Ziegfeld Follies,* and just for good measure, I told him I was Mary Eaton's sister.

Murray was a tall, angular man, and he was looking over his shoulder with an arched expression, his body almost turned away from me as I spoke to him. I said that my specialty was tap dancing and asked if he could use a tap dance instructor. I had a strange feeling that he was measuring me from a great distance. He tended to avoid eye contact; he did not convey any sense of being dismissive or disinterested, but he was certainly distant. Without any further discussion or questioning, he said, "Why yes, I think we can use another tap dance instructor. You can start in the morning at ten." He led me over to the receptionist, introduced me, and told her to start booking me for pupils the following morning. And that was it. There was no discussion of pay or expectations or anything else. No orientation, no training, no introductions. I walked out into the sunlight of Manhattan with a lighter heart, offering an unspoken thanks to the good Lord and to my famous sister Mary.

The next morning, I was shown to my studio on one of the upper floors, where the other instructors were all males teaching ballroom dancing. The first week I was there, I worked a total of eighteen hours, and I was supposed to turn in my billing in order to be paid. I did not know what to ask for, but Eleanor Walsh, one of the instructors who had befriended me, said that they were paying instructors one dollar an hour. So that is what I asked for and that is what I received. Those eighteen hours were the fewest hours I would work in a week for many years to come.

My bookings quickly increased, and soon I was working from ten o'clock in the morning to ten o'clock at night, and on Saturdays from ten to six, with thirty minutes for lunch. There was only one other tap dance instructor in the studio, and soon he left and I had more than I could handle.

While I had no further conversation with Arthur Murray about my teaching, his wife, Kathryn, came in the second week and said that she would like some lessons in tap dancing. She had a couple of lessons with me and did not come back, so I assumed that she was checking me out for her husband.

My students were varied. I taught mostly children, but I had a few adults, including some businessmen and some young women who simply wanted to know how to tap dance. It was great just to be working, and we were eating good meals again. Knowing that there was a check coming in every week and that I did not have to worry—week to week—about the next job was a wonderful relief. I was sleeping well at night—even in my two upholstered chairs with a stack of magazines between. But more than anything, I had that wonderful feeling that I was doing something really well. I felt good about myself, and I felt in charge of my own life. Really for the first time in my life, I felt in charge. Soon we were able to pay the back rent and get Papa a room upstairs so that we could have more space and greater comfort.

One day, I was called out to the desk to meet a beautiful young lady who wanted to see me about learning to tap dance. She was identified only as Princess dePolinac from France. She reminded me of a Renoir portrait—gorgeous red hair, blue blue eyes, cream-colored skin, the most perfect complexion— what a lovely human being she was. She just thought it would be fun to be able to tap dance, although she would be in New York for only two weeks. So we worked together daily for two weeks, and she made great progress and loved every minute of it. When she had to leave, she told me that it had been a wonderful experience and she had enjoyed it immensely. She asked, "Where can I send you a gift?" So I gave her my address on Eighty-fifth Street. Well, that day a uniformed chauffeur in a magnificent limousine delivered a case of Moet-Chandon champagne. There in that tacky brownstone front, with everybody on that entire melancholy block broken-down and destitute, we had this case of expensive French champagne delivered as a gift from the Prince and Princess dePolinac of Paris, the distinguished representatives to the United States of Moet-Chandon, the largest house among the shippers of illustrious French champagne.

For the following several months on Saturday nights, I would cook steaks, and we would set up a bridge table and cover it with newspapers, and Papa, Charlie, and I would dine and drink Moet-Chandon champagne. We couldn't—or didn't—drink a whole bottle, so we would put a stopper in it and put it back in the icebox to save till the next Saturday night. Of course, after a week, it was no longer filled with stars, but it tasted good enough to us. We knew nothing of champagne. We just knew we were *privileged*.

In the late spring of 1937, somehow Herb Brown found out where I was living and my phone number. On a Friday morning, just before I was leaving for the studio, he phoned saying that he was in town and would very much like to see me. I was quite surprised at the call. I agreed to see him at his hotel after I finished work—which would not be until 10:30 P.M. On my way to the hotel, I thought to myself, "Why am I doing this?" Then I thought, "I'll see what happens one more time with this 'lost cause.'"

I arrived. After the small talk about what I was doing, he suggested that I might do better in Hollywood and why not go back to California—perhaps we could work something out. No proposal, just maybe we could work something out. I had been there about fifteen minutes. I rose and walked toward the door and said, "I'm not interested." I walked the short distance to the elevator, and when the elevator door opened, I walked in, turned around, and saw Herb standing at the open door of his room. That was the last time I saw Herb. As the elevator door closed, I said to myself, "The curtain has come down on this episode of my life."

I was glad that I had this one last meeting. All the way back to my brownstone home, I felt free as a bird. It was like a new birth. I was happy with my teaching. My income was increasing a little each week with new pupils, and the commissions on renewed courses were coming in. Most important to me was the feeling of self-confidence and self-esteem that had been developing within. Yes—it was a new birth, and I was not going to take a backward step.

The next day was Saturday. When I arrived at the brownstone about six-thirty in the evening, after teaching my nine and one half hours, Charlie had the bridge table with newspaper cloth and paper napkins all set. I cooked the steaks, and Charlie poured the champagne. Charlie, Papa, and I drank a toast to the future, and for the first time in many years, I felt that I had won. Inwardly, I knew I was determined to work for that future with all my heart and mind and spirit.

⦿ ⦿ ⦿

Arthur Murray had started in the business of teaching dancing in New York in 1924. He was from East Harlem and had originally studied dancing with Vernon and Irene Castle, for whom he worked for a while as a dance instructor. He opened a studio of his own in Atlanta, Georgia, and then moved back to New York in 1924 to get a larger clientele and begin a national mail-order business. He developed his famous floor diagrams, showing foot movements, and began what seemed like an improbable task—teaching dancing by mail. What he learned was that the mail order was a prelude to a customer coming into the studio for instruction, so it greatly increased the number of pupils—that is what he called his dance students: pupils—coming to the New York studio. Almost from the beginning, he had an extraordinary marketing orientation, and his business grew by leaps and bounds. Famous names like Eleanor Roosevelt, the duke of Windsor, John D. Rockefeller Jr., Winthrop Rockefeller, Harvey Firestone, Cornelius Vanderbilt, the Kennedys of Boston, and Elizabeth Arden, all made their way to Murray to learn ballroom dancing. Before he was through, there would be over five hundred studios in the United States that bore the name of Arthur Murray—and there were others in England, Germany, South Africa, Bermuda, Australia, and Puerto Rico.

As more and more big bands appeared, making records and playing in hotels and nightclubs, social dancing became increasingly popular. Glenn Gray, Guy Lombardo, and Leo Reisman were among the earlier bands shaping America's popular taste in music and dance. Before long, there was a tremendous flowering of big bands: Wayne King, Eddie Duchin, Freddy Martin, the Dorseys, Duke Ellington, Benny Goodman, Count Basie, Artie Shaw, Glenn Miller, Harry James—and the list goes on. Along with the big bands came a whole generation of new singers, who crooned love songs into microphones and brought dancers to the floor to hug to music, even if they couldn't really dance. Eventually, for the white collar set, in order to be sophisticated and popular with the opposite sex (as all Arthur Murray ads proclaimed), you had to be able to dance. Then when the Latin dances came along—particularly the rhumba—and Latin bands like Xavier Cugat became popular, a greater demand for dance lessons was created.

So even while I was teaching tap dancing, my eyes were on those instructing ballroom dancing, and I knew that was really what I wanted to learn more about and teach. I thought the dancing was beautiful, and the Murray methods were clear, intelligent, and fun to teach. Ballroom dancing also reflected a kind of lifestyle—manners, customs, and a way of relating to others—that I found attractive. I felt that the dance studio was a special place, and it was the place I wanted to be.

There were often classes for instructors there on my floor, so I asked Mr. Murray if I could sit in whenever I had the time in order to learn more about how the ballroom instructors approached their task. He said, "Of course, if you wish. Go ahead, anytime you want." So I did as often as I could, taking the instruction along with the other apprentice teachers. Additionally, since I was the only female teacher on that floor, whenever one of the male instructors needed a partner to demonstrate a step, he would come and ask me if I could help. This is how I met Cy Andrews, the dance teacher who would later become my business partner and my very good friend. Over a period of time, I was learning a lot about the teaching of ballroom dancing and the particular approach that Arthur Murray brought to that enterprise. He actually had a tremendous impact on ballroom dancing in the United States, as well as developing new and original methods for the teaching of it.

He focused his method on two very simple movements that he called the magic step. Most ballroom dancing, he said, can be reduced to two kinds of movements: a walking step and a side step. Combining these two, you had the basis for the fox-trot, the rhumba, the waltz, and any number of other dances—all you did was change the rhythm and add variations in combining the two movements. It made dancing so simple for people to learn. Once you mastered the magic step, you could get instant gratification by adding the variations and suddenly finding yourself doing a beautiful dance. Everyone can take two sliding steps forward—left, then right—and then step to the side with the left foot, bringing the right foot alongside it. As we would repeatedly say, "Walk, walk, side, together." At the most elemental level, that was Arthur Murray's contribution to social dancing. Starting there was easy for most pupils, and the rest was adding simple refinements. Watching how people could become so much more graceful, hold themselves in more poised and pleasant postures, and develop the manners and practices of polite social dancing was a truly gratifying experience for me. To me, it was an art form that added elegance, interest, and entertainment to one's life. Unfortunately, over time Arthur became too greedy, and he started putting more effort into the sales program than into the dancing. And some of the beauty and excitement of the studios was lost—but I'm getting way ahead of myself.

Soon I had virtually given up teaching tap dancing and was teaching ballroom dancing full-time. I loved it and had a natural talent for doing it. I don't know that I ever said I loved being in show business, but I truly loved the dance studio and what we were doing there. We stayed very busy most of the year, but things slowed down considerably in the summer months. It was then that Cy Andrews—one of the great guys of the world—asked me if I would go with him to Spring Lake, New Jersey, to a summer resort as junior host and hostess to provide entertainment throughout the summer for the guests. The management provided us with room and board for our work in entertaining the guests. We would also have a studio for the guests to take dancing lessons from us. This would be our income for the summer months. There were many children at the summer resort, and we had to provide for the children as well as the adults. Cy did not like to work with children, so I agreed to do that in addition to working with adults every day. Although it was hard work, it turned out to be a very pleasant and profitable way to spend the summer.

Lunch at the Stork Club
with Arthur Murray, 1938

Dancing with Arthur Murray
in the Detroit studios, 1939

Then Arthur suggested that Cy and I take some time during the winter to go to Florida, to teach at the Flamingo Hotel in Miami, during what was the high season there. It was always easier to get extra teachers in New York than in other places, and Arthur was interested in getting instruction into resort hotels. So off we went to Miami during the month of January in 1938. That was another successful experience, but it too was terribly hard work with very long hours. While there, we met a good many automobile executives from Grosse Pointe, Michigan, who were vacationing in the warmth of southern Florida. They were wonderful pupils, bright and well educated, relaxed, and rested in the casual ambiance of Miami. It was my first experience in working with industry executives and their families, and that experience, as it turned out, helped to shape my future.

During the season there, having met so many people from the Detroit area, Cy had become convinced—and he convinced me—that there was a great opportunity in Detroit for an Arthur Murray studio. While we were still in Florida, Cy got in touch with Arthur Murray and asked him to think about having a studio in the Statler Hotel in Detroit. By the time we returned to New York, Cy and I were excited about the possibility of having our own studio in Detroit. We knew that we could not get ahead simply remaining as dance teachers, and the time seemed right to make a move. Up to that time, no Arthur Murray studio had been established outside of New York, so what Cy and I were planning would be a first.

After our return to New York, when Cy spoke with Arthur about pursuing the idea of a studio in the Detroit Statler, Arthur stunned Cy by saying, "Yes, it has already been arranged. Just go see Mr. Hennessy at the Statler office." Hennessy was something like the chief operating officer for the chain as well as a leading stockholder. He was a jovial, red-faced Irishman, with a fatherly, friendly manner. As we walked into his New York office, he greeted us warmly and asked what we wanted to see him about.

Well, Cy steered me to a chair directly across the desk from Mr. Hennessy, thinking that a gal might have more success in dealing with this powerful corporate figure. It was obvious that he wanted me to take the lead, and so I plunged into my first innocent, ignorant, and blissful experience in the business world—a world I never felt comfortable in even after years of experience. I said, "Cy and I would like to open an Arthur Murray studio in the Detroit Statler, and we understand that Mr. Murray has made the arrangements with you for us to do that." Mr. Hennessey sat there quietly for a few seconds, a quizzical look on his face. "Nothing has been arranged," he said. "Murray mentioned he might like to try a studio in the hotel, but there was no real discussion about that." I looked at Cy, who had blanched considerably, and neither of us knew what to say.

Finally, I turned back to Mr. Hennessey, who now looked amused at our nonplussed state, and plunged into a narrative of what Cy and I wanted to do. When I finished, he said, "That's sounds all right to me. What about the financial arrangements?" I quickly said (since Cy and I had discussed the matter), "We thought the hotel should have five percent of the gross." Mr. Hennessey looked disappointed and said, "I think that fifteen percent would be about right for the space you'll need." Pulling a phrase from Papa's negotiating vocabulary, I said, "Well, let's split the difference, Mr. Hennessey. Let's make it ten percent." I think he was so amused at my struggling efforts and obvious discomfort that he quickly said, "Okay, Doris. We'll make it ten percent. When do you want to start?" We told him we could leave right away, and in fact that is what we did.

Over twenty years later, in an article in the *Saturday Evening Post,* Kathryn Murray told the story this way:

> Cy Andrews and Doris Eaton, one of our resort dancing teams, were the first to ask Arthur if they could open a franchise studio. Doris Eaton had been a musical comedy star and while teaching for us in Florida had met the Henry Fords and other Grosse Pointe families. She and Cy Andrews had decided that they could do well with a dance studio in Detroit. They promised to follow Arthur's advice and instructions and give him ten percent of the gross. Because he had confidence in their ability, he agreed.

We set out once more in Cy's old rattletrap Ford to arrange for space in the Detroit Statler for our studio. I had that excited feeling that Detroit was my new Blue Bird, a new opportunity to find success and happiness. Cy's wife, who was also a dance instructor, and another male teacher would be standing by, ready to join us when the arrangements were made. I remember that trip and how determined we both were to make it work. Naturally, we were anxious and uncertain about how long it would take us to get started, and the big question was whether we could hold out long enough to get the studio established and make it succeed. We had no idea of how quickly that question would be answered.

On the evening we arrived at the hotel, even before we went to our rooms to unpack, we went by to see the Terrace Room. It was an elegant room where dining and dancing took place. It was an enormous room, large enough to hold about three hundred people, and there was a band of twelve musicians playing, a typical society dance band of that era. But we were stunned that only about four of the tables in that huge room were occupied. It was an astonishing sight, even a bit depressing, to see this huge, lovely room so nearly empty. Cy said, "Why don't we get checked in and change clothes and meet back down here." So we did. When we returned and were seated, the band started playing, but no one got up to dance. Cy said, with an impish grin on his face, "Shall we dance?" And I said, "I'd be delighted."

They were playing a fox-trot, and we danced the last half of the number. When it was over, those at the few occupied tables applauded, with appreciative smiles on their faces. The bandleader asked us what we would like to hear next, and Cy said, "How about a rhumba?" Well, the bandleader almost fell off the bandstand. He had this pained expression on his face, and it was pretty obvious that he did not know the rhumba, which was just beginning to be popular in this country. So he said, "How about a waltz?" And we said "Okay." We waltzed and got some more applause and smiles as the only dancers in the room, and we sat down. An older guy at one of the other tables came up to us and said, "That is the loveliest dancing I have ever seen. How did you learn to dance like that?" So we explained to him that we worked for Arthur Murray and that we were going to open a dance studio within the next day or two. He said, "I am going to be your first customer." As it turned out, he was.

We put an ad in the paper, and—to our great surprise—a line formed outside the office the day after the ad appeared. There were fifteen to twenty people waiting in line to sign up before we ever opened. Cy and I had all we could handle, so we sent an SOS for the others to come immediately, and our studio was suddenly a reality. From the very first day, it was a successful operation, and every day, it grew larger.

It is still hard for me to believe how quickly the business became such an overwhelming success. We received a lot of press coverage in Detroit, as if our coming were a major event for the city. In the first news articles announcing our new venture, other than being called "a star of the *Ziegfeld Follies,*" I was referred to as "Mary Eaton's sister." Even though Mary had not performed in several years, she was still well known. By the end of May in 1938, I had a weekly column in the *Detroit News,* which I called "On Your Toes." It was a dance advice column, in which I would describe certain bad habits or poor techniques that characterized many would-be dancers. Here is a sample:

> As he begins to dance, the left arm begins to pump. Up and down, up
> and down, sometimes in rhythm; more often not. His steps are wide

and far apart. Over the floor he goes in leaps and bounds. And the Pump Handle never stops. His partner is by no means the sole sufferer. Everybody in his orbit is in danger . . . it's lucky if there are no serious casualties. . . .

I ended each column with some advice on overcoming the bad techniques. I invented a lot of names for problem dancers: the pump handle, leaping Lena, the clinging vine, the knee-knocker, lazy daisy, the strap hanger, the spine cracker, and so on. Most who read the column had some recognition of the transgression, either as the victim or the perpetrator. It was a very successful way to communicate the value of proper dance methods and techniques. More and more people sent letters describing dance problems they had encountered or asking for advice of one kind or another. And our business kept getting bigger and bigger.

Every Monday evening at eight in the Terrace Room, we gave demonstrations of the various dances—rhumba, tango, shag, conga, fox-trot, and waltz. Our demonstrations really amounted to a floor show, and they became very popular. We started a champagne contest in which I, along with a male instructor, would demonstrate a certain step and then invite anyone from the audience to come up and try the step with us. After several different patrons came up, we would have the audience applaud to select the one who had learned and performed the step the best. The winner was given a bottle of champagne. That became an enormously popular program, and before long, that huge Terrace Room was filled every evening, and we had more and more pupils.

Mr. Hennessy frequently visited the Detroit Statler, and he was intrigued with the success of the studio and the turnaround in the number of customers now thronging to the Terrace Room. Although he insisted that we keep it between the two of us, he wanted me to teach him the fox-trot. We had only one teaching session, which he seemed to enjoy greatly, but he never took another lesson with me. After several years, when he rarely visited the Detroit Statler, I would visit with him whenever I was in New York, and we had lunch together on a number of occasions. It was the first business relationship that I had in my new career, and it was the best one I ever had.

We were fortunate that during our first year in Detroit, a new dance craze hit the country and brought to us a great amount of attention. It was the Lambeth Walk, which originated in England and was popularized in this country by the Broadway musical *For Me and My Gal*. Suddenly, everyone wanted to do the Lambeth Walk, which someone called "the perambulating rage of the country." It was an up-tempo walkabout, ending with the dancers slapping their knees and shouting "Hoi!" Not much of a dance—rather silly really—but we got a lot of publicity out of teaching and demonstrating it in many of the private clubs where we often gave dance exhibitions. Everyone in Detroit knew we were there.

In the fall of 1939, the hotel brought in Xavier Cugat and his orchestra, and the dance floor was filled with people doing the rhumba—almost all of them were or had been our students. There was something about the Latin dances that gave to such evenings a special aura that was romantic, festive, and colorful. The *comparsa* was the Cuban name given to the conga chain that brought all the dancers to their feet to weave in and around the tables throughout the Terrace Room. It was a good way to get everyone into the act and to realize how much fun you could have with those Latin numbers.

Within our first year, the Terrace Room had become the place to be, and if you were going to be au courant, you had to know how to dance the Latin dances. The Statler manager told us that the remarkable success of the Terrace Room was directly due to our studio and our promotion, and he was very appreciative. It was not too long before we had the whole second floor of the Statler, and we went quickly from four to ten instructors.

Soon after we opened our studio, our students were having some difficulty in finding other clubs in Detroit to go to because the bandleaders would play rhumbas too fast or too slow or simply incorrectly. So I called about six of the local bandleaders and had a special class for them, demonstrating the proper rhythms and tempos of the Latin dances. Pretty soon, there was a boom of Latin dances in the nightclubs of Detroit, and everyone was dancing the rhumba, the tango, and the conga. The hotel continued to bring in touring Latin bands. Enrico Madrigeura and Fausto Courbelo were two favorites that came into the Terrace Room. For more than a decade, Detroit was a center for Latin dances, and we had Arthur Murray teachers coming to us from all over the country to learn how to teach them.

On New Year's Eve, December 31, 1938, a ticket to the Terrace Room celebration, which included a demonstration of ballroom dancing by the Arthur Murray Dancers, was the hottest ticket in town. The party started at 10:00 P.M. and cost the whopping amount of ten dollars, to dance out the old year and in the new, with Jack Marchard and his Society Orchestra. Once again, among those who jammed into the room that evening were a majority of our pupils, including some of Detroit's most influential leaders and a good many of the corporate kings from the automotive industry. We became a part of the high-society party circuit, with hostesses frequently requesting that we send exhibition dancers to entertain at their parties. We never turned anyone down because we invariably got new students that way.

During the thirties, Henry Ford had brought to Dearborn, Michigan, the distinguished dance teacher Benjamin Lovett from Boston to teach his workers the traditional dances he taught in New England. Lovett was the top dance teacher in Boston, teaching the old, traditional dances brought here from Europe or developed here in past centuries. Lovett showed up one day at our studio, and he said to me, "I am really intrigued with some of the dances you are doing, and I would like to learn more about them." I asked him if the Latin dances were the ones that interested him, and he said that they were, but that he would like to keep it very confidential because he did not want Mr. Ford to know he was coming to the studio. So for about a six-week period, I privately taught him the various Latin dances, which he seemed to greatly enjoy and learn very quickly. We both enjoyed talking about dancing and getting to know each other. He was very dignified, urbane, and soft-spoken, obviously highly cultured and well educated.

One day, we received a formal invitation from Henry Ford to take our teachers to a dance demonstration in Greenfield Village, which Ford had built along with the Ford Museum to preserve Dearborn's rural past. The demonstration was to be presented by Mr. Benjamin B. Lovett on January 22, 1939. There was a huge building there that had been named Lovett Hall in honor of this extraordinary dance teacher, and the demonstration took place in the large ballroom of that hall. Mr. Ford was there and had his picture taken with the group of our teachers who attended.

There I saw for the first time the lovely dance patterns that had developed during the nineteenth century or earlier, presented here with the correct musical accompaniment in a dignified atmosphere befitting their performance. There were eighty dance students (Ford employees) who danced with precision and grace, in perfect time with the orchestra music. They paraded before us the authentic polkas, *la varsovienne*, the five-step schottische (Mr. Ford's favorite dance), a charming minuet, the rye waltz, and many other dances of equal interest. It was a thrilling exhibition. After it was over, Lovett announced that the Arthur Murray teachers would now demonstrate the contemporary ballroom dances, and Mr. Ford stoically got up and walked out of the room. I was stunned because he said nothing at all. He just walked out.

Later, I learned a good deal more about Mr. Ford. He was a staunch pro-hibitionist and had strong moralistic attitudes about drinking—and social dancing. He opposed any establishment—such as a nightclub or dance hall—where social dancing took place. He disapproved of the physical closeness of the one-on-one face-to-face dances, and therefore he doubtless had a rather low opinion of what we taught in our studios. His prudish attitude was shared by many religiously conservative people (including Mama's parents) when social dancing became popular earlier in the century, but it surprised me to learn how strongly Mr. Ford felt about it. Such attitudes were very much a part of his extraordinary efforts to reclaim the past by bringing Benjamin Lovett to Dearborn. He was not only trying to preserve the old, he also really wanted to do away with the new.

It is ironic that I would later teach Mr. Ford's grandson, Henry Ford II (son of Edsel) and several of his great-grandchildren all of the social dances. We often did instruction at the Grosse Pointe Little Club, where we taught the children of the automotive executives. I recall that Henry Ford II came to the Detroit studio when he was just a college student home for his Christmas break and wanted to improve his dancing. I taught him a few lessons myself and then assigned another teacher to take over. When it came time to pay for his lessons, the young Ford asked me politely, "Miss Eaton, would it be all right with you if I send you a check?" I told him with some sense of amusement that I would certainly trust him to do that. Soon I received the following letter, dated January 14, 1939, on his Yale University stationery, with the check enclosed:

Dear Miss Eaton,

Thanks a lot for the lessons and I'll be back sometime to learn what I didn't get a chance to get last time. Quite frankly my rhumba isn't so hot. Enclosed find my check.

Regards, Henry Ford II

Later on, I learned that the elder Henry Ford was a most eccentric anti-quarian. He was in love with the past, and he wanted to change the modern world into the Dearborn of 1870, the world he knew as a boy. (A strange passion for the man who was leading the world into a new age!) He had ear-lier bought the old Wayside Inn in Massachusetts and restored it to what it was when new. It was while he and Mrs. Ford were there in Massachusetts that he saw a demonstration of traditional dances led by Mr. and Mrs. Benjamin Lovett. He was so taken with these wonderfully graceful old-fashioned dances that he hired Benjamin Lovett and his wife to come to Dearborn to establish a dancing school there for his associates and employees.

It was fun talking with Mr. Lovett about dance. Listening to him was like hearing the words of the master, and the words came with an authority and certitude that stayed with me for long after. He was a principal advocate of dances involving large groups in various formations and they had to take place in large airy rooms—much superior to couples on a crowded dance floor in a cabaret. He believed that dancing should inspire the group spirit of fun and be carried out with the proper decorum and the proper space and always with the appropriate music. The whole undertaking should emphasize "rhythm of movement, beauty of pattern, the spirit of play, and grace of deportment"— that was the message of Benjamin B. Lovett. He made such an impression on me that in my future teaching of dance instructors, I always emphasized the history of the dances and those basic principles.

Lovett also shared the belief that properly learning to dance was an effective cure for shyness, self-distrust, and awkwardness—something I believed very strongly, as did Arthur Murray, who capitalized on these qualities in his advertising. Properly learning dancing also involved instruction in dressing properly, personal hygiene, good grooming, courtesy in relating to one's fellows, grace and delicacy in one's dancing position. All this was in addition to learning the precise steps and rhythms of the dances, with the proper music.

I was struck by the fact that even though we taught very different dances, we had precisely the same emphasis in our dance studios. To me, these were indispensable virtues, and I was proud of what we could accomplish in instilling those virtues in the lives of our students. I felt a deep kinship to Benjamin Lovett, because we shared a great respect and reverence for the dance. He was my kind of guy, and I'm very glad I had the opportunity to get acquainted with him and share ideas about dancing. I still laugh when I think of the clandestine way in which he came to our studio, and it was obvious why it was so important that Mr. Ford not find out.

By the end of the thirties, Joe was back with the CCC, although he was now a commissioned officer and enjoying new responsibilities. His experience was preparing him for a successful military stint to come and an enduring love for military life. Charlie, too, was back in California trying to make it in motion pictures, but he was really floundering around and getting nowhere. Mama and Papa were both in California, living there on Olympic Boulevard, but these were not happy days for either of them.

In late June of 1939, I received a telegram from Pearl that Papa had been found critically injured on a Los Angeles street, where he had apparently fallen and struck his head on the pavement. By the time they got him to the hospital, he had died from a cerebral hemorrhage. As was usual for him, he had been at a newspaper plant visiting with the workers there until after midnight, and he was apparently walking to the bus stop to go home. To my knowledge, alcohol was not involved—Papa rarely drank much, and there was no indication that he had been drinking that night. It was not the first time he had fallen; once in the subway in New York, he had fallen and broken his arm. Evelyn thought that when he was feeling miserable, suffering as he did from migraine headaches, he was unstable on his feet and not very careful about what he was doing. It seemed incredible to me that an otherwise healthy man, not yet seventy years old, could kill himself by falling down on the street, but that was the only explanation given for his fatal injury.

I left immediately for California to be with Mama. When I went to the funeral home to see Papa, I was surprised to see that he had grown a mustache and he looked so different. I knew there was much about him that I would never understand, so much of his life was spent outside the family circle—from the time that we moved to New York until the day he died. How I wanted to talk with him about all those years and learn what personal thoughts and feelings he had about it all. Most of all I wanted to tell him that I loved him even if I did not fully know him. Papa is one of the enigmas of my life.

Mama decided to stay with Mary in Hollywood, but I feared then that it would not be a very good arrangement. Mary was obviously drinking heavily, and her second marriage by this time was filled with conflict and problems. Chuck Emory would soon divorce her, and that would have devastating consequences for Mary.

I returned to Detroit with a heavy heart. I had serious concerns about Mama's future, and I didn't think I could rest easy until I got her to Detroit. Suddenly, it seemed, so much was going wrong with the family. Evelyn had been divorced and was increasingly unhappy with her life. Pearl was happily married and had started a dance studio of her own on Ventura Boulevard, but she, too, had started drinking excessively, and her collection of pill bottles was growing larger. It was very hard for me to understand how this could be happening to my family.

We had managed the successes and the material rewards of the twenties without giving in to the excesses of the day. And it may be that the demands and rewards of show business—along with that strong sense of being good and dependable troupers—did not create the need for such escape or dependency. When it was over—when the stage lights, the applause, and the next show were no longer there, and neither were youth and beauty and hope—it was very hard to cope with the inevitable sense of loss and emptiness. I wept for my poor sisters, and I had an ominous feeling that things were not going to get better for them. Soon these haunting feelings would lead me back to California to bring Mama to Detroit, and Mary would go once more to a rehabilitation center to be treated for alcoholism.

Like my older brother, Robert, my two younger brothers went to war, 1942–45.

Charlie and Joe joined me in my Arthur Murray Dance Studios in Detroit, 1940.

Joe served on General Eisenhower's staff, London and Paris. He rose to the rank of lieutenant colonel.

Charlie served in the Army Air Corps in Italy and Africa. He rose to the rank of major.

After the war, back to our dance studios

Joe and Doris

Charlie and Doris

Joe and Charlie at a studio
party for students, 1946

Reconstructing old social dances for our own television show

Joe and Doris dance the Pavanne from the *Court of Queen Elizabeth I*

Doris and Joe waltz to "Casey Would Waltz with the Strawberry Blonde and the Band Played On"

Doris and Charlie dance the Chicago Toddle

CHAPTER THIRTEEN

DANCING IN DETROIT

In that same year, 1939, I contacted both Joe and Charlie and urged them to come to Detroit to work in the dance studios. There were many women instructors, but men instructors were much harder to find. I knew they both had the talent and the personality to be very good in the business, and they agreed to come. Charlie had already started working as a dance instructor in Los Angeles at a studio owned by Eleanor Walsh, one of the first people I had met at the Murray studio in New York. At first, Charlie wasn't terribly happy with the idea of being a dance teacher, finding it hard to give up his hopes for future success in show business, but he adjusted well. Soon both Joe and Charlie were excellent dance teachers. Because of his early and very notable success as an actor, Charlie, who was not yet thirty, continued to think of himself as an entertainer rather than simply a teacher. He incorporated a lot of his funny little shticks into his teaching methods, and they served him well, particularly in working with large groups. He would at times have over a hundred students in classes that he taught at the Detroit YMCA. He became a master at teaching large groups, but whether it was one student or a hundred, Charlie was always on stage.

Charlie had his most famous dance students even before he came to Detroit. While working for Eleanor Walsh, he encountered one evening—in the men's room of the Cocoanut Grove, to tell the whole truth—two young men on the brink of stardom whom he had first met on the set of *The Ghost Talks*. They were John Wayne and Ward Bond, two close friends who had played football together at the University of Southern California. Wayne, who had been a prop guy on the set when they first met, asked Charlie what he was doing. When Charlie said he was teaching ballroom dancing, both said they wanted Charlie to show them how to rhumba. So they came to his studio and had one long rhumba session. That was about the time John Wayne made *Stagecoach* and went on to become a superstar. Ward Bond didn't do so badly either.

A year or so after Joe and Charlie had come to Detroit, the Japanese bombed Pearl Harbor, and we were suddenly in World War II. Joe was about thirty-four and Charlie thirty-one, and both felt they should join in the fight.

They had been commissioned as officers in the army reserves after they arrived in Detroit, so when they went into the army, both became commissioned officers and both went overseas.

Initially, Joe went to Camp Bowie, Texas, where he was made company commander of an infantry company preparing to go overseas, but he was later transferred to the Quartermaster Corps and sent to Fort Sam Houston to take command of an all-black company—the armed services were still segregated at that time. This new outfit was a bakery unit that Joe called "a rolling bakery company." It was deployed to serve the fighting units. Soon Joe and his bakery company were on their way to England. After arriving there, Joe met an officer whom he had known in the United States, who advised him to apply for a transfer to London, where the Allied Command was being established to plan for the second front. He said that they had a dire need for administrators and they could really use Joe. So that is what happened. Joe was transferred to a military police battalion, where he was in charge of training and security for the headquarters of General Dwight D. Eisenhower. He eventually reached the rank of lieutenant colonel. Later, he was sent to Paris, after the liberation of the city, to help establish the headquarters for the allied command in the final days of the war in Europe. He was awarded the Bronze Star and was very much the military man. After his release from active duty, he remained in the army reserve throughout his career, and was eventually awarded a lifetime reserve appointment.

Charlie, who served in the Army Air Corps, became adjutant of the Sixteenth Reconnaissance Squadron, stationed in Tunisia and later in Foggia, Italy. The mission of his unit involved the detection and jamming of German radar in order to make ineffective the radar-controlled antiaircraft fire. His unit, which became known as the Ferrets, flew dangerous missions over enemy territory, carrying out an essential role in the defeat of Germany. During the war years, Charlie reached the rank of captain, and at the war's end, he was promoted to major. Following his return to the United States, Charlie remained at the Pentagon in Washington throughout 1946, completing a detailed history of the Ferret operations during the war, for which he received a special citation. I was proud of both of my brothers and anxious to get them back to Detroit.

From the time we arrived in Detroit, we had made every effort to become a visible and positive part of the community. We did a lot of work with the Detroit Athletic Club, and I taught children dancing at the Detroit Golf Club. We did programs at the Children's Orthopedic Hospital and the YWCA.

Throughout the war years, we went on a regular basis to the veterans' hospital at Kalamazoo, to teach dancing to veterans who had lost limbs in the war. It was deeply rewarding to us and was enjoyed so much by the veterans. It helped them to overcome their reticence and deal with the reality of a lost arm or leg in a social situation. They were terrific young men, and we were thrilled by the progress they made.

Some of the industrial leaders we had met in Miami at the Flamingo Hotel when Cy and I were teaching there involved us in a variety of social activities, as well as continuing to be involved themselves as students. One of them was the CEO of General Motors, Albert Bradley, who became a dance student of mine, and it was said he would even leave board meetings in order to make his dance lesson on time. He never missed one and became a very good dancer.

Far from having an adverse effect on our dance studio, the war seemed to create a greater need for the kind of relaxation and escape that both men and women found in dancing. Jobs were abundant in Detroit, and people had more money to spend on leisure and relaxation. The demand for dance lessons continued to grow, and it was not long before we had thirty rooms for studios and thirty-nine instructors. Early in the war years, over one million people were enrolled in dance classes in the United States, a clear indication that the war had brought an end to the depression. In the movie *The Fleet's In,* which featured the Jimmy Dorsey orchestra, Helen O'Connell and Bob Eberly sang, "Arthur Murray Taught Me Dancing in a Hurry." And when Jimmy Dorsey's band with his two talented singers came to Detroit, the Arthur Murray studio received a great deal of free publicity because of that song. We soon began to add studios in different Michigan cities, and added two more in Detroit itself.

Occasionally, we designated an evening army day, when we had no one but uniformed soldiers in for dance lessons, and a navy day for sailors. We also had USO events where all service personnel could come and dance with local volunteers. Once a week, we went to Kalamazoo to give dance lessons to wounded service men. So those days were very hectic, crammed with activities and commitments, and I loved every minute of it. I was in charge of my life and more satisfied with what I was doing than ever before. Cy was looking after the business side, so I could concentrate on the dancing side—the showbiz side, that is what it was. It involved creativity, performance, directing, and producing—all the things necessary to enhance the dancing and to present a style of life that involved elegance, refinement, and the spirit of play. My self-esteem was never higher, and my sense of professional satisfaction never stronger.

By the end of the war, we had a vastly enlarged dance business, with 107 instructors. We had moved out of the Statler in 1944, into well-located space that allowed us to expand both staff and studios. There was by then a vastly changed Detroit. By 1943, the population of Detroit had grown to about two million, which was a 500,000 increase in a three-year period. For the duration of the war, Detroit was a war-related industrial city—what President Franklin D. Roosevelt called the "arsenal of democracy." Some went so far as to say that we won the war *in Detroit*—meaning that it was the industrial might of the nation symbolized by Detroit that triumphed in the war effort.

People came from all over to work in the factories. In the beginning, there was a white migration mostly from the South, and then southern blacks started coming in huge numbers. The numbers finally exceeded the job opportunities, and the infrastructure of the city really wasn't able to support the rapid growth. All kinds of social problems began to develop—resulting in the riots of 1943—but the worst urban problems were still some years away.

When the war was over in 1945, Joe took over the Toledo studio for a while and then returned to Detroit and resumed his work as a dance teacher and studio manager. He brought with him a talented dance teacher named Lucille, whom he would soon marry. (They were still married when Joe died in 1998.) When Charlie came back from Italy, and after his work at the Pentagon to complete his extensive report on the antiradar program, he was asked to take over the Baltimore Arthur Murray studio, which he did for almost two years. He returned to Detroit in late 1947.

By the time Charlie came back to Detroit, the Latin dances had become the rage. I felt a strong need to learn more about the dances in the places where they had originated, and so Charlie and I decided to visit Cuba, Brazil, and Argentina to see what we could learn. Joe would remain in Detroit to run the studios. My partner Cy, without whom I would never have tackled the Detroit franchise, had decided to join the central office of Arthur Murray and also run the Toledo studio, and so we had amicably ended our partnership. Cy was a great friend and a fine partner. Our interests complimented each other's because I always wanted to be in the dance studio, while he wanted to handle sales and the business side. Joe fit right into the role that Cy had carried out. When Charlie and I were gone, Joe ran the whole operation, which he could do very well.

Our first visit was to Rio to learn about the samba. Most Americans knew the samba through the movies of Carmen Miranda, which led to an interpretation of the dance as a high-spirited, fast-stepping dance. Carmen Miranda, who was Portuguese, was a diminutive and highly animated dancer who wore outlandish fruited headdresses and really introduced the country to Latin America with such movies as *Down Argentina Way, That Night in Rio,* and *Weekend in Havana.* She had her own peculiar approach to the dances, such as her highly charged samba. But we discovered in Brazil that the samba was often danced with elegance and grace—a truly lovely dance. The beautiful song "Brazil," imported to America in 1942, was the quintessential samba song, but in Brazil, it was not played at the tempo of a jitterbug, but rather as a graceful, flowing dance.

We also learned that social status was an important determining factor in how the dance was approached—from the grace and elegance of the upper crust to the frenetic and passionate excitement of the largely African underclass population. That contrast was not always evident, but I think the observation is generally valid.

With the help of a Brazilian guide, we visited several huge dance halls where the ordinary (and generally poor) citizens thronged. The government provided these dance halls as a public service, and it was obvious that they served a hugely important role. Those who danced there—though economically deprived—always showed up in their finest attire, and their efforts to emulate the upper crust were obvious in their mannered decorum and restrained dancing. The dances were slower, with less body movement than in the privately run "peasant" clubs, and we were told by one of the managers, "If we let them cut loose and dance faster, they would wreck the place."

Charlie and I were not permitted on the dance floor in these large public halls, but we were allowed to observe from a balcony. The motion on the dance floor was a fascinating mosaic of waving movements with everyone moving together like a well-rehearsed dance company. It was really very impressive.

We danced in all the private clubs, with the rich and the poor, and we always danced "their way," learning all of the variations of the dance. Often they would form a large circle around us and watch us with great delight and obvious pleasure, surprised that we could dance like they danced. We danced "with the natives" through many nights, and that is how we became increasingly authentic in our approach to Latin dancing.

In Buenos Aires, Argentina, we had a most enjoyable time, but we did not learn much new about the tango. That dance had been well known throughout Europe and the United States and had been taught for years in the Arthur Murray classes, so we were very familiar with it. Nonetheless, dancing with Argentines at all levels of society certainly helped us learn the nuances of that exciting dance. We also took dance lessons for several days and observed a variety of formation dances—the Argentine approach to line dancing.

In Havana, Cuba, we discovered some interesting variations to the rhumba. We not only found some novel approaches to take back, we also discovered a country where dance thrived, where it was revered as a central part of the culture. We would later establish a part-time studio there, in the Hotel Nacional, where Charlie developed a highly successful vacation-dance program.

The rhumba was really a basic dance with a number of colorful variations: the bolero, the *danzón,* and the *son* (which rhymes with "loan"). It was a wonderful, rhythmic, and sensual dance that even in Havana itself had variations that were related to the social and economic levels of that pre-Castro society. We saw all varieties, from the elegant to the passionate, in the posh casinos and in the poorest of the peasant clubs. We experienced what I like to call the essence of the dance, its ethnic origins, its cultural importance, and its social significance. While Charlie stayed in Havana several months at a time during the first few years, many of our most talented teachers would go there for shorter stays. As a matter of fact, the prize for the winners of our semiannual dance competition among teachers was a trip to Havana to work in one of Charlie's vacation-dance programs. I made annual trips to Cuba over a seven-year period, and over time, Detroit made a unique contribution to the Arthur Murray chain as the center for the teaching of authentic Latin dances.

Later, as the mambo and the cha-cha-cha originated out of the combination of American jazz with Cuban rhythms, those dances swept the United States as the rhumba had done a decade earlier. We were prepared for that, and we kept Arthur Murray, Inc., abreast of what we had developed in Detroit. For several years, we held workshops both in Detroit and in New York for dance instructors from across the country.

In 1948, ten years after we had started the Arthur Murray Champagne Hour, we (Joe, Charlie, and I) returned to the Terrace Room of the Statler to start a Tuesday evening program we called "The Arthur Murray Dance Interlude." We presented all of the Latin American dances to very appreciative audiences. Of course, by that time, we had many students who would come every Tuesday night—ordinarily a slow night for restaurants—and fill the Terrace Room. It was a touch of show business that we had held onto, performing for appreciative audiences without worrying about whether there would be another job waiting for us.

About this time, I learned that a Ziegfeld Club had been established in New York. For some reason, they had not been able to locate me until then, although the club had been started in the mid-thirties, initially organized as part of the publicity for the movie *The Great Ziegfeld*. Bernard Sobel, who was a longtime publicist for Ziegfeld, tells the story in his book *Broadway Heartbeat*. He started it as a "publicity stunt . . . but also a wish-fulfillment ideal, a club that will celebrate Ziegfeld's memory and serve also as a charitable organization for indigent Ziegfeld girls." He goes on to say that every time he ran into a former Ziegfeld girl, he would tell her about the club and ask her to pass the word along to others.

Over the years, the club developed into quite a successful organization, and I started attending the annual gatherings, which featured gala floor shows—early on produced by Ned Wayburn—with *Follies*-quality entertainment. After I had attended for several years, I had the temerity to suggest that instead of hiring expensive entertainers to come in each year, we—the former Ziegfeld dancers—should provide some of the entertainment ourselves. Initially, my suggestion was received with great skepticism, but I volunteered to do the "Mandy" routine I had done as Marilyn Miller's understudy in 1919, and everyone agreed to try it. So that year, at the Hotel Pierre, I did that dance number, and it was a great success. However, I discovered that I was the only one of the "ol' gals" willing to do it, so the reliance on outside entertainers continued.

Actually, the fun of the event was less in the entertainment than in the reunion of old friends and colleagues. Once more dressing up in Ziegfeldian style, with sparkling jewelry and magnificent gowns, we drank a champagne toast to the glory of times past. Of course, we were no longer as young as in those glorified days, but the spirit and glamour and gaiety were very much alive. Friendships were happily renewed, and some of the less fortunate of the former Ziegfeld girls were helped by the club's generosity. The annual ball raised a lot of money for various charitable purposes, primarily for hospitals, and over the years, the total amount became very substantial. Now, of course, seventy years after Ziegfeld's death, we are a vanishing breed. There are not many of us around, and the annual ball, which in time became an annual luncheon, will soon fade away. Thanks to the good Lord, I have been able to dance each of the past few years at the annual luncheons. The club still has an office in New York, continuing its good work, thanks to the tireless efforts of a fine man and good friend named Nils Hanson.

Speaking of those annual balls reminds me of an innovation we developed in Detroit that we called the Medal Balls. These were gala annual affairs for students and staff alike, in which we awarded bronze, silver, or gold medals to the students who had mastered different levels and types of social dances. These were formal occasions, held in the huge ballroom of the Masonic Temple, and were very well attended by our present and former students. At our largest ball, we had about 1,500 in attendance.

It was always my purpose to cultivate the highest sense of decorum and social grace with respect to the dance, to have fun, and to enjoy the elegance and the style of formal occasions. We required black tie and evening dress of all those attending. It was a lifestyle that had begun to fade from American life by the sixties, but for most of the fifties, it was part of the celebration of the good life in music and dance.

Beginning about 1950, I started a thirteen-week television series that I continued for a seven-year period. I loved doing it, and it turned out to be our best marketing tool. It was quite popular in Detroit, and I remember on our first show we had the fine actor Edward Arnold as our guest. While I could not always lure celebrities to the program, I did manage to arrange to meet and have pictures taken with celebrities visiting Detroit. I can recall meeting Tony Martin, Thomas Mitchell, Peggy Wood, P. G. Wodehouse, Nina Foch, Lauritz Melchior, and Eddie Bracken. The pictures were often featured in the newspapers—not as paid ads but as feature articles. It was great for the business. Of course, my old friend the fine actor Frank McHugh came to Detroit specifically for a visit, and I was so pleased to see him.

Throughout much of the fifties, Charlie spent parts of each year in Havana, conducting his vacation-dance programs, which were very successful. He had an apartment and studios in the Hotel Nacional, with a small staff to assist him with the dance groups, which would come in for a two-week stay. The largest group had seventy-four students eager to learn the rhumba and samba. He went several times on Caribbean cruises that centered around Arthur Murray dance lessons aboard ship, while sailing to the Virgin Islands, Jamaica, Martinique, or Curacao. And he later conducted the first Arthur Murray international dance competition, bringing both professional and amateur dancers from various countries to Havana. It was the Castro-led revolution that eventually terminated those programs, but while they lasted, they were wonderfully successful. They were Charlie's masterpiece.

It was, incidentally, some Arthur Murray dance lessons on a Caribbean cruise in 1938 that would eventually and indirectly cause another major change in my life.

CHAPTER FOURTEEN

PAUL

When we completed the arrangements to open the first Arthur Murray branch studio in Detroit, Murray gave Cy a list of names of people living in Detroit who had paid for Arthur Murray lessons on cruises and still had lessons remaining. Cy had given me the list to work on, so one day, I was making routine calls to some of these individuals. I came across the name of Paul H. Travis, who had paid for dance lessons on a cruise to Rio in 1938. I called him and asked if he would like to come to the studio to take the lessons he had already paid for. After a few minutes of meaningless banter, he audaciously asked if I would go to dinner with him at the Detroit Athletic Club, where we could discuss the matter. Well, I had a very strict rule about teachers not dating students, and why I just didn't refuse with some polite explanation, I don't know. I was a bit taken aback by his brash invitation. I tried to convince him that it would be appropriate for him to come to the studio; we could meet, and he could then decide whether he wanted to complete his lessons. He argued that it would be better for us to meet first and then he would consider going to the studio. I said, "Just a minute." And I turned to Cy, whose desk was next to mine, and said, "Cy, this guy wants me to go to dinner with him at the DAC, and he won't come to the studio unless he meets me first." Cy looked unimpressed and said, "Well, we know a lot of people at the DAC. Sounds like a pretty safe place to me." So I agreed to go, and Paul said he would pick me up at the Statler at six o'clock.

Paul Travis, I learned, was a graduate in engineering from Cornell University, who had recently gone into business for himself manufacturing automotive parts. In his senior class, he was selected as "the student most likely to succeed" and was immediately hired by the Kelvinator Company in Detroit, where he worked in sales for two years. He was so successful that they fired him. They fired him because he was earning so much in commissions that the other salesmen were complaining about him. Later on, I would learn that Paul always did things his own way and just wasn't cut out to be a "company man." He never suffered fools wisely, and I imagine he told a few supervisors what he thought of them.

He told me that after he was fired, he sat "on the park bench with the other bums for a while," unable to find work in those depression years. Eventually, he was introduced by one of his lawyer friends to an executive of Woodall Industries and was given a job scouting out possible manufacturing sites for them, as well as selling jobs to existing manufacturers. In two years, after being once again very successful, Woodall fired him. Fired, again! This time, Paul concluded that he was not made to work for someone else, and if he could make money for others, why couldn't he do the same thing for himself? And that is what he did, beginning a small operation in half of a friend's double garage. He hired a machinist to work with him, and he manufactured parts for cars that he could then sell to the automotive companies.

The first invention he constructed in that garage was what came to be known as the "door check," the catch that holds a car door ajar. After completing it, he put it on the shelf to think about it for a while, and he filed for a patent on it. A year after receiving his patent, he decided to manufacture it himself. He first sold Ford on the idea, then Chrysler, then General Motors, and from that time on, Paul retained the patent on the door check. In time, he developed improvements in the glove compartment and the sun visor, which he also capitalized on. Later, when he had become very successful, he liked to say, "I have only three customers: Ford, General Motors, and Chrysler." Well, I didn't learn everything about him at that dinner, but I had a lot of laughs.

Paul fancied himself quite a dancer, and he loved to do this big dip step. I asked him, "Where on earth did you learn that?" He said at Cornell, so I started calling it the Cornell Dip. In fact, he was a very good dancer, and he obviously enjoyed his artistry. He agreed to continue lessons, and I arranged for him to have one of our best teachers—an attractive redhead with beautiful teeth and gorgeous green eyes. Paul never missed a lesson.

I saw him in passing at the studio, but he never called me to go out again until a year had gone by. One evening as I sat working at my desk, the phone rang and it was Paul. "What are you doing?" he asked. Well, I happened to be working on an essay for a composition class I had enrolled in at Wayne State University, and I told him what I was doing. "What are you going to do when you finish?" he asked. "Well," I answered, "I thought I would go to a movie." "Can I go with you?" he asked. I said, "Sure, if you wish." So he picked me up at the Statler, and we went to the late movie. The movie ended around eleven, and he drove me back to the hotel. End of second date.

After that, I saw him casually around the studio when he came for lessons. At times, he would come into the office and sit at Cy's desk, while eyeing me with those quizzical eyes of his, but he did not ask me to go out again. After six months, he called on a Sunday morning. "What are you doing?" he asked, a question that became his standard opening line. I told him I was catching up on some paperwork, and he said that he had been invited to a brunch at Mrs. Vernor's, of the Vernor Ginger Ale family. Her son had become a friend of Paul's at the boat club. (Paul was a champion rower.) For some crazy reason, I never said no to Paul's off-the-wall invitations, and so I agreed to go. We spent a long, lovely afternoon at the Vernor's, and as he drove me back to the Statler, he asked if I would like to get something to eat and I said that would be nice. He said, "Okay, how about going to the White Castle for hamburgers." I said that wasn't quite what I had in mind. "I want a full, complete meal." I saw that sly half-smile on Paul's face—his typical substitute for laughing—a look that never changed over the years. Paul was very expressive without a lot of physical movement. When he was amused, his face would light up, his brown eyes would dance with pleasure, and that little half-smile of his would reveal his playfulness. Sometimes, in a group, he would look around at others with that quizzical expression on his face, as if to ask "What's going on?" But of course, he always knew.

It was much more difficult in the early days of our relationship for me to know what he was thinking. He never directly revealed a lot about his inner thoughts and feelings, and as far as I could tell, all of his relationships were essentially on his terms. That is just the way it was with Paul. Early in his manufacturing business, he had a partner, but there were disagreements, and even when there were not, Paul did not like explaining to someone else all of his actions, so they dissolved their partnership. Paul never had another business partner after that.

After that long Sunday, we started having dinner together more often, and sometimes on Sundays, we would drive to a farm he had bought near Everett, Michigan. I remember that one evening, he asked me if I wanted to go by to see his "factory," and he proclaimed, "I doubled my work force today!" As I soon learned, he had gone from one employee to two, and from half a garage to the whole garage. But he would soon buy a small factory and begin to expand the manufacturing activity. Then in 1942, he bought at auction the Rochester Paper Company, which he would build for the next twenty-five years. He manufactured everything for automobiles requiring foundation board, such as door panels, glove boxes, and sun visors, and by the mid-sixties, he was doing ten million dollars in sales annually.

Paul was an ambitious, aggressive builder, driven to be successful. He enjoyed the challenge of making anything better than it had been before. The most meaningful gauge of his success was money. He loved to make money, although he never liked spending it. He was frugal and careful, never taking on new ventures until he had studied every detail and looked at every angle. Once he made a decision, he was always upbeat, optimistic, and confident. He was never in a sluggish, down mood; instead, he was always being filled with energy, strong opinions, and great self-confidence. He kept well concealed the fact that under his aggressive, tough guy facade there was a sensitive, gentle heart.

Well, this eccentric relationship that started with three dates over a two-year period became a blossoming romance throughout the forties, and we were finally married on March 19, 1949. He was forty-nine, and I was forty-five. Each of us had had an early unsuccessful marriage, and we had certainly not rushed into the second. As a matter of fact, I had reached the point of believing that this relationship was going the way of my earlier relationship with Herb Brown—which was nowhere. I began to doubt that marriage would really come about. I had been thinking quite a bit about this when Paul called one evening and said in his matter-of-fact way, "See you at the DAC in thirty minutes." I said, "No, you won't. I have plans for dinner." And I hung up. I did not hear from him again until the next evening, when he called and said in quiet, distinct, and measured words, "When do you want to get married?"

Even though I told him I would marry him, I felt great uncertainty that he really wanted to get married. I discussed my doubts with the wise minister I had selected to perform the ceremony, and he convinced me that Paul and I were mature individuals, that I should accept Paul at his word, and that we were both very independent people but we each felt incomplete without the other. Life doesn't offer certainties, but there are certainly things worthy of taking a chance. "Plan the wedding," he said, "and then if he doesn't show up, you'll know." Well, he showed up.

This was our wedding night: At 7:30 on a Saturday evening, I walked across Grand Circus Park, in front of the Statler Hotel, with Mama, Joe, and Charlie. When I walked back forty-five minutes later, I was holding onto Paul's arm. We were married! I had arranged for a wedding cake in our suite. There was just the family and Howard Davidson, Paul's best man. After a short time, Howard drove us to the train station, where our trip to Miami and on to Bermuda would begin.

At the station, the porter took our bags, we said goodbye to Howard, and we started following the porter, who had our reservations in the Pullman car. Paul had told me many times about his travels as a salesman and sleeping in the Pullman car. He made it clear that he always took an upper berth because it cost less. I had learned that he was a frugal person. Well, I was following behind the porter, and we were walking through the Pullman car. I began to be a little apprehensive and was watching to see where the porter would stop. When he stopped midway through the car by a double berth, I confess I held my breath. Were we going to spend our wedding night *in an upper berth?* But the porter had stopped just to rearrange our luggage and then continued to the end of the coach, where we entered a very nice drawing room. I was breathing again. The porter set down our baggage, and Paul tipped him well and closed the door. I was on my honeymoon with someone I loved dearly.

When we returned, we moved into a lovely old two-story farmhouse on land that Paul had purchased near Rochester, Michigan, where he would eventually own over eight hundred acres and would raise in turn cattle, sheep, and eventually turkeys—a flock of twenty thousand—and his own processing plant. I had about a thirty-minute commute to the Detroit studio and Paul something less than that to Rochester. In time, we built a large, enclosed porch on the back of the house, with a glorious view of the rolling green fields. It was a wonderful place to live, and Paul—being Paul—was always thinking about how to make the farm as profitable as possible.

Paul did not enjoy the same things that many affluent people do. He spent little on clothes or other personal items. He did not drink or smoke or enjoy fancy dinners. He never understood why people traveled when they were not forced to. His fun was in his work. He certainly enjoyed making money, but more than that, he enjoyed leaving something better than when he found it. That was his whole life—building, doing, creating—and he always did it his way.

Another change in my life, 1949

Leaving the church with my
husband, Paul H. Travis

In my suite at the Statler Hotel, Detroit. A little family
wedding reception. Left to right: Howard Davidson
(Paul's best man), Paul, Doris, Charlie, Mama, Joe,
and Lucille.

And we danced and danced

Doris and Paul, an
evening at the Detroit
Athletic Club, 1951

Doris and Paul on our
television show, 1954

The next generation

Lucille, Joe Sr., and Joe Jr.

Doris with Joe and Lucille's daughter Diane, preparing to become a beauty queen of the future

Diane Eaton and Joe Eaton Jr., following in the Eatons' footsteps— exhibition at our studio ball, 1961

CHAPTER FIFTEEN

MAMIE

By the mid-forties, Mama was with me in Detroit. When I visited California and saw the seriousness of Mary's alcoholism, I knew that Mama could not stay there. Mary agreed to go to a rehabilitation center, and Mama came back with me. Initially, she had a room in the Statler adjoining mine, but soon the hotel manager provided us with a two-bedroom suite so that we could have a sitting room. Mama, who was just over seventy when she came to Detroit, enjoyed all of the activities of the dance studio, and we lunched together daily in the Terrace Room. The teachers in our studio were like an extended family for her, and when our showbiz friends came through town, it was always a gala reunion.

Once when Skeet Gallagher and Max Hoffman—actors we had known in New York—were appearing in Detroit, I invited them to have lunch with Mama and me in the Terrace Room. Skeet had appeared with Mary in *Lucky,* a show that also involved Pearl and Charlie, and starred in *City Chap,* with Pearl. He had become a good friend of the family and was now in partial retirement, making only a few appearances. He died at age 65, just a few years after his visit to Detroit. Mama loved show folks, and that made it an important occasion for her. She really "dolled up" for those two guys, and wore a large-brimmed hat with a blue feather, black gloves, the works. I was sitting with Skeet and Max when Mama entered the Terrace Room, pausing at the top of the stairs leading down to the sunken dining room. She stood there beaming, as if she were back on Broadway among the stars. Skeet jumped to his feet and went to escort her to the table, while she waited there like the very special lady that she was.

Throughout her advanced years, Mama remained an engaging social creature, as long as she had her health. She overflowed with good will and acceptance and never saw a stranger. During our showbiz years, she had become a favorite "Mom" to some of the twenties' most luminous talents—performers, writers, composers, musicians, producers—and for her, these were years of happiness and fulfillment. With hard work, Mama had slimmed down a lot during those years and was always so neatly and attractively groomed that she readily fit in among the "beautiful people" of Broadway. She was so different from Papa, who often felt misplaced and ill-at-ease and never really adapted to the showbiz culture.

What appealed to our Broadway friends (other than her extraordinary cooking) was the fact that there was never anything about her that was phony or artificial or egocentric. In a field where phonies and affectations abounded, she never sounded a false note. While she put a high value on proper behavior, she was never a prude, nor was she easily shocked by the often ribald language of entertainers. She was, as the phrase goes, "a regular gal."

Mama always had an inner strength that allowed her to cope with some pretty bad times. She simply took things in stride and had a way of quietly holding on until she could work things out. There was no gloom or doom or guile in her. When necessary, she stood her ground and fought for those she loved, without ever becoming ugly or strident. She was never at a loss for the right words to assert her position and push her point. It is true that she was ambitious for us and tireless in her efforts to help us all succeed. But she never viewed her efforts as sacrificial. I believe she felt deeply rewarded for what she did, and she never thought that she was giving up something to serve her children. For her, it was simply her primary mission in life, her reason for being on this earth.

She would never remind us that we were deeply indebted to her (in the way that Evelyn did in the later years). The truth is, she had been everything to us: a loving mother, an effective manager, a companion, a mentor, and a role model for us all. She became quite a celebrity herself, with many articles and newspaper columns written about her, but she never lost her down-home Southern modesty and generous warmth that could melt even the rock-hard hearts of some of Broadway's toughest producers. She took to show business like it was her natural habitat, and she loved the customs and folkways of that special world. And in Detroit, she found the dance studios and the related social activities reminiscent of those glory years on the Great White Way.

I know that Mama must have suffered terribly to see Mary's decline. Mary had steadfastly cared for both Mama and Papa most of her adult life, and her love for them was always openly expressed. I still have a copy of a letter to the editor that Mary wrote to *Collier's* in 1925, after an article about Mama suggested that her children might be "sacrifices on the altar of their mother's ambition." Mary wrote: "I answer for one of the children. I might have been a waitress in a Childs restaurant, an $18-a-week stenographer, or I might have found a meal ticket and some clothes by marrying early, if I had not been blessed with an ambitious mother who has been willing to help me get the training a real stage career requires." Mary always gave Mama credit for her success on the stage, and she never doubted for a moment that she had a responsibility to care for her. Unfortunately, Mary was no longer in a position to do that.

Mama and I never stopped worrying about Mary, and I tried to keep in contact with her. During the time she was in the rehabilitation center, she met an actor who, I believe, was also being treated for alcoholism, Eddie Laughton. They developed a close friendship, perhaps out of mutual need for support, and would soon get married. It was hardly a match made in heaven. Eddie may have been a nice guy, but by that time, they were both pretty well down and out. They visited us in 1946, while Eddie was looking into the possibility of a comedy act being developed by someone in Detroit. I will never forget when Mary arrived at the Statler in a taxi; the doorman called to let me know she was there. I immediately went down to greet her, and to my great sadness, I discovered that Mary was very drunk. I took her around to the rear of the hotel to take her upstairs. She could hardly stand.

There were moments during that visit when Mary seemed like her old self. She visited with Mama, and they reminisced about the New York years and had a good time together. Mary enjoyed learning about what we were doing in the studios, and it was obvious that she had never lost her love of dance. But when she went with me to the studios, she wore a veil over her face—even through that veil, she looked beautiful—and she seemed to tire easily. I suspect now that she was not only tired, she wanted to return to her room to have a drink. Once when I took her back to her room, I noticed an open bottle of Scotch next to a chair. She seemed exhausted, and I helped her into bed.

That visit was the last time we would see Mary alive. In 1948, when Eddie came home late one evening, he found Mary dead. The cause of death was listed as "severe metamorphosis of the liver." Indeed Mary's liver had every reason to be in very bad shape, but I have always believed that the immediate (and accidental) cause of death was a combination of sleeping pills and alcohol. It was such a sad ending for my sweet and beautiful sister. Mama and I went to California in a state of great sadness, and we were met there by Pearl and Evelyn to make arrangements for Mary's burial at Forest Lawn next to Papa. The response from the show business community was overwhelming. Even though it had been eighteen years since Mary's last appearance on the Broadway stage, dozens of the biggest names in show business sent flowers or

Mamma and Joe Jr.

cards to the family. She had not been forgotten by them. We had enough flowers to spread throughout Forest Lawn, which is what we did with them.

Pearl was the executor for Mary's estate, but by that time there was nothing left of great value—just a few fur coats and some jewelry. Both Pearl and Evelyn suspected that Eddie had taken the most expensive jewelry, which he denied. After considering taking him to court, Pearl let it go, and Eddie just disappeared. I ended up paying Mary's unpaid bills and the funeral expenses, which I did without hesitation. One could never balance the books with Mary, so great had been her generosity to us all.

Mary certainly deserved to have a longer career and a better chance in movies. With better management and listening to the right people, I am sure that her name would be a lot better known today. But, sadly, she made some bad decisions that ultimately proved disastrous. Brother Joe was more succinct in his appraisal of Mary's decline. He said, "She married three drunks in a row."

I always remember Mary from those earlier days when we were together on the road or sharing a room or a stage or coming down from the high of an evening's performance. We were not sisters who shared everything, but we didn't really need to. We simply enjoyed being with each other. Her light burned brighter than that of her brothers and sisters. She had more talent. More beauty. More success. And in the years since her death, she has always been very much with me. I recall that poignant thought from *The Blue Bird,* as the brother and sister journey to the wonderful land of memory where no one dies as long as they are remembered by someone on earth. When Mytyl asks as they walk through a cemetery, "Where are the dead?" Tyltyl answers, "There are no dead."

When Paul and I were married in 1949, I arranged for Mama to have a very large and beautiful room in the Statler, so I saw her regularly, continuing to have lunch with her daily. Also, Joe and Lucille had a little boy, Joe Jr., whom Joe would take by to spend time with Mama, and it was great for both of them. Charlie was back in Detroit by then, so he also saw Mama often. After her children were married, Evelyn came to stay with Mama for a while, and I rented an apartment for them. But this arrangement did not work out well for either Mama or Evelyn, so after two months, Evelyn left to return to New York, and I moved Mama back into the Statler.

A few years after Paul and I were married, Mama began having physical problems that were no doubt related to the accrued effects of giving birth to seven children. She had surgery and afterward needed the kind of care she could not receive in the hotel, so I faced the agonizing decision of putting her in a nursing home. I recall that day when I took Mama to what I thought was an excellent nursing home. She lamented, "I gave birth to seven children, and there is no place for me to stay with any of them." Well, I did not feel good about that, but with the kind of care she needed, I had no alternative. Soon after she entered that nursing home, where I visited her once or twice a week, I received a call from her, and she asked, "Will you please come and get me? I can't stand it here." So I went to see her. It was in the early evening, and one of the aides came in to give her a pill. I asked what it was, and she told me it was a sleeping pill. It was early evening, and I couldn't understand why they were giving her a sleeping pill. It became obvious to me that it was a way of quieting everyone down early in the evening, and I wasn't about to leave Mama to that kind of treatment.

Luckily, I found her a place in the home of a woman who was a Christian Scientist and who cared for only five or six women. Mama felt in the company of friends, who could share with each other their spiritual beliefs, thoughts, and meditations and the rich experiences of their lives. It was a very good atmosphere for her, and she received wonderful care there until her death in December of 1956. Her last three children, Joe, Charlie, and I were with her. We had been called that morning by Mrs. Wampler, who told us that we should come because Mama seemed to be fading. We three stood beside her bed as she turned her head toward us, opened her eyes for a second, smiled faintly, and stopped breathing. She was eighty-three years old when she departed on her last and best trip.

CHAPTER SIXTEEN

NO MORE RAINBOWS

On Tuesday, September 9, 1958, Morris Goldberg delivered Pearl's daily food order from nearby Gibson's Delicatessen to her apartment at 1426-B Manhattan Beach Boulevard. He had come to know her well from his daily deliveries, and found her to be both friendly and generous. He particularly liked her wisecracks and robust laugh.

But on this day, she seemed different. She appeared dazed and somewhat disoriented, and Goldberg was worried about her. On Wednesday morning, when she did not make her customary call for food to be delivered, Goldberg's worries intensified, and he went to see about her. When she did not respond to his knocking and calling out to her, he entered the apartment and found her lying naked on the floor beside her bed in a pool of blood.

Goldberg immediately called the Manhattan Beach police, who conducted a homicide investigation. My dear sister had been severely beaten around the head and torso, and a later autopsy showed that she had died from the head wounds. The police questioned the neighbors, but few knew much about Pearl, and one even called her a recluse. Neighbors said that she was almost never seen outside her apartment. However, someone reported that a few days before her death, Pearl was seen somewhere with over a thousand dollars in cash. The police searched the apartment thoroughly and found no cash at all, so they concluded that she was killed at the hands of someone who robbed her. The murder was never solved, and we know nothing more about her death than what I have said here.

While the news of her death in such a brutal and shocking way was a devastating blow to me, I believe I had been grieving for her a long time before it happened. I knew she was locked into a self-destructive life of pills and alcohol, and while I tried to give her moral support, I could see that she was fighting a losing battle. I never expected her to die at the hands of a murderer, but for years, I had this ominous feeling that her struggle would not have a happy ending. After Mama had gone through the sadness and grief of both Robert's and Mary's deaths, I thanked the Lord that she would not have to go through that again with Pearl's terrible fate.

For some reason, unimaginable to me now, I could not leave Detroit at the time of Pearl's death, so Joe went to Los Angeles to look after everything and help Pearl's daughter, Dossie, who was flying there from New York. Joe, thankfully, packed up Pearl's personal belongings that Dossie wanted me to have—her scrapbooks, her writing, pictures, letters, and so on. Most of what I know about Pearl's last few years I know either from the things Joe shipped back to Detroit or from letters that Dossie later gave to me.

Pearl's death at age sixty came six years after the death of her husband, Dick Enderly. He was only fifty-six when he died suddenly of a heart attack at their home in Encino. It was as devastating to Pearl as Millard's death had been to Mary, and it brought a drastic change to Pearl's life. Not only had Dick's corporate responsibilities defined much of their social life, he was also an officer of the prestigious Jonathan social club, a member of the Yacht Club, the Los Angeles Petroleum Club, and an exclusive golf club. They had lived a life of almost constant social activity—dinners, receptions, parties, travel. Suddenly, with Dick's death, none of that had relevance to Pearl's life, and she felt utterly lost and alone. The social drinking—often excessive social drinking—that was so much a part of their life for twenty years now became for Pearl a solitary practice, and as the years passed, it became more and more insidious.

For a while after Dick's death, Pearl tried selling real estate, taking a course that, according to her, she passed with flying colors. But her heart really wasn't in it, and she ended up "just playing around with it." One year, she worked for the Special Los Angeles Census as a census taker, but that too was a passing thing of no real interest. What she really wanted to do was get back into show business. She wrote in a letter to Oscar Levant in the mid-fifties, "They say once a ham always a ham—whoever *they* are."

She discerned that for her, the only way back to show business was through writing. She had tried writing various things during the years she and Dick were married, but now she threw herself into it totally. She wrote short stories, biographical fiction, essays, comedy sketches, idea pieces for movies, and any number of songs, both words and music. Most of what she wrote was left in pencil on yellow paper in a first draft or in fragmentary condition, but some things she apparently did complete and send off to a wide variety of publications: *Reader's Digest, Charm, Cosmopolitan, The American Weekly,* and *Life.* Some of her notes indicate that she sent an article about Mama to *Billboard,* but I've never found such an article. She did make several starts at writing about the Eatons getting into show business, and some of that is printed here in Chapter 2. At times, she fictionalized the family, as if she were writing a biographical novel. As far as I am aware, nothing she wrote was ever published. In my judgment, her writing was almost good, but she was not an accomplished writer, although she was clever and inventive. Her remarkable and spontaneous wit, which was so evident when she spoke, did not come across in sparkling fashion in her writing. While she was probably the brightest Eaton, she was not well educated, and in an effort to make up for that, she had started reading a good deal. Her notes list Ernest Hemingway, William Faulkner, F. Scott Fitzgerald, and Luis Bromfield.

One of her songs, which she called "Don't Beat Around the Bush," she liked well enough to have professional orchestrations made for full orchestra. She may have sent that orchestration off to both Arthur Freed and Oscar Levant. It would seem that she certainly intended to, but I have no way of knowing if she actually did. Dossie's son Michael remembers as a boy hearing a demo record of the song, but no one picked up on it, and her efforts went unrewarded.

Periodically, in the years after Dick's death, she would go on drinking binges that could only be stopped by her being hospitalized at the Cedars of Lebanon Hospital. (My guess is that when Goldberg saw her the Tuesday before her death, her disoriented behavior was the result of a binge she was on.) She was in and out of Alcoholics Anonymous, and I know she was desperately struggling to stay sober. I remember corresponding with her, not long before her death, trying to give her encouragement and hope that she could lick this terrible problem. Except for one time when she came to Detroit, we had not seen much of each other over the years. I wanted her to know that I was in her corner, hoping and praying that she would succeed. There is no evidence that she continued her writing during the year or so before her death, and that may mean that she had just given up.

As I look back at my sisters' lives, I often wonder why I was the only one to land on my feet after we left show business. There may not be an easy answer to that, but in reflecting on it, I think an important factor was my going back and forth between New York and California. I never got into the Broadway routine of work and play the way that Mary and Pearl did. Each of them was often in the limelight, the center of attention, and highly regarded as Broadway personalities. I always felt that I was in the background, and to tell the whole truth, I never believed that I was on the same level as my sisters—Mary as a Broadway star, Pearl as dancer-director-choreographer. From the outset, Mary was a star, never dancing in a chorus and always having work. Pearl, while never a star on Broadway, was highly popular, well-known, and well connected. The two of them seemed a pair, and I could never make it a trio.

That is why I went back and forth between the coasts looking for that star-making role. I spent far less time on Broadway than my sisters. From that experience of being apart from them, I gained a kind of independence, learning to stand on my own two feet without the protective shelter of the family. I spent a lot of time alone, reading and thinking in strange hotel rooms. And I spent a lot of nervous energy worrying about whether there would be a next job. While my sister's careers appeared to be soaring, mine just wasn't going anywhere. Finally, after struggling through half of the thirties, I wanted to leave show business. It was my decision, and I never looked back.

On the other hand, my sisters' careers suddenly ended at a time when they had risen to the top—or very near the top. Their lives up to that time had been in large measure a wonderful and successful run. Even with all the hard work, it was for them a ball that just went on and on—with music and gaiety and celebrity. Even when there were dark days or stormy times along the way, they would soon have rainbows of glory streaming from another accomplishment. There was always the next role, the next show, the next season. Then suddenly, when it was over and there was nothing, just nothing, all those rainbows disappeared.

I can see now that I was more fortunate than my sisters. Whatever personal strength I had came from values other than those of our showbiz world. My worth and my self-regard were not tied up in the glamour and excitement of the stage, and I never resorted to drowning my sorrows in alcohol. Pills and booze never appealed to me—beyond a glass of sherry or an occasional glass of wine with dinner—and I don't take medicines even to this day. Thankfully, Paul never drank at all or did anything to excess, so we lived a very stable and normal life. As a matter of fact, none of the three men in my life—Joe Gorham, Herb Brown, and Paul Travis—ever drank. Interesting.

I always felt I had a purpose in this world beyond the lights of Broadway or Hollywood. Even when I was pretty beaten down, I was able to draw strength from spiritual sources; it was faith and belief that kept me going. I often wrote to Pearl about that, knowing she was trying to rescue herself through Alcoholics Anonymous and knowing one of the first steps is to recognize a strength external to yourself—"a higher power" that needs to be in charge. She would never have felt so lost and lonely had she been fully able to accept that fundamental belief. She tried, bless her heart, but for whatever reasons, she couldn't make it.

My religious views have always been a private matter with me, but they have been a very real and sustaining part of my life. Throughout our show business years, Mama and I received letters from Aunt Jane Locker, the wise and loving Christian Science practitioner who cared for Joe as a boy. Her letters were filled with encouragement, practical wisdom, sage advice, and little lessons about God's love. As I have mentioned before, she was my spiritual guide in the way that Evelyn had been my intellectual guide, continually giving me reading lists and admonitions about improving myself. Mama, too, taught me a great deal about life and living. When we traveled together on trains in the early days, Mama always had along a *Book of Psalms* and a copy of *Science and Health, with Key to the Scriptures* by Mary Baker Eddy. She thought through a lot of things on those trips.

I recall that after visiting Aunt Jane in the mid-thirties, I started going to the Christian Science Reading Room and attending testimony meetings to hear how other people had coped with their problems, how they found guidance and direction, and how they turned their lives around. Religion to me was more about learning how to live in this world rather than in the one hereafter. It was a search for wisdom and guidance, and for me it was very useful. So I eventually said to myself, "Okay, I am through wallowing in self-pity, and with God's help, I will get work doing something." After all, as that great philosopher Jimmy Durante said, "I'm flat on my back, so there is no way to go but up."

When I applied for work at the Arthur Murray Dance Studios in New York, it suddenly dawned on me that I did have valuable knowledge and skills that could be applied to other pursuits. My prayers for God to show me the way were being answered. If the doors to show business were closed, I just had to find other doors that would open. Teaching dance seemed a natural, and not being burdened with any grief about my lost career—and confident now that God would guide me—I experienced true joy in finding a new direction for my life. As it turned out, the most personally rewarding years of my life were not in show business, but in the dance studios teaching what I knew best. I have never forgotten that transition, and to this day, I often look back to that pivotal time and thank God for lifting me out of that mire of despondency and anxiety and opening the way for a wonderful future. It was the greatest blessing of my life.

My beloved sister Evelyn

Evelyn's three children
appeared in Broadway
plays. Clockwise from top:
Edwin, Evelynne, and
Warren

CHAPTER SEVENTEEN

EVELYN, THE MAGNIFICENT BITCH

In the early fifties, Evelyn's three children—Edwin, Evelynne, and Warren—became involved in teaching social dancing in the Detroit studio when there was a lull in their show business careers. They learned quickly and worked well for me for several months, and afterward, Evelynne and Warren went with Charlie to Havana to help with his vacation-dance programs. All three of Evelyn's children were attractive and engaging, and they became excellent teachers. Later, Edwin taught social dancing in Glendale, California, when his acting career appeared to be going nowhere. Warren did not much care for the role of dance teacher. He was very clever and creative and was more drawn to the sales and advertising areas of the business. He was a talented graphic artist as well as a very good writer. Later in New York, when he was trying to write a novel—which he was calling *Dancing to Life*—he took a job with Arthur Murray, creating and developing different advertising approaches.

Evelyn, who was called "Mummie" by her children, had been preoccupied with her role as stage mother all of her adult life. When she was about sixty years old, she suddenly found herself with an empty nest. It was a distressing time for her, no longer being so directly involved in the lives of her children. Having been divorced from Bob Mills for several years, she now found herself very much alone. She showed some resentment toward her children when they took time out from acting to learn the teaching of social dance. She thought they should be in New York or Hollywood, pursuing acting jobs. But even when Edwin and Evelynne tried to resume their show business careers, they chose to be independent of their mother, no longer subject to the relentless pushing that Evelyn had applied all their lives. They loved their mother, but they could no longer tolerate her constant efforts to control them. Every discussion between the children and their mother started out in a calm and rational way and invariably ended in harsh, hurtful, and overly emotional confrontations. After all three children married, they each made it clear to Evelyn that they wanted to lead their own lives. It was a turn of events for which Evelyn was not prepared, and she took it very hard.

It is truly sad that Evelyn was so unrelenting in her demands on her own children, even when they were very small. She wanted them to be the best actors possible, and if they did not show up well in an audition, she was on them with such rage and disapproval that it was clearly—in today's language—child abuse. At the same time, she was fiercely protective and made sure that no one took advantage of them. I recall her talking about a play that Edwin was in with the famous actress Eva Le Galliene, and she thought that the actress was trying to keep Edwin from looking good. She said, "That Eva—what's her name—Le Galliene kept intruding on Edwin's lines, and so I told him just to stop speaking when she started and wait quietly until she stopped and then go back and continue with his lines. And he did that to perfection, and it shut that bitch up. She didn't step on his lines any more."

She felt the same way about the much beloved Helen Hayes, with whom Edwin worked on the radio show "Mayor of the Town." "She was a bitch too," Evelyn said. "All other actors were there to be subservient to her." What struck me about Evelyn's harsh opinions was the extent to which intense hostility colored her perceptions and judgments. Even her language had become charged with anger. Obviously, in the final analysis, she had found that the vicarious satisfactions she had derived from her family's show business successes had not been fulfilling. Her singular efforts on others' behalf had brought her no personal sense of accomplishment, and instead there was a haunting sense of ultimate failure that she could not escape.

In what is perhaps the last letter that Warren wrote to his mother, he said, "Sometimes when we talk, issues become clouded, emotions get in the way, and we wind up not knowing what is what and who is who in our wonderful-awful-brilliant-stupid-crazy-curious misunderstandings. . . . We become fractious, intolerant, and ill-humored. . . . We constantly wage war on each other because we are waging war in each of our private selves."

Evelyn later said to me that she had three children and they were all "mental offbeats." Well, they really were shaped to a great degree by the relentless demands placed on them by Evelyn and her extreme efforts to get from them the kind of behavior she demanded. Eventually, as adults, they simply wanted to escape their mother's domination, and they became part of a younger, freewheeling group whose lifestyle was far different from what Evelyn wanted for them. It bothered her terribly that all three of them drank and smoked too much, but what really took the wind out of her sails was their loss of enthusiasm for show business. She was helpless to deal with that reality.

She could preach to them about their vices and try to change them, but she could not transfer to them her intense love for the theater and acting—indeed, she knew that her overbearing efforts to do so had backfired. In the early fifties, Warren in his letters to his mother—he was in New York, she in Los Angeles—tried to coach her on how best to get along with Evelynne and Edwin, and he often criticized her for her self-pity and her pervasive sense of failure. He told her that she had created for herself her own "tomb of loneliness." Yet he stressed his determination to rescue her from that drab existence and take her with him abroad to wonderful places—as soon as the world discovered what a great writer he was. Sadly, that day never came, and the relationship between Warren and his mother became characterized by tension and conflict, until they no longer communicated with each other. Around 1970, Warren apparently drifted into depression and despair, and in the cruelest blow of Evelyn's life, he killed himself. Incredibly, it was a tragedy compounded by the earlier death of Evelynne from a viral respiratory infection in 1964, prior to her fortieth birthday. For Evelyn, her grief was so mixed with chronic anger, self-pity, and bitter disappointment that the last years of her life were terribly unhappy ones.

Earlier, in 1952, Evelyn had come to Detroit to stay with Mama. I rented an apartment for the two of them, and I felt good about having Evelyn close by. I knew that her strong love for Mama would be therapeutic for both of them. Well, that is what I thought, but it didn't turn out that way. I had clung to a rather idealized view of Evelyn from my childhood. For me, she was a nurturing, mentoring, loving mother-figure, who inspired me to learn, to read, to appreciate art and literature and theater. And while I had experienced in the thirties Evelyn's hostile and moody temperament, it was hard for me to see what others in the family had long known: that Evelyn was a controlling, driven person whose sense of well-being was derived from others doing her will. While she was trying to encourage us all to achieve a kind of quality and beauty of mind and soul, her manner interfered with the message and was written off as "her constant bitching."

Initially, after arriving in Detroit, Evelyn enjoyed being around the dance studios and the social activities associated with them, but I soon began to notice that she was very impatient with Mama and increasingly gruff and dismissive in her behavior toward her. When I went by Mama's apartment in the evening on my way home, Evelyn would latch on to me and want to talk and talk about what she had read or was thinking or recalling about the showbiz years. It became difficult to leave, as she seemed to have a desperate need to talk about things in which Mama—at that stage of her life—apparently showed no interest. Evelyn became a caged animal, restless and unhappy, and she obviously wanted to get back to "where the action was." It was a lifelong characteristic of hers, but now her relentless need to become involved in the lives and careers of her grown children made it impossible for her to stay away from Broadway or Hollywood.

I worried quite a bit about her. During her stay in Detroit, I could clearly see that same kind of intolerant behavior that she had expressed toward Bob. Their arguments had seemed to go on forever, ended finally by their divorce. I visited with Bob in San Francisco soon after their separation, and he broke down and cried. He said their fights had become more frequent and more violent, and he could not please Evelyn no matter how hard he tried. Bob, incidentally, left the insurance business, became a shoe salesman, remarried, and had other children.

Now with Evelyn in Detroit, Mama began to suffer the brunt of her insensitive and increasingly abusive behavior. Evelyn seemed so filled with anger and resentment that her often-expressed love for Mama was obscured by her extreme bitchiness. She had become a sad—even tragic—version of the Evelyn I once knew. The Evelyn who had sacrificed—and that is the right word, "sacrificed"—so much for the rest of us was now one of the unhappiest people I had ever known.

It was about this time that Evelyn—for reasons I've never understood—changed her name to Eve Warwick. Maybe it was a symbolic gesture to change her life or a rejection of the life she had led to that time. Since the stately old Warwick Hotel was just east of where we once lived in New York, I guess that is where she got the idea.

After she left Detroit to go to New York, she got a job as a key clerk at the New Yorker Hotel. Edwin and Evelynne were in and out of New York but were spending more time on the West Coast, and Warren, out of show business, was living in Manhattan. Evelyn was still searching for something—perhaps a whole new life—to replace her lost life as her children's manager and driving force. It was as though she was striking out on her own with a new identity and new goals. But in reality, it was the beginning of a very lonely, bitter, and isolated period of Evelyn's life.

Whenever I was in New York, on business with Arthur Murray, Inc., I would go by to see her at the New Yorker. She worked evenings, and she was there always with an open book. She read incessantly, and she never missed absorbing everything printed in *Variety*. She always knew what was going on in the entertainment world, and I think she never gave up the idea that she would once again become engaged in some kind of work in show business. I could see then that she was increasingly bitter and unhappy, at a stage of her life when she had dreamed of having achieved success and artistic fulfillment, at least vicariously through her family. I felt great sympathy for her.

I have always believed that her anger and resentment began back on Rhode Island Avenue in Washington, D.C., when she was cast in the role of "second mother" in the family. As the family grew, Evelyn's responsibilities to the household became greater and greater. Papa didn't want her to go to high school at all, but Mama insisted she go for at least two years. But even during those years, she helped with the cleaning and cooking and caring for the smaller children. She even served as midwife when Charlie was born and the doctor had not yet arrived. She was alone there with Mama and had to deliver the baby and care for him. As a high school student, she had to study late at night after all the chores were completed. Only then could she escape into literature and languages—she was studying both French and Latin—and that was the only redeeming moment of her day.

I am sure that the cruelest blow to Evelyn's interests was when Mama decided to go on the road with Pearl, Mary, and me, leaving Evelyn (who was just twenty) at home to look after the others. Charlie went along with us, but Joe, who was only six, and our cousin Avery, also six, were her responsibility for several months, as were Papa and Uncle Bobby. Evelyn later said that it was her greatest ambition in life to get Mama out of the day-to-day burdens and drudgery of taking care of house and family into a better life. Well, she had managed to do that, but it was not part of her plan to inherit those burdens and that drudgery for herself. She never really got over it.

From about the age of sixty on, Evelyn's awareness that her life and all her dreams had slipped away produced an increasing self-pity and a brooding anger that came to dominate her personality. I was often stunned by the vitriolic language she used, often about her own children's lack of consideration and appreciation toward her. She said such things as, "They live in their own little warped world, and they treat me in a hideous, shabby, tragic way." Or, "You wouldn't believe the rotten, lousy, stinking things they say to me." She called her daughter, Evelynne, "a sadist and a crawler and a double-crosser."

When she was not asked by Evelynne to come to be with her when her first baby was born, Evelyn wrote her to say, "I will never get over the insult, belittlement, and rejection of your forcing me to miss one of the few precious and priceless moments of life. I am starved for a little of your attention, which you hatefully refuse to give." As some of Warren's letters reveal, Evelynne and Warren both believed that if Evelyn were there at that time, she and Evelynne's husband, Eddy King, "would be at each others' throat constantly and her visit could have very bad consequences."

Even when Evelyn wrote her most blistering letters to her unappreciative children, she would close by saying, "Remember always how much I love you, and everything I have done I have done for you."

The following letter, which I have only slightly edited, is a good example of how preoccupied she was with what she saw as the family's and her children's rejection of her. It was handwritten front and back on Statler Hilton stationery, probably while she was on duty as a key clerk. She was sixty-seven years old.

Saturday, April 30, 1960
Dearest Doris,

Received your interesting, informative letter. Glad and happy for you and yours that everything is working out so beautifully for you.

Now about my plans—I haven't any and never intend to have any, as far as I can see (which is not very far maybe). . . . At the moment my feelings or sensibilities or consciousness or thoughts (the state of my being) seem to have come to a halt, a stop, a stand still. The green light is very dim right now.

When I review my bleak past, and every day my bleak present, trying desperately not to face my bleak future—bleak is a mild word to use. How my life could be so fouled up for sixty years (starting at five with screaming migraine headaches) through two generations (using as I thought idealistic efforts to demonstrate the good life—which the members of both generations called domination, bossing, cruelty and God knows what else they did not say out loud) without giving me one minute's satisfaction for my trying or any signs of peace of mind and joie de vivre for the future—all of that is beyond my understanding. . . .

I am not looking for sympathy. . . . All I can say is that I tried and tried and tried. But that didn't seem to be enough. I just go from one grief to another. It seems fantastic. It doesn't make sense. I don't understand. For sixty years I have tried "to run and not be weary," "To stand still and see in the salvation of the Lord which He will shew to you today," "To stand porter at the door of thought." Well, I am still running but I am very weary. I stand still and I just get static.

To me one of the most precious gifts in life was to have two families to work for. First, your own, consisting of father, mother, sisters and brothers; and, second, (not less in importance) your family of husband and lovely children. Well, as far as I can visualize, understand, or see, both of my families went the limit on side-stepping precious human relationships we could have had with each other. Both families have become strangers . . . reminding me of the saying in the Bible "Who is my father, mother, sister, or brother?" and I might add, "Where are my children?"

All of you (both families) have passed me by or passed by me and I had the feeling or (strange) notion that I was the best pal any of you ever had. . . . I think I tried more earnestly than any of you to try to reap a full-rounded rich life for all of us. If I goofed or muffed I did not selfishly mean to. I hope I live long enough to reason out what I have been lacking in understanding. . . . I hope the nightmare of mortal living will turn into a dream-boat of happiness for all of us before we go our separate ways.

Love, love, love,

Evelyn

Many years later, when she was eighty-four years old, living on the West Coast, her fiery anger was still there when she talked about her sacrificial life. She continued to express extreme resentment at the intrusion of responsibilities of home and childcare that diverted her from her own wishes and ambitions. With her full awareness, I taped a few of our conversations, because she could often recall events and people that I could not. These are her frank and unvarnished words from a rambling conversation:

I was forced in my half-assed way to do all that domestic crap to keep the show business thing moving. I had all the dirty work, the hard-hat stuff. . . . Houses, houses, houses. The houses got bigger and bigger as the kids just kept coming. I hate houses, gardens, trees, and mountains. I love concrete. Give me a small apartment above the streets of New York. That's my idea of a home. I know I'm a cynical cynic. But I spent my whole life trying to eliminate the things that held me up. It was all a drag to me. My only passion was for reading and literature and the theater. You know, in the beginning was the word—and that is as far back as you can go. The word. That is what's important in life; that is not illusion. That is truth. The world is illusion. Most of life is a phony ritual that someone made up once and everyone fell for it. Women got put in that thankless role as domestic slaves, and did it for fifty thousand years. Now they talk about liberated women; well, I was born a liberated woman, and that's the way I'll die.

The other Evelyn, the one I remember as a loving sister and mentor as I grew up, had a profound effect on my life. The development of knowledge and refinement, being well read and sophisticated, becoming an educated person—all that was terribly important to her. She constantly talked with me about reading and learning. She supplied me with books, and when she traveled with us on the road when I was a child, she made it all an educational experience. It was she who instilled in me the desire to get a college degree. Even though limited in her education to her high school years, she was inherently an intellectual. She loved ideas and discourse, and she felt perfectly at home with Broadway's brightest and cleverest people. She was not witty and quick the way Pearl was, but she was the deepest. At her best, she thought more profoundly and was more serious and analytical than anyone else in the family.

I think Mary's stardom exacerbated her problem with Evelyn, who developed a brooding animosity toward Mary because of what she perceived as her unwillingness to open doors for her children. Evelyn was working tenaciously to keep all three of her children active on the stage. As she put it:

> I got precious little help. I was always clutching, clutching, clutching to keep my children going. I not only took them to auditions, I coached them on what to do and how to do it. It was hard work, but I knew that once you start in show business you can't let up. You just have to keep it going. It was the same way back in the beginning. It was I who went to Mr. Harris [Sam, the partner of George M. Cohan] and convinced him to audition Mary. I told him she was going to get better and better, so he should hire her now and her stock would appreciate. So Harris talked Cohan into auditioning Mary. That is how Mary got started in *The Royal Vagabond.* I went home from Harris's office and had a miscarriage in the bathroom. I threw it into the trash can. It would have been a boy.

That final shocking statement, it seems to me, was in her eyes a measure of her sacrifice for the family. In pounding the pavements looking for work for us, in her tireless efforts to convince producers to give us a chance, she sacrificed her unborn child. It was five years before she had another baby.

Evelyn had more theatrical intuition and brains than all of us put together. She would have made a keen and successful theatrical agent, but such thoughts never went into her personal development. Her thoughts and efforts involved only her family. In the years that I was traveling back and forth between New York and Hollywood, Mary and Pearl were having great success on Broadway, and it was they who received Evelyn's unwanted advice and criticism. Throughout the showbiz years, there were increasing tensions in the relationship between Evelyn, on the one hand, and Mary and Pearl, on the other. Evelyn thought that Mary was too frivolous and self-centered and that Pearl was too fun-loving and vulgar. What was offered as sound advice and sound admonitions were dismissed as verbal attacks and bitching.

In retrospect, had my sisters been more willing to listen and to think about what Evelyn was bitching about—not their success but how they were handling it—their show business careers may not have ended so soon or so abruptly. More importantly, they might have found the courage and strength to redirect their talents after they realized their careers had come to an end.

The last twenty years of Evelyn's life were stung with unbelievable tragedy and grief. In the sixties, Evelynne became increasingly estranged from her mother, up to the point of her untimely death in 1964 and there followed the cruel blow of Warren killing himself. Then, as if the family were cursed beyond belief, Edwin developed a brain tumor and was seriously disabled by the "successful" surgery. Evelyn cared for Edwin after his brain surgery, and since he was divorced and had custody of his son, Riley, she cared for Riley as well. I purchased two small houses for them in Los Angeles, one for them to live in and the other to rent out to generate the funds for the house payments. There was little at the end to brighten her days and reward her dogged efforts on behalf of others. Every few months, I would go to visit her and Edwin. It was sad to see them have so little in their lives after the supreme efforts both had put forth for so many years. Evelyn's one solace was her regular trips to the public library, a habit she had formed early in life when she had to give up high school. At that time, she had surmised that it was unlikely that any of us would ever get more than a public school education. This did not satisfy her growing ambitions for progress and achievement for us all. She had dreams even for Papa. I remember her early in my childhood trying to get Papa to start learning how to write. In his work, he set type and he proofread the best journalistic writing. She felt that he could have acquired a good knowledge of the English language and how to present ideas. I used to hear her say, "Write, Papa, write. Just try. You can do it." But he never tried.

Some years later, it was she who convinced Papa to become Mary's agent when Mary started talking with Ziegfeld about the *Follies*. It was a great leap for Papa, who had been a passive spectator to the showbiz life of his family. But Evelyn also wanted something better for Papa. She wanted him to feel a part of what was going on with his family and she had faith in his ability to protect Mary's best interests. So he agreed to do it, and for five or six years, he negotiated all of Mary's contracts. His only experience had come from working with newspaper unions. It seemed a formidable task for him to deal with the most respected and successful producer on Broadway. But, as it turned out, Ziegfeld liked him, and they got on well together. And it was to Papa's good fortune that Ziegfeld was very generous toward his stars. (He might have had a rougher time dealing with the Shuberts.) Papa got a great deal of personal satisfaction and pride out of having an important role in Mary's career, and it was Evelyn who brought that about.

At each visit, in those later years, I realized more and more what grit she had, what courage she expressed, facing a hopeless future, to keep on doing every day what needed to be done in taking care of the house chores, caring for Edwin, and struggling with his son, Riley, who in his young teens had become uncontrollable and would do nothing constructive in getting his education or in finding suitable work. I learned later from Edwin that Riley at times was physically abusive to both of them. Evelyn never let me know of that, saying on one occasion that the black eye she had was because she had bumped into the door. I knew better.

Inevitably, in our conversations, we would reminisce about the family's success in show business, and we would ask, "What happened to Mary's and Pearl's inspiration, dedication, and hard work? Had the sudden rejection by the theatrical world in which they had been so popular been so traumatic to them as to create a lack of self-esteem, a loss of self-confidence that they had once enjoyed, a fear of failure in any future endeavors?" I remarked in one of these discussions, paraphrasing a popular song, "I guess the smoke of their cigarettes got in their eyes." And Evelyn responded in a harsher tone, "Yes, and the alcohol got in their brains and bodies, and it ruined their minds and talents." She was, of course, correct, as she had been in so many of her observations and criticisms.

In those family reviews, we would visualize what Mary and Pearl could have accomplished in Hollywood had they had enough determination to redirect their talents. With their reputations and experience, they could have created a whole new world for themselves—perhaps in developing a professional dancing school. As I did in social dancing, they could have found great satisfaction in developing and teaching young people to perform in the professional theater. What beautiful productions they could have developed, giving to their students their first taste of Broadway at its best.

Throughout the seventies, I had many precious moments with Evelyn on my various visits. Just as when I was a child, she continued to express ideas and thoughts to help me in my intellectual development. She would refer to her "files"—an accumulation of articles on various subjects she had gathered through the years—and she would pull out some of the most recent articles and authors she thought I should read. I followed many of her suggestions, and as always, they helped to stimulate my thirst for education, a thirst she had so patiently and conscientiously tried to inspire in me many years before. I am sure that where she may be now—and it has to be in heaven, for she deserves it—she is happy to know that her baby sister finally acquired a college education.

When she passed on in 1980, in a ward of a Los Angeles hospital, Edwin was being cared for in a nursing home. Not one member of her beloved family was present. Her grandson, Riley, was off on his own, and her one granddaughter, Julie—Evelynne's daughter—lived some distance away and knew nothing of her condition. Evelyn was utterly alone. I was unable to go immediately to Los Angeles because my husband, Paul, was having heart surgery. Two days later, I was able to leave for Los Angeles to take care of her funeral. Several months later, Edwin died, and I repeated the trip. Evelyn and Edwin are buried side by side on a little hill in the Glendale Cemetery in Glendale, California. Last year, 2001, I repeated the journey, this time to bury Edwin's only son, Riley, who like my brother Robert died too young from drugs and alcohol. Sadly, he died in a city-operated vagrant's house in Los Angeles. He is buried just a short distance from Edwin and his long-suffering grandmother, another pitiful lost soul.

My visits with Evelyn, during her last years, were not all sad or bitter. Evelyn had a great sense of humor. Her love of life and its possibilities enabled us both to enjoy often a good laugh at us human beings and our peculiar antics. We could escape the darker thoughts for a while and retreat into the happier world of pleasant memory and shared joys. Eventually, however, a cloud of disappointment would tinge our reminiscing over our loved family members, and the sadness and frustrations would return. At one point, she said, "I wish I had done it all differently. I wasted my life, and I can never get it back." A poem that we both had read in our early school days, by the New England poet John Greenleaf Whittier, titled "Maud Muller," expresses our feelings. After considering the beautiful future the two main characters might have had together, the poet concludes with: "For all sad words of tongue or pen/The saddest are these: It might have been."

I loved and respected my brave, self-sacrificing, ambitious sister. She was, indeed, a magnificent bitch.

⬣ ⬣ ⬣

As a final bit of irony in the Eaton-Ziegfeld saga, I recently became aware of an article in the *New York Graphic* of April 23, 1933, in which it was stated that my sister Evelyn was the last person to sign a contract with Flo Ziegfeld before his death. The contract was for her daughter, eight-year-old Evelynne, to play the part of the child, Kim, in Ziegfeld's revival of *Show Boat*. I wish she might have known this bit of theatrical history before she passed on alone in that Los Angeles hospital. It might have given her a moment of satisfaction, knowing that like her three sisters, she had made it with Ziegfeld.

CHAPTER EIGHTEEN

ANOTHER RISE AND FALL

By the fifties, Arthur Murray Studios of Michigan, of which I was the president and owner, consisted of eighteen studios. There were three studios in Detroit, and one in each of fifteen other cities—Ann Arbor, Bay City, Birmingham, Dearborn, Flint, Grand Rapids, Jackson, Kalamazoo, Lancing, Muskegon, Point Huron, Pontiac, Saginaw, Travers City, and Wyandotte—each with its own manager. I had the franchise for the entire state, and no one else was permitted to open an Arthur Murray studio in the state of Michigan. In no other state was there such an exclusive arrangement. Arthur Murray had given me permission to subfranchise in these various cities, from which I was to receive a percentage of their gross. Under my new franchise agreement, Arthur Murray was to receive seven percent of the total gross of the Michigan studios.

I felt very good about the success we had enjoyed, particularly in the great boom period from the end of World War II to the mid-fifties. It was an exciting time for social dancing, and I was proud of the high reputation the Michigan studios had earned. The long period of affluence, when the baby boomers were still young children and their parents were enjoying the postwar boom—with a new home and a two-car garage and a frequent night out on the town—was certainly the heyday of our business. But by the late fifties, we were beginning to notice a drop in the number of new pupils coming in and an alarming increase in the number of problems that had begun to develop throughout the franchise.

The lure of television and home stereo equipment was beginning to keep more people at home and out of the clubs. The big band era was virtually over, and only a few dance bands remained on the road. More importantly, music was changing. Bill Haley's "Rock Around the Clock," Chuck Berry's "Maybellene," and Elvis Presley's "Hound Dog" ushered in the rock-and-roll era—big time!—although none of us thought it would last very long. Like the Hula Hoop, we thought it was another fad that would go away soon. Of course, we were wrong. By 1958, nine of the top ten singles of the year were rock-and-roll songs. There was only one nonrock song to make the top-ten list: "Volare," sung by Domenico Modugno. It was a beautiful fox-trot that I had put on our studio sound system.

Then in 1960, Ernest Evans, who was much better known as "Chubby Checker," recorded a song called "The Twist," and the dance that he introduced became a national sensation. Along with that dance would soon come the proliferation of discotheques, where people could go to do the twist and other new rock-type dances to recorded music. In the discos, dancing without touching became the style of a whole new generation of young people. As rock music came to dominate the popular music field, discos with high-decibel electronic sound and psychedelic lights replaced the sedate clubs of the forties—and social dancing was relegated to an aging generation. At about the same time, black singing groups, such as the Cliftones and the Coasters, brought in a new song style called "doo-wop," and in our own city of Detroit, the Motown sound was born.

As Bob Dylan put it, "The times they are a-changing." In the years to come, there would be folk rock, hard rock, funk, blues rock, jazz rock, progressive rock, country rock, bubblegum, and heavy metal. God, help me! It became a different world. Our stock in trade—the rhumba, the fox-trot, the tango, the waltz—was becoming passé to the vast baby boomer population.

Along with the revolutionary changes in music, it was obvious that important social changes were also taking place. The civil rights movement was well underway, and Martin Luther King Jr. would soon make his "I Have a Dream" speech in Washington, D.C. In Detroit—which had become the fifth largest city in the United States (with Philadelphia having moved into fourth place)—we were on our way to becoming the country's first city with a majority black population. White families started moving out to the suburbs, and many did not want to come into the city at night, as the crime rate began to rise. We actually closed the downtown studio for a few months, moving to a northwest location, but we reopened it when our pupils insisted they would stay with us in the downtown location.

During the fifties, Kathryn and Arthur Murray had a weekly television program, "The Arthur Murray Party," which eventually became a popular national program on NBC. Kathryn was the vivacious emcee, and Arthur was the often ill-at-ease host who would give a brief dance lesson to a guest celebrity. Today, we would call it an infomercial, because its primary purpose was to increase the visibility and attractiveness of Arthur Murray dance lessons—and perhaps to increase the wealth of the Murrays. It certainly made Arthur Murray a household name. While it never had the effect of counteracting the declining number of pupils coming to Arthur Murray studios, it may have slowed the rate of that decline. Who knows?

With all of the social changes, I knew by the end of the fifties that we had an uphill battle to keep our studios busy, and I let it be known that I would sell the franchise for a million dollars. I actually had some conversations with potential buyers, but I never got an offer. I learned that all over the country there were Arthur Murray Dance Studios for sale, and it seemed that there were more sellers than buyers. So I made the decision to do whatever I had to do to maintain the success of the franchise.

Many of the franchise owners in the Arthur Murray chain had become increasingly disenchanted with the New York office. We were troubled by the extent to which greed appeared to be the dominating pattern in all the corporate policies, without much concern for the plight of studios in changing times. There did not appear to be any leadership with regard to changes and adaptations that would help us cope with the new world we were living in. There was only the constant admonition to sell more lessons.

About this time, I started receiving more and more complaints from pupils of the various Michigan studios, pupils who did not want to complete their lessons and wanted refunds. Often, I learned that their decisions to enroll in extensive dance programs were the result of an effective sales pitch that offered an exaggerated list of benefits stretching over many years into the future. Some were disappointed with the reality of their lessons, but others simply were having financial problems and had gotten in over their heads. Arthur Murray, Inc., in all of the sales communications from New York, had been encouraging the sale of these very expensive multiyear packages that came to be known as lifetime lessons. It was a program I never agreed with, and I often conveyed my feelings to the New York office. It was a program that would eventually have disastrous consequences for the entire nationwide chain.

Arthur Murray, Inc., had also established a loan company—as I recall, it was named Educational Credit Company—where students could borrow the money to pay up front for their contracted lessons. So Arthur Murray was not only getting the benefit of the exorbitant dance packages, he was getting the interest from millions of dollars in loans. It was not unusual for such packages to cost $5,000, and the New York office showed no concern for the long-term liability incurred by the studios that had to provide the services.

The studios in Michigan were built on carefully developed principles and high moral and ethical standards. I was very proud of that, and I had worked vigorously to enforce a high quality of teaching in all the studios. Our training programs for our teachers were well developed and rigorous. Joe was a superb manager, competent, dependable, and my rock. Charlie handled the training program with great success. He always had this incredible ability to get along with people, to charm them and entertain them. He was always a stand-up comic, but he could also teach.

What was of paramount importance to me and to the best of our dance teachers was what we called the "product." First of all, that meant the best dance instruction money could buy, but we believed that we did more than teach a person to dance. As I have said before, we believed that we had a positive impact on the lives of the individuals and couples who came to our studios. We worked very hard to maintain an atmosphere of fun, elegance, propriety, and sophistication. We stressed proper dress, manners, and social poise. And we enhanced the social lives of our pupils through delightful, fun-filled social activities: weekly parties, special events (such as nightclub tours), dance contests for both students and teachers, and elegant balls. Just like the ads claimed, we built self-confidence and self-esteem. We really did believe that we accomplished these things, and we took pride in our achievements. We loved what we were doing, and so did our students.

After the Michigan studios initiated annual dance competitions among our own statewide studio chain, we eventually started hosting annual contests involving studios in the Arthur Murray chain from coast to coast. Year in and year out, the Michigan studios won the lion's share of the medals in the competitions involving both students and teachers.

As time went by, I became increasingly upset with the preoccupation of Arthur Murray, Inc., with those long-term sales programs while seeming to ignore the dance instruction and the mounting problems of the franchise studios. How to increase the gross in the shortest amount of time was the constant concern, not how to cope with the immense social changes that had been thrust upon us. We continually told the New York office that we did not approve of the lifetime sales program. We thought the whole idea was fraught with danger, and we resisted as long as we could. But ultimately we had no choice but to go along, since all of the direct communications from the New York office to our studios emphasized how effective the program would be in increasing sales and in providing lucrative commissions for the staff, including teachers who signed their pupils to additional contracts. We even decided to form our own Detroit loan company to finance loans for our pupils, but I finally closed that down after several months. It was a game I did not like playing.

For one who had great reverence for the dance, I found myself immersed in this hotbed of salesmanship. We could have been selling encyclopedias or brushes or vacuum cleaners. Salesmanship—that was Arthur Murray's career-long interest. He had studied business, psychology, and advertising at Georgia Tech in a two-year program. Writing advertisements and figuring out schemes for selling were what really drove him. His greatest innovation—mail order dancing lessons—was phenomenally successful, largely because he knew how to sell them. He learned early that the best way to get people to respond was not to convince them that dancing was fun but to sell them a remedy for their inferiority complex, their lack of self-confidence, or their social awkwardness. The slogan "Learn to dance" was totally ineffective, while "How to Become Popular Overnight!" had a magnetic appeal, as did "How to Overcome Your Inferiority Complex." That was what he sold. He came up with the picture of a young man with a beautiful girl on each arm, under the caption "30 Days Ago They Laughed at Me!" No doubt about it, he knew how to sell and how to make money.

I remember in the first teacher's meeting that I attended in New York, Arthur Murray spoke of the sales program. He said, to my astonishment, "The only real profit to be made in teaching dance is with the untaught lessons." That struck me as being very strange at that time. Why wouldn't you want people to complete all their lessons? Teaching people to dance was what we were supposed to do. But it soon became obvious that the whole sales strategy was to sell people more lessons than they would use. He knew that most people would lose interest and drop out somewhere along the way. He counted on it, and he made a fortune because of it.

By 1957, he had pushed the envelope as far as possible with the lifetime lessons, putting a huge burden of untaught lessons on the studios throughout the country. Bad publicity began to appear in newspapers coast to coast, and dance studios were made to look like con operations fraudulently extracting money from defenseless victims. The *New York Post* did a seven-article series on what it called "Arthur Murray's $65 million empire." The examples they used involved a blind man, a female minor, and an emotionally disturbed veteran, all of whom had started out to take a few lessons and wound up with huge indebtedness. It was not long after that when we began to hear rumors that

Arthur Murray was trying to "dump the business." (He actually did in 1964, when George Theiss took over the company.)

As I said before, my new franchise agreement with Arthur Murray called for me to pay seven percent of gross receipts from all my studios to Arthur Murray, Inc., of New York. In turn, there were a number of obligations that Arthur Murray, Inc., had to the Michigan studios. New York was to do nationwide promotion of the dance lessons, establish rules and methods with regard to the teaching of dance, furnish studios with materials to be used in the sales program, audit the books of all studios, and insure that proper procedures were being used by studio management and the instructors.

However, it became obvious that Arthur Murray, Inc., was not providing the services that the studios needed. In particular, there was no national publicity program advertising the studios. So in the absence of a national promotion, we did our own advertising throughout the state. We had our own television series featuring students and teachers dancing, demonstrating all the social dances that we taught. We did what we could to promote the services of the eighteen studios throughout the state, and in Detroit, we continued our dance demonstrations and worked diligently with a number of prestigious social groups—trying to keep our visibility as high as possible.

As one who detests the intrusiveness of current telemarketing practices, it is painful to confess that at the insistence of Arthur Murray, Inc., we established in Michigan a "telephone room," for which I hired a supervisor and twenty callers, who were making hundreds of calls every evening between five and nine o'clock, offering three half-hour lessons free of charge. Not many other businesses had yet started that irritating telemarketing practice, so it was unusual in those days for people to receive such a call, and it became our most effective sales effort.

The push from New York to sell the lifetime dance lessons became almost obsessive. The pupils, as I've said, had to pay up front for the lessons; they could then claim their lessons at any time at any Arthur Murray studio in the nation. The constantly increasing liability that was being built up with the untaught lessons was very troubling. A person could pay in Denver, for example, and then come to Detroit for the lessons. When we billed the Denver studios for the lessons we taught, we would not usually get paid. We therefore found ourselves in the position of teaching other studio's commitments with no income coming in.

The liability of untaught lessons had infected the entire chain nationwide, at a time when social dancing was sharply declining in popularity. Indeed, the

Florida chain was destroyed by the huge number of paid-up lifetime pupils who had moved to Florida and showed up to claim their "prepaid" lessons. There was no way the Florida studios could provide those services without income, and they were getting no help from the New York office in seeing that the sales income was properly distributed throughout the chain. One franchise had the money, another had the expense of teaching the students. The latter had little success in getting the money from the former.

By 1958, in Detroit, the problems were clearly beginning to outweigh the rewards, and each day was another painful gauntlet that had to be run. That year, I had to take over four of the Michigan studios whose finances were in chaos and whose indebtedness was staggering. Invariably, the problems centered around a poor or dishonest manager who had let things get completely out of hand, or an ambitious one who simply left to seek greener pastures. The problems were popping up all over, and I felt like the little Dutch boy trying to keep the holes in the dike plugged up. It reached a point where I was afraid to get out of bed, not knowing what jolt of bad news I would receive on that day.

On a day in 1960, that jolt was the federal government and a bill for back taxes and interest totaling $100,000. The government claimed that an interpretation of the tax law back in the forties by our bookkeepers was incorrect and that I had to pay the taxes plus the interest for the intervening years, something over ten years. Since the taxes were for the time that Cy was my partner, half of the bill was really his, but by that time, he had been let go by Arthur Murray, and he was having a very difficult time getting along.

Cy was living in Detroit, looking around for something to do. I did not think it would be a wise move for him to come back to the studio where he had been co-owner, and I think he understood. Cy was a great guy, and I hated to see him down on his luck. I had loaned him five dollars one day, and he paid me back with a check. Well, his check bounced, so I knew he would be of no help with the tax bill, which I paid myself. It almost did me in, but I paid it.

About this same time, the Federal Trade Commission showed up, and it was obvious that they were seriously investigating Arthur Murray, Inc. They asked a great many questions, and we gave them as much information as we could. The concern of the Federal Trade Commission had to do with Arthur Murray's overselling, overpromising, and then failing to perform. It was a little too late to save the studios from that misbegotten sales program, but it was an inevitable consequence of the selling frenzy.

Had I fully realized early on how great these problems would eventually become, I would have happily given away the franchise with all its studios to whomever would accept it. Looking back at it now, it was the showbiz story all over again, a long season of success, followed by a downward plunge into failure and disappointment. I did not know when to get out. Like George Santayana said, "Those who cannot remember the past are condemned to repeat it." Once I took a battery of tests that helps you decide on a suitable vocation or course of study, and among the other things it told me about my temperament was the statement "Has a tendency to stick to lost causes." Well, I guess so. After twenty successful years in the teaching of dance, I entered a decade-long season in hell, probably the worst ten years of my life, trying to salvage a lost cause.

What happened to me is complex and has many different parts, not the least of which was my own limitations as a business manager. In 1948, I bought Cy's interest in the Michigan studios, when he was lured away by Arthur Murray to work for the New York office. I became the sole owner of the franchise, which at that time consisted of ten studios. I remember proclaiming to Paul—facetiously but also with some pride—"I own Michigan!" For several years to follow, the growth in studios and students was phenomenal. I was sub-franchising to new managers at such a rate that the quality control began to slip. I always believed that I was dealing with good managers who were persons of integrity and competence, and over the years certainly most of them were. However, there were some bad apples in the group that would in time cause me great misery and grief.

By the early sixties, I had twenty-two lawsuits against me by disgruntled pupils at the various studios. Some believed that they had been promised more than they were receiving. Others had simply gotten in over their heads financially and were demanding refunds. In cases where it seemed clear that they had a legitimate grievance, I agreed to give them a refund. In other cases, the courts ruled that we had to refund the fees.

The lucrative commissions being paid by Arthur Murray for the sale of lifetime packages were too inviting for some studio managers and teachers to ignore, and everyone was trying to sell the big packages. Some unscrupulous managers would offer prospective students the moon. I learned that in one case, someone was promised six special Life Time parties a year, in addition to all regular studio parties, a free trip to Cuba on a dance vacation, free escort to parties outside the studio, invitations to special dance exhibitions of all the dances taught by Arthur Murray, every medal ball free for life—all that in addition to unlimited lessons. Of course, not only was this a highly unrealistic list and an absolutely dishonest enticement, it was the kind of liability that would inevitably become mine and not the local studio's. By that time, the corrupt manager was long gone.

Often teachers would dump their students onto other teachers so that they could spend their time off their feet, selling lifetime packages. Indeed, many aspiring teachers who went through our expensive training program "jumped ship" and went out to make their living in the "business" of dance teaching on their own. Even though we had contractual agreements with them to teach for us after their training, it was too expensive and complicated to try to enforce those agreements.

I had established a trust fund into which each studio was to deposit the funds for the untaught lessons, and money would be returned to the branches as the lessons were taught. However, this practice was never well received by the managers, and the money sent to the trust fund was only a fraction of what should have been paid. In addition to the failure to forward the funds, there was the added problem of inflation. When the legitimate benefits of the dance courses were offered, the costs may have been manageable, but in a few years, the costs of teaching those courses had gone up significantly but the liability remained. It was a plan designed for disaster.

With the continuing decline in the number of pupils and my horrific discoveries that some of the departed managers had left behind them huge indebtedness, I began to fall behind in the payroll. At one point, I was three weeks behind in paying the teachers and other staff, and I had started borrowing money to keep the franchise going. I was also far behind in sending the seven-percent royalty to Arthur Murray, Inc.

During the late fifties and early sixties, I borrowed a total of $250,000 from Paul, who eventually became thoroughly disgusted with trying to help me instigate intelligent business principles in my studios. Paul had been working very hard over these years and had put together a small empire of factories—starting with the one he purchased off the auction block in Rochester, Michigan—which eventually grew into five different specialty operations. He was a successful, intuitive business man, and he never let his problems discourage his efforts. Each of his victories established him more securely, and he was clearly a unique, self-made man of the automotive industry.

When he first started in the direction of acquiring small factories, I was "in the bucks," and I loaned him $30,000 to help buy his first building in

Detroit. He had a partner in that venture who was an accountant and who kept the books for the operation. In almost no time, Paul paid back my loan with interest. Even when he suffered the devastating blow of seeing that first factory burn down within the first year, he picked up the pieces and moved on. He dissolved his partnership with the accountant and never again took on a business partner. He liked going it alone, and it was not long after the fire that he bought the Rochester property at auction and began to build his little empire.

I understand his disillusionment with the business tactics developed in the Arthur Murray chain. They got worse each year. The tentacles of the monster organization in New York choked us all eventually. When they had squeezed out all they could—and had become exceedingly rich—they withdrew, leaving the badly wounded studios to die—which is what happened to studios all over the country.

The strain of the decline of my studios caused difficulty in my relationship with Paul. Especially after I had gone into debt to him for the $250,000, which weighed on me like a ton of lead. That is when his faithful employee Al Giuliani, who was the comptroller of Paul's companies, said to me, "Thus far and no farther." He helped me to start making the cuts and changes that were necessary if I was to survive and to start repaying Paul. I closed studios and began to fight back against the New York Arthur Murray group. Those last several years nearly cost me my marriage, and I don't blame Paul. He had done all he could to help me. I was just in so deep, and I was so frantic, it was a miserable time. Every morning, I prayed that I would just get through the day.

I struggled desperately with the management side of the business: the personnel problems, financial statements, mounting bills, management decisions, hiring and firing, and so on. So when Al Giuliani came in to help, I was willing to do whatever he told me to do. I wrote to all my creditors explaining to them that I could not at that time pay what I owed them but that I would begin to make small monthly payments as soon as possible and continue to do so until the entire debt was paid. The payments would vary from month to month, but I would keep them informed on a monthly basis about how much I could pay. They all went along with me—even the telephone company, so critical to my business—and eventually they were all paid, but it took ten years of my life working day and night just to get out of debt.

The good will that we had built over the years in Michigan had allowed me to make those arrangements with my patient creditors. That good will was based on what we had done in Michigan—not what the New York office had done. What was going on now nationwide in the late fifties and throughout the sixties was causing a deterioration of our good name and services in Michigan. The number of lawsuits against the studios throughout the country was horrendous, and newspaper articles started to appear about customers being ripped off by dance studios (not just Arthur Murray, but Fred Astaire Studios and others). The affiliation with Arthur Murray, Inc., had become more of a liability than an asset. So after consulting with Al Giuliani and our Detroit attorneys, we decided to stop making the franchise payments. Arthur Murray, Inc., was not fulfilling any of its obligations to us and was imposing policies with which we could not agree. We began to receive threats from New York about losing our franchise if we did not pay the franchise fees, but we held fast to our position.

We organized a meeting with studios from a number of other cities outside of Michigan—Chicago, Baltimore, Denver, Atlanta, Toledo, and several more—and learned that all of us felt alike about what the New York office was doing—and not doing. We, as a group, met with the New York office to express our discontent and New York promised to make changes and provide all of the obligated services. But, they insisted, the franchise fees and all the back fees must be paid immediately. Most of the other managers capitulated and paid the fees, but we did not. New York delivered on none of the services they had promised, but nevertheless, they attempted to cancel our franchise in 1962.

To his great credit, Al Giuliani—who had carefully documented all of the failures of Arthur Murray, Inc., with regard to obligatory services, and particularly their failure to perform the auditing function—convinced the very famous New York attorney Louis Nizer to take the case. Nizer had written the best-selling book *My Life in Court,* and had handled many high-profile cases, including the highly publicized Billy Rose divorce case. At that time, he was probably the best-known attorney in the United States. We sued Arthur Murray, Kathryn Murray, and Arthur Murray, Inc., for $1 million plus the cancellation of all back franchise fees for the harm done to the Michigan studios. In turn, the Murrays sued Arthur Murray Studios of Michigan, Inc., and Doris Eaton Travis for $5 million plus all back franchise fees. Al Giuliani worked closely with a Mr. Zimmerman from Nizer's office, and they compiled and indexed over eight file-cabinet drawers of data, documenting every failure of the New York office to meet its obligations to us, and the other behaviors that we deemed detrimental to our dance business. Louis Nizer told Giuliani that it was the best-documented case he had ever represented, and he glowed with confidence in our ultimate victory.

Well, I guess our case was daunting enough for the other side to want to settle out of court, and that is what happened. Arthur Murray, Inc., agreed to pay the Arthur Murray Studios of Michigan, Inc., the lawyers' fees (about $150,000), agreed to a contract allowing us to continue using the Arthur Murray name, and agreed that no back fees would be paid and no future payment of franchise fees would be paid for a ten-year period. It was a sweet victory, and it saved the operation. At last, Arthur Murray Studios of Michigan, Inc., was able to start the process of getting out of debt. That could never have been possible without the agreed upon settlement that no franchise fees would be paid for ten years.

Joe, who had been managing the east side studio in Detroit throughout these years while serving as a district manager for Arthur Murray, came to the downtown office to help me start digging out. Joe had suffered heart problems throughout his life since having polio (infantile paralysis) as a child, but he worked tirelessly for me. He had all of the attention to detail that eluded me, and over the years, he composed, printed, and mailed newsletters to all of the various managers in the Michigan group, in an effort to give them encouragement, ideas, and information to improve their operation. Charlie had been managing the northwest Detroit studio, and he also came to the downtown studio, where he handled all of the training classes.

Joe and I, over an extended period of time, visited each studio to evaluate the magnitude of the untaught lessons problem and assess the overall operation. One by one, we closed down the studios, resolved the leases, and made arrangements to send teachers to a local hotel to complete the untaught lessons commitment.

The three of us—Joe, Charlie, and I—had the formidable task of keeping the morale high and building a sense of optimism, while conducting what was basically a salvaging operation. We trimmed down our expenses while trying to keep parties and events going and giving high-quality service to our students. Thank God for some very dedicated and talented teachers who stuck with us during this period. We had gone from 103 teachers at the peak to 20 in the last few years. The good teachers loved what they were doing, and we all worked well together. And I plodded along in the slow, grinding process of paying my creditors, including the $250,000 I had borrowed from Paul. It was not easy, but the job got done.

When at last I had managed to pay off all of the indebtedness of the studios, I was able to sell the franchise to Ron Anderson, one of our former teachers from the Grand Rapids studio. By that time, the Michigan franchise had been reduced to a single studio in Detroit. One by one, I disassembled the chain I had built. That was not a pleasant task. It was a terrible period for me. With a bittersweet sense of relief and disappointment, I began to plan my last medal ball.

Paul did not come to my last medal ball. He was still angry about the whole affair, and he never wanted to have anything to do with the dance studio business for the rest of his life. There was still a wall between Paul and me. I tried to ignore it, but it didn't go away for quite a while. So I went ahead without him. The ball was a small affair compared with the many extravaganzas we had put on a few years back. As fate would have it, the ball took place in a ballroom of the Statler Hotel, where it had all started in 1938, when Cy and I opened the very first branch of Arthur Murray Studios of New York. That venture took some courage and determination, and for the first twenty years, it gave to me the best years of my life.

I had rented a room in the hotel to spend the night there following the ball. Frankly, I did not know whether I still had a marriage or not, and I did not know what my next move would be. I didn't want to think about it until this last medal ball was behind me. You know, "After the ball is over . . ."

The entertainment began with Ron Anderson and me dancing an English waltz, and then there followed all of the dance demonstrations and the awarding of medals. Soon it was time for me to give my farewell speech and introduce the new owner of the studio. Well, I choked up during the speech, and it took several seconds for me to regain my composure. I did get through it finally, and they brought me a beautiful bouquet of red roses. When the speeches were over and everyone was once again on the floor dancing, I eased out of the ballroom and went to my room. My career at Arthur Murray's had come to an end. For the first time since childhood, dancing was no longer a part of my livelihood.

CHAPTER NINETEEN

"MOURNING INTO DANCING"

t was dancing that saved my marriage. The last several years in Detroit had been very hard on my relationship with Paul. For almost a decade, I had struggled with the indebtedness of the Michigan studios and the declining demand for social dance lessons. I was reducing the chain of studios from eighteen down to one, which was a torturous process. At the same time, Paul was going through his own business agonies, experiencing painfully mixed feelings about selling his "baby," the Rochester Paper Company, which he had built from almost nothing, eventually acquiring four additional mills as subsidiaries. Unlike the sacrificial way in which I was selling the dance studios, Paul was selling a very profitable business and making a large amount of money. But it was still an emotional and stressful loss for him, having been his pride and joy for twenty years.

During that painful period, we didn't have much to offer each other except our fatigue and frustration, and too often, anger smothered affection. Eventually, a wall had been built between us, and our lives had become virtually separate. It was hard to see how we could get back together again. I was working very late and would often arrive home after Paul had retired for the night, and he would leave early in the morning, while I was still sleeping. Although we hardly saw each other, each morning he would bring my car from the garage and park it by the door for me. That single act of kindness I viewed as a fragile thread of hope that someday the anguish for both of us would be over, and we might be able to recover the precious elements of our once happy life together. After a time, I found myself spending more evenings alone in a hotel in Detroit rather than driving the thirty miles to the farm, knowing that Paul and I would not see each other anyway.

In 1968, Paul purchased a 240-acre ranch near Norman, Oklahoma, planning to raise quarter horses. He had become convinced that the smart money was in breeding quarter horses instead of the Appaloosas he had started raising in Michigan. It was a lovely spread of ranch land in an area known as the "ten-mile flats"—a long stretch of level grasslands perfect for horses. Paul would later increase his land to 880 acres, buying adjoining parcels of land as they became available.

I began the laborious process of closing out my downtown studio in Detroit. Ron Anderson, who had purchased the franchise, did not want to keep the downtown studio, preferring to take over the space in the northwest part of the city. Working with Joe and Charlie, I spent the better part of a year going through and cleaning out a thirty-year accumulation of records, costumes, pupil files, and hundreds of recordings—old seventy-eights and the newer forty-fives. What a painful process that was, constantly reminding me that once again an exhilarating and highly successful period of my life was ending in disappointment and sadness.

Joe was not in good health and was ready to retire. His wife, Lucille, and his two grown children were also pleased that he was retiring, and they all looked forward to it. On the other hand, Charlie, who was then only fifty-nine, was more troubled by the closing of the studios. He had grown up in the theater and had never wanted to leave show business. He had successfully brought his talents as an entertainer into the dance teaching business, and since he had never married, his whole social life was centered around his work. So throughout that final year, as we sorted through the remnants of the past three decades, Charlie had this rising sense of loss and a growing aware-ness that he had nothing to do and nowhere to go. Ultimately, he decided to remain in Detroit, where he had friends and where Joe and his family would be nearby.

In early 1970, Paul and I moved—lock, stock, and barrel—to Norman, Oklahoma, and began our new life. I must confess that I did not know at that time whether we would even stay together. On the one hand, I was relieved to have the terrible burden of the past ten years off my back, and on the other, I was filled with anxiety and pain at the sad state of my relationship with Paul. But I knew that I wanted to make a supreme effort to find a way to resolve our differences and make our separate lives one again. So as Paul was setting up the ranch, acquiring high-visibility stallions and brood mares, I looked for ways to become a part of the operation. Before long, it became obvious that a bookkeeper was needed for the business of the ranch. Records needed to be kept on all of the horses, personnel records on the ranch employees, and of course, all the financial records necessary to the business. So with some basic lessons from Al Giuliani, Paul's Michigan accountant and friend, who contin-ued to handle Paul's financial affairs, I learned to keep the books and became a working partner with Paul.

I also began to learn the horse business and quarter horse racing. Believe me, it was a whole new culture for me, with its own vocabulary, traditions, and folkways. The horse people and the racing people were openly friendly, down-to-earth, and highly skilled. Many were superb horse traders, with keen knowledge and the kind of savvy to make good deals. When they encountered Paul, they may have believed that they had found a real patsy, a neophyte in the horse business ready to be taken. But Paul had carefully prepared himself. He not only had the necessary knowledge of the horse business, he had the instincts of a master salesman. They met their match in Paul, and he made some very lucrative deals.

I traded in my upscale business attire for blue jeans and cowboy boots, and I learned to talk about horses the way we once talked about performers—the greats, the near-greats, the also-rans. Paul had purchased with the ranch two great stallions—Three Chicks and Tiny Watch—and he had brought one with him, named Pannabar. He would eventually own between twenty-five and thirty outstanding mares. Other mares were brought to the ranch for stud service, so that at times, as many as sixty mares would be on the ranch. My job was to keep records on each of them, and I enjoyed the feeling of being a useful part of this new adventure.

Paul's horses would soon be winning races at Ruidoso, New Mexico, starting with Miss Three Wars, the offspring of Three Chicks and Miss Leo War. Miss Three Wars won the Rainbow Futurity and finished second in the Kansas and All American, each time losing to the great stallion Easy Jet. With such early success, our horse business was off and running.

Although Paul and I were working well together, the wall between us had not yet been entirely removed. It finally began to fall when we went to a dinner-dance club in Oklahoma City and had fun dancing together again for the first time in many months. Paul was an excellent dancer, and we blended well as a couple. People would come up to us to tell us how much they enjoyed watching us dance, and Paul enjoyed the compliments he received. Women loved to dance with Paul because he led so well and always knew exactly what he was doing. It was clear to me that the one precious heritage that we had from the Detroit days was our knowledge of and love for social dancing. So I sought out opportunities for us to dance together. Paul even agreed to go to an Arthur Murray Dance Studio with me—one of the few still operating in the diminished national chain (and that one would soon close). We both loved the ambiance of the studio, and it was always fun to learn new dances or relearn old ones. There we met a couple who were taking lessons—Charles and Marlene Peppers—with whom we became good friends and started going out dancing together as often as we could.

Then came the horses—another new direction

Paul and Doris with Miss Three Wars
and her trainer, Tom Warren

A successful horse breeding and racing career for my husband

Paul's quarter horse Miss Three Wars won
the Ruidoso Rainbow Futurity in 1969.

Places for social dancing were very limited in the Oklahoma City area, but about this time, country-and-western dancing was becoming popular, not only the round dancing, like the two-step, but all manner of line dances—Slappin' Leather, the Duchess, Cotton-eyed Joe, and so on—and they appeared to be great fun. Paul and I started going out regularly to learn the line dances, and soon we were truly enjoying each other and once again having fun together. Dance step by dance step, the wall came tumbling down.

We had started going to the University Club, at the University of Oklahoma, where they had a western band playing at that time. Once or twice a week, we would be there with a growing group of faculty and staff members, learning the new dances. Soon I found myself, irresistibly, teaching the dances to others, and Paul would help me out. We did this for several years, eventually moving on to teach other dances: the fox-trot, the rhumba, the tango, the waltz. Paul, when he was in his eighties, received such positive comments from everyone on his skillful dancing that it made him feel youthful and alive. Life had become good again.

Shortly after Paul and I had revived our pleasure in dancing together, and especially with the fun we were having with the country-western style, the thought occurred to me that here we were in an entirely new setting—here in the former wild, wild west. Drawing on my old showbiz experience and the many presentations and parties I had devised for the students of my dance studios in Michigan, I suggested to Paul, "Let's give a party for all our new friends." Since he had attended many of those Detroit parties and often was part of the entertainment, he responded with "Okay. Let's go."

We decided that since we were now "westerners," we could make it a real old-fashioned "old, old golden west" party with the old western dance hall atmosphere. So I got busy and worked out the whole idea in detail. Most of the entertainment was performed by several of the guests. It is always more fun at this type of party if the guests get into the act. On the date set for the party, November 16, 1983, everyone was ready for it, and this is how it unfolded.

Above the entrance to the door of the ballroom was a sign stating "Travis Elegant Saloon." The tables were arranged in a large circle, leaving ample room for the dance floor. After dinner, the entertainment began. It started with four dance hall girls doing a take-off of the famous cancan music, a dance style right out of Montmartre in Paris. However, I did not use the cancan music, but instead used the tune that was heard in just about every saloon in the west. It was written by two Americans and was called "Ta-Ra-Ra Boom-Der-E"—often sung as Ta-Ra-Ra Boom-Dee-A. The country-and-western band I had engaged for the evening played the old tune with great relish, while the girls—four students from the dance department of the University of Oklahoma—kicked up their heels and flaunted their many ruffled dance hall costumes. It started the floor show off with a bang.

Next came an act of the barbershop type, harmonizing by three of our guests with excellent voices, who had quite a reputation locally for their delightful singing of the old songs as well as the new. They kept to the old favorites of the west in this performance. Of course, "Sweet Adeline" was one of them, and the other guests loved it. Following this was a solo number by the female member of the band. She sang that old heart-wrenching "She's Only a Bird in a Gilded Cage." But as she was halfway through the song, there burst out of the area that was our stage two frantic dance hall girls screaming as loud as they could while being chased by two male guests (previously selected by me, of course). They ran all around and in and out of the guests' tables, finding their way back to the backstage area, the males still in hot pursuit. All the while, our soloist in the band kept up her mournful rendition of "Bird in a Gilded Cage" and never missed a beat.

I had been teaching social dancing to a group of our friends, four couples, for several months, and I suggested that they take part in our show. There was some hesitation at first, but when I told them that they had already learned the dance step they would do in this dance, they all agreed to participate. So we began our rehearsals for an old French court dance called *la varsouvienne*. This old French dance had also found its way to the golden west, but there it became known as "Put Your Little Foot Right There." From my study of the history and patterns of the old court dances of Europe many years ago, I taught them the dance formations in the style of the French court. They danced it sedately and elegantly.

We had a little fun during the rehearsal because my students were really my professors. This is how that happened. One day, I repeated my often stated desire for a college education. Paul said to me, "I've listened to you moan and groan about not having a college degree for too many years. The University is only fifteen minutes from this ranch. Now either put up or shut up." Well, I guess that was all I needed. I procured the General Education Development Test program to achieve high school equivalency status, studied for one year, and in the fall of 1980, I enrolled at the University of Oklahoma and began one of the truly great experiences of my life.

But now here's the rub. Of the four couples I was now rehearsing, three of the gentlemen were my teachers in college. Paul Sharp had been president of the University and a professor of history. He was now retired but continued to teach occasionally. J. R. Morris had been provost and interim president and was now teaching psychology. Kenneth Hoving was dean of the Graduate College and vice provost for research, and he served as my academic advisor. With his guidance, I studied philosophy, English, and history—finally settling on history as my major. Because Dr. Hoving wanted me to have a well-rounded liberal education, he was quite insistent at times in telling me what courses I should take. However, when he included physics in one of my programs, I put up quite a resistance. I asked, "When and where will I ever need physics? He answered, "For a well-rounded education, you need to know what physics is all about." The very word scared me, but as usual, he won. If it were not that the final exams and scores are a matter of record in the university student archives, no one would ever believe that I got an "A" in physics. My professor said, "It was a skinny A, but it was an A."

But now I was the teacher of my teachers. What a group. I had fun lording it over them during rehearsals, saying that they might be the great intellectuals of the University but that I was now the teacher and in charge. We all had some good-natured laughs about the turnaround. At the party, they with their wives all performed their dance without a flaw. I was so proud of them. When it was over, the group gave me a lovely sweater with the word "TEACH" on the back of it. I shall treasure it always.

But on with the show! Next came Paul's and my contribution to the floor show. I had reconstructed the dance patterns of a beautiful old waltz called the three-step waltz. There was a particular pattern that identified the three-step movement from which the waltz got its name. Paul was exceptionally good at waltzing. It was his favorite social dance, and he enjoyed learning this old-fashioned rendition of it. He danced with his usual precision and warm dignified expression. He was eighty-three, and I was seventy-nine.

What a heart-satisfying moment it was for me to be giving a dance exhibition with Paul again—just as we had done so many times in my former dance studio activities, including his appearances with me several times on the local television show I produced for seven summer seasons. Our television show was confined to the presentation of social dances old and new. All of the dance routines were performed entirely by our staff and students—with Paul making guest appearances as my partner.

The climax of the entertainment was a little dramatic (so-called) skit on the stage area. The curtains were parted to reveal a big double bed, presumably in a bedroom. From one side of the stage, one of the dance hall girls came on stage in a long flannel nightgown, slightly shivering, and said "Great guns, what a night!" and got into the bed and under the covers. When she was settled, dance hall girl number two came on from the other side of the stage— also in a nightgown and shivering—and said "Great guns, what a night!" and went to the other side of the bed and got in under the covers. A few seconds passed, and dance hall girl number three came in and repeated the action. A few seconds later, girl number four came on in nightgown and shivering and repeated the action. The audience was quiet. There was about fifteen seconds of suspense. Then, suddenly, the covers in the center of the bed were thrown back, and a male figure in flannel nightgown and the proverbial stocking sleeping cap on his head sat up and blurted out, "Great guns, what a night!" He then looked from side to side, snuck back under the covers and pulled them over his head, at which time, the curtains were pulled back together. The hilarious point was that the man in the bed was not only a guest at the party, but he was the reigning sheriff of the county. Of course, everybody knew him, and the audience roared.

The funniest incident in the whole preparation for this skit was the following: I had asked the sheriff's wife if she had any objection to the sheriff doing this skit and explained what he would do. She said she didn't mind at all. So I approached the sheriff to see if he would do it. I explained the setting and then asked, "Do you object to getting in bed with four dance hall girls?" His answer came back quick as a flash, "No-o-o problem."

From then on, I began to plan two parties a year. Each March, we would celebrate our accumulating wedding anniversaries combined with my birthdays, as they were just a few days apart. In November, we would celebrate Paul's birthday. It became such a wonderful way to get together with everyone, and the guests seemed to enjoy the opportunity to visit with each other this way. Paul attended his ninety-ninth birthday party. It was a happy time even though he was in a wheelchair. The theme of that party was "Hats in Time." Everybody had to wear a hat of their choice—old or new. I had gone through our wardrobes and pulled out all the old hats of mine and Paul's that I kept these many years. As part of the entertainment, I put on Paul's and my hats from different moments in our lives and gave a brief remark as to the fashion styles of those periods in which we had worn them. And so we gave our last exhibition together, our hats doing the dancing.

As the years rolled on, Paul and I gradually rediscovered our early love. In his last few years, as he became less active, we grew closer. He left us in the earliest hours of June 24, 2000. He had grown less talkative in the last few weeks. Two nights before he passed on, I was beside him in his bed. He said to me, "I love you a tremendous amount. I love you," and he took my hand and kissed it. Those were the last words he spoke to me.

I had intended to give him a centennial party, and I did, but as a memorial. I returned to the theme of that very first big party—the "OLD, OLD, OLD GOLDEN WEST." Even though it was seventeen years later, many of the guests from that first party were there. Once again, there were four dance hall girls dancing to "Ta-Ra-Ra-Boom-Der-E," the barbershop singers, and two couples from the original group dancing *la varsouvienne*. One of my former teachers in my dance studios in Michigan, Earl Tyrie, had come to live with us for a while as a companion to my brother Charlie, with whom he had worked closely on many special events. I taught him the three-step waltz, and we danced just as Paul and I had done so many years before. We all knew that Paul was there with us in spirit. We had a happy time, as he would have wanted us to.

〜 〜 〜

What I did not expect to happen at my age was a surprising renascence in my show business career—sixty years after I had left it "for good." But in the fall of 1997, five of us original *Ziegfeld Follies* girls were asked to be guests at the reopening of the New Amsterdam Theater on Forty-second Street. The Walt Disney Company had purchased and successfully restored the theater to its original atmosphere of elegance, beauty, and refinement. The ABC television program *20/20* featured us "girls" in a nostalgic look back at the Ziegfeld era, and as part of the taping, I did a few dance steps for old times' sake on the newly rebuilt stage. (I'm not bragging, but I was the only one of the group who could still dance.) Then in the spring of 1998, I was asked to return along with the other original Ziegfeld girls to the New Amsterdam to participate in an AIDS benefit sponsored by Broadway Cares/ACTORS EQUITY FIGHTS AIDS. This was a more elaborate affair. I was to dance with a chorus of gypsies from several different Broadway shows for an audience made up of show people—actors, dancers, singers, directors, and so on.

We five Ziegfeld girls were introduced on stage, and as we were walking off, I stepped out of the line and—after a brief preplanned exchange with the orchestra conductor—danced the same soft-shoe routine to Irving Berlin's "Mandy" that I had danced on that stage in the 1919 *Follies* as understudy to Marilyn Miller. I had practiced, of course, for a few weeks before this event, but I must admit a moment of "opening night nerves" as I moved down the stage on my music cue. But I have learned a lot about how to face crises in my life since I danced on that same stage at age fifteen, so I said to myself, "This is it. Do it." And I did it, thank heaven, with no difficulty.

There was a roar of applause when I finished the routine, a standing audience clapping and shouting. I had never had a moment quite like that in the theater in all my times there. Gradually, the audience quieted down with a little gesture from me indicating that there was more to come. The orchestra resumed, and the waiting chorus began their routine while I danced over to join them. At a certain music cue, we all went into that famous basic step of tap dancing called the "time step." Where the energy came from for that more demanding tempo, only the good Lord knows, but I did it, and again the audience roared! I finished my part and was escorted off into the wings, where the production crew, stagehands, and fellow performers, bless them all, congratulated me enthusiastically, while the audience continued its thunderous ovation. What a moment! This is what show people spend their whole careers hoping for. At age ninety-four, I thrilled to every second of it. One of the producers, Scott Stevens, was quoted in the press as saying, "In the ten year history of the Easter Bonnet shows there's never been an ovation like that." One of the young chorus dancers was overheard saying to a fellow dancer, "She was awesome."

I had no idea how much notoriety my dancing would cause, but it made scores of local television stations across the country, as well as *USA Today, U.S. News and World Report,* and ABC's *Good Morning America,* and I received a call from Rosie O'Donnell that led to two appearances on her show—including my doing another dance routine with an all-male chorus.

What a thrill all of that was for this old Ziegfeld girl. It was all so unexpected, and to think that more people saw me dance on the Rosie O'Donnell show than had seen me in my entire show business career. I had unexpectedly and at long last fulfilled my mother's ambition for me to become famous—at least for my allotted fifteen minutes.

There were, in the following months, some other unforgettable moments. I was named Oklahoma's Ambassador of Good Will at the 1998 Oklahoma Hall of Fame ceremony and again danced on stage, re-creating an old vaudeville sister act I had seen as a child. My "sister" dancing partner was the late Alma Wilson, who was then chief justice of the Oklahoma Supreme Court and a member of the Hall of Fame. We danced to the great, old ragtime song "Hello My Baby," with the well-known Oklahoma bandleader and singer Joe Webster as our backup singer. We were told that we were the hit of the show.

In the spring of 1998, I received a call from Nils Hanson in New York, a good friend and the guy largely responsible for my renascent career. I had begun to call him my New York agent, because that is what he had become. His phone call was to ask if I would be interested in doing a scene in a Jim Carrey movie called *Man on the Moon,* based on the biography of the late comedian Andy Kaufman. I said I would consider it, and I ended up returning to Hollywood in the fall of 1998 for my first motion picture in seventy years. I filmed only a brief dancing-comedy scene with Jim Carrey, but what an adventure of mind, soul, and body to be working on a Hollywood set after all these years— and with an Academy Award winning director, Milos Foreman. A grand experience. In between takes, I was able to squeeze in another TV appearance on the Howie Mandel Show. It was great fun teaching this popular young comedian the dance that had started the jazz craze years ago, "Ballin' the Jack."

I've returned to New York five times since 1997, for benefit performances, including dancing each year in the Easter Bonnet AIDS benefit. Once I shared a dressing room in the New Amsterdam with Broadway legend Gwen Verdon and superstar Bernadette Peters. And in another charity affair called "There Is Nothing Like a Dame," I danced with the two original stars from Joe Papp's *Chorus Line,* Donna McKechnie and Priscilla Lopez. In April of 1999, Charlie and I attended the annual Ziegfeld girls' luncheon, where I—as honorary president—took over the duties of our much-loved president, Dana O'Connell, who was unable to attend. As part of the entertainment, before crowning Bebe Neuwirth as Miss Ziegfeld for 2000, brother Charlie and I did "Ballin' the Jack." Charlie put on a brown derby, and I put on a fancy hat and a feather boa. The audience seemed to love these two old original *Ziegfeld Follies* performers doing their thing once more. That same spring, Charlie appeared with me in the Easter Bonnet show, also doing "Ballin' the Jack." In 2001, I was back again at the Easter Bonnet show, this time dancing modern swing with a whole chorus. I wore a bright yellow dress, after the one worn by the leading lady in the musical *Contact.* My partner was a young man, Eric Sciotto, who was a featured dancer in *Annie Get Your Gun.* We had a ball. In April of 2002, I danced the Charleston at the Easter Bonnet show and was joined on stage by Rosie O'Donnell. That's as good as it gets.

In 2003 I did a bit in which I taught the Black Bottom to Sutton Foster, who was starring in the hit Broadway show *Thoroughly Modern Millie.* In this appearance I gave her a quick runthrough of the steps of the Black Bottom, which she learned quickly. And then with the music, we danced it together. It was fun for both of us, and the audience gave us another standing ovation.

It has been wonderful for Charlie and me to relive these thrilling and ecstatic moments on the bright side of show business. Lord knows, the Eaton

Charlie and Doris in the Easter Bonnet Show, 1999, New Amsterdam Theater, New York

Doris with one of Broadway's leading dnacers, Eric Sciotto, in the Easter Bonnet show of 2001

family knew enough of the dark side. Charlie, particularly, suffered the double blows of his failed career in show business and then seeing his whole world collapse around him with the sale of the last dance studio—going through almost a year of anguish while we cleaned out all the memorabilia of the downtown studio. It was the place where we had spent so many creative and productive years. Then with my having left Detroit, Charlie was living alone in a small house in an unpretentious neighborhood to which he was a stranger. It was a soul-tormenting episode in his life. Charlie by nature is a people-person, and he had been surrounded by people all of his life, and now his loneliness became intolerable. I cannot blame him for finding a small bar close by and going there to seek a little company. Of course, drinking was a part of the camaraderie, and then it became a mental and emotional crutch to take home. By the end of the sixties, I became alarmed at what I saw happening, so I stopped giving him money and sent him to a rehabilitation center.

The neighborhoods, both Charlie's and Joe's (which was not far away), deteriorated to the point that you could not take trash to the alley without the danger of being attacked by hoodlums. I was able to move both of them to a lovely new condo complex north of Detroit, in Troy. The surrounding atmosphere for living was vastly improved, but the loneliness for Charlie was not. He saw Joe, whose health was failing, once or twice a week, but Joe soon became unable to look after the condo or Charlie. Then Charlie was injured in a fall on the pavement and had to go to the hospital. It was obvious that he was no longer able to live alone, and so being a veteran, he was sent to a nursing home. While he found some friendships there, he felt terribly abandoned—just as Mama did when I took her to a nursing home. Mama and Charlie had always been very close when Charlie was growing up, and that closeness continued in later years. He was her last baby, and she knew it. Charlie had the feeling that Mama would always be there for him, and now he felt that he had no one. I could not tolerate the estrangement and unhappiness that Charlie felt, so I brought him to Norman to a nursing home close to our ranch. After a year, Paul built an apartment onto our ranch house for Charlie, who moved in in March of 2000. Charlie celebrated his eighty-ninth birthday on June 23 of that year, and Paul left us a few minutes after midnight of that day.

The mental and emotional strain of the past twenty-four years are gradually being erased, and Charlie is returning to the bright and cheerful person he was before the closing of the dance studios. He and I are closer than ever, and now happily, he always has people around him. There is a song we hear at Christmastime on the Lawrence Welk television show, which I believe was written by the singer Ken Dilo for his daughter. The first line is "Oh, to be a child again." It would not surprise me if that were the feeling Charlie has whenever he thinks of Mama.

Now there is only Charlie and me of the seven Eatons. We are having happy times together again as we did when we were children traveling on the road in *Mother Carey's Chickens* so many years ago. Charlie has never lost that sense of childhood wonder and discovery, nurtured by his early life in the fantasyland of the Broadway theater. After all, he played in *Peter Pan!* I surmise that he still thinks that all the world is a stage and that we—the people he deals with every day—are the somewhat peculiar characters playing around on it. He is kind, thoughtful, not wanting to be a burden to anyone, and he contributes his keen sense of humor to his observations about the crazy antics of the world we seem to be living in. He is still able to engulf us in laughter. How very grateful I am that it has worked out for Charlie and me to be together in these precious years of our lives. Sadly, brother Joe, who died in December of 1998, is not here to enjoy this time with us. He did, however, live long enough to know that—for a fleeting moment—an Eaton was back on Broadway, dancing her heart out once more, just the way we did a long time ago.

☟ ☟ ☟

Earlier in this book, I questioned how I, of all the Eatons, survived the twists and turns of our collective and individual lives. I believe that it was because in 1936, when my life was given an entirely new direction, I—in some feeble sense of gratitude to God for His deliverance—became determined to devote more study to understanding how He had helped me and why. Since then, I have conscientiously studied the Bible and *Science and Health with Key to the Scriptures* by Mary Baker Eddy. I have tried to let these teachings, as far as I could understand them, be my guide. They have given me the courage, hope, and determination to be the best and most that I am capable of being.

Psalm 30, verse 11, states: "Thou hast turned for me my mourning into dancing: thou hast put off my sackcloth and girded me with gladness." This verse has literally come true for me. My passage seemed slow and painful at times, but it has happened.

A QUIET REFLECTION

Through my many years, I have often expressed my most inner sentiments through the rhythm of poetry. That is a kind of dancing with words. This is my "Requiem" for my family.

Years ago when life was new,
Our hearts all full of play,
We danced and sang and earned a place,
In the glitter of Broadway.
We worked so hard and took our share,
In moments with the best,
The time so full of tempting things,
We hardly stopped to rest.
To rest and weigh the way things were,
Or how a change might come,
We danced the whirlwind here and there,
And then we learned how numb,
Our judgment of tomorrow's course,
'Twas just a kind of blur,
Each day so full of pleasantries,
We liked them as they were.
We did not note the signs around,
That pointed to the dangers,
For after fifteen glory years,
To Broadway we were strangers.
In stages all descending,
Life turned bleak for family members,
Talents shown in bright starlight,
Were now just dying embers.

But who can know at start of life,
To tell the end of trying?
We're born, we live, we work, and play,
And never think of dying.
Perhaps we can't do more,
Than what our changing concepts let us,
If that be true then there's no blame,
For anyone to tell us.
But like the song on Paris,
Which sparked such memories dear,
I'll take those words to comfort me,
When thoughts bring loved ones near.
I'll cherish them as then they were,
When hearts were "young and gay,"
No matter how life changed them,
I'll remember them that way.

Thank you for reading our story. Remembering the sentiment in the last line of *The Blue Bird,* which started our sojourn into the fantasyland of show business, let me encourage you with this: If you have lost your Blue Bird of Happiness temporarily, keep searching for it. I am sure you will find it "bye and bye."

Doris Eaton Travis

1908   Pearl (age ten), Mary (age seven), and Doris (age four) all study dance at Miss Cora Shreve's Dancing School, in Washington, D.C., appearing in Shreve's periodic dance productions.

1911   Evelyn takes Pearl, Mary, and Doris to try out for parts in the Shuberts' road company production of *The Blue Bird*. All three are hired.

1912–1914   The Eaton children appear in a number of Poli stock company shows in Washington, D.C., and Baltimore, including *Mrs. Wiggs and the Cabbage Patch* and *Little Lord Fauntleroy*. Joe at five is sometimes listed in the program as Josephine to play girl parts. Mary and Doris often play boy parts.

1915   Poli gets the Shuberts' permission for a Washington production of *The Blue Bird,* and they choose Mary and Doris for the two leads. The play is a huge hit, and the Shuberts decide to do a New York revival and road show, with Mary and Doris in the leading roles and Pearl in an ensemble dancing role.

1916   After four months on the road, *The Blue Bird* returns to New York. All along the way, Mary and Doris receive high praise for their performances. After a four-week run, Pearl is hired for the Winter Garden chorus for *Robinson Crusoe, Jr.,* starring Al Jolson. The Eatons decide to move from Washington to New York. Mary starts studying ballet with Theodore Kosloff. Doris and Charlie travel with Mama doing plays for the Poli stock companies.

1917   Pearl and Evelyn are in the chorus of the Shuberts' *The Passing Show of 1917* at the Winter Garden. It is Evelyn's only attempt at performing. Evelyn marries and does not continue in show business, except to scout out parts for her siblings and later her own children. Mary appears in *Follow Me* with the great Anna Held, but is forced out of the cast because she is only fifteen.

1918   Mary dances in a ballet performance in a show called *Intime,* in Washington, with President Wilson in the audience. She receives raves. She then does *Over the Top,* on Broadway, with Justine Johnstone and Ed Wynn. It is the debut on Broadway of Fred and Adele Astaire. Pearl is hired for the chorus of the *Ziegfeld Follies of 1918,* starring Will Rogers, W. C. Fields, and Lillian Lorraine, along with newcomer Marilyn Miller. Pearl is also made assistant to the famous dance director, Ned Wayburn. Doris is hired for the *Follies* road show (at age 14, she takes the name Doris Levant and passes for sixteen). She is made understudy to Ann Pennington.

1919   Pearl starts dancing in Ziegfeld's *Midnight Frolics,* at the New Amsterdam Roof. Doris is a specialty dancer in the *Ziegfeld Follies of 1919,* starring Eddie Cantor and Marilyn Miller, for whom Doris is the understudy. George M. Cohan sees Mary dance and hires her for *The Royal Vagabond.*

1920   Ziegfeld talks Cohan into releasing Mary so that she can star in the *Ziegfeld Follies of 1920.* Doris is a *Follies* principal now, and Pearl continues in the *Midnight Frolics.* Doris makes two movies at Astoria, Long Island, *At the Stage Door,* with Billie Dove, and *The Broadway Peacock,* with Pearl White.

1921   Charlie is in the *Ziegfeld Follies of 1921,* at age ten, in a skit with W. C. Fields. When Charlie drops out to make a movie at Astoria, Long Island, Joe takes his place. Mary again is one of the stars, while Pearl is one of the specialty dancers and assists with dance direction. Doris and Mama go to England; Doris makes a movie, *Tell Your Children,* directed by Donald Crisp and primarily shot in Egypt.

1922   Mary stars in the *Ziegfeld Follies of 1922,* while Pearl is asked by Ziegfeld to evaluate all of the dancing applicants. Pearl later goes on the road with the *Midnight Frolics,* its only road tour. Doris goes to Hollywood to star in the *Gorham Follies.*

1923   Mary is featured with Eddie Cantor in *Kid Boots,* produced by Ziegfeld and a huge hit. Pearl goes on the road with the *Follies* as a specialty dancer, which is her last job for Ziegfeld. Charlie at twelve plays the Palace, doing the balcony scene from *Romeo and Juliet,* with ten-year-old actress Miriam Batista.

1924 There are four Eatons on Broadway in four different theaters: Mary in *Kid Boots,* with Cantor; Doris in *The Sap,* with Raymond Hitchcock; Pearl in *Annie Dear,* with Billie Burke; and Charlie in *Peter Pan,* with Marilyn Miller. Pearl starts with Texas Guinan as a specialty dancer in one of New York's swankiest speakeasies, the El Fey, working after the theaters close. She continues to dance in other clubs throughout the twenties.

1925 Doris is a featured performer in *No Other Girl,* with Eddie Buzzell and Mary Lawler. Her dancing draws rave reviews. Charlie is on the road in *The Naked Man,* with Henry Hull and Ann Morrison. Doris gets the leading lady role in *Big Boy,* opposite Al Jolson. Later, she goes on the road in the John Cort production of *Suzanne.*

1926 Mary stars in the Charles Dillingham production *Lucky,* with Charlie also in the cast and Pearl working as stage manager—the first woman stage manager in Broadway history. Doris returns to Hollywood and stars in the *Hollywood Music Box Revue,* with Morton Downey. Nacio Herb Brown composes "Doll Dance" for Doris, which is a huge hit. Doris writes lyrics for the score. Evelyn's three children —Edwin, Evelynne, and Warren—are all active in show business and will have successful but short-lived careers as featured players on the stage, in radio, and the movies.

1927 All three sisters are on Broadway again at the same time: Mary is having her biggest hit with *The Five O'Clock Girl,* with Oscar Shaw. Doris is in the long-running *Excess Baggage,* with Miriam Hopkins, Eric Dressler, and Frank McHugh. Pearl is in *She's My Baby,* with Bea Lillie. Charlie is on the road with *Don't Count Your Chickens,* with Mary Boland. Later, Charlie has a role in *The Royal Fandango,* starring Ethel Barrymore and Edward G. Robinson.

1928 Doris films *An Affair of the Follies,* with Billie Dove. Charlie creates the role of Andy Hardy in the play *Skidding,* with Walter Able. He leaves the cast to go to Hollywood to star in Fox's first full-length talking picture, *The Ghost Talks.* Doris returns to New York to do *Cross My Heart,* in which her syncopated tap dancing stops the show.

1929 Doris introduces the song, "Singin' in the Rain," written by Nacio Herb Brown and Arthur Freed, for the *Hollywood Music Box Revue.*

She then enters a Franchon and Marco production, *The Serpentine Idea,* and leads a dance troupe of thirty dancers. Doris makes two "talking" films: *The Very Idea* and *Street Girl.* Mary films *Glorifying the American Girl,* at Astoria, Long Island, produced by Ziegfeld. She also makes *Cocoanuts* with the Marx Brothers. Pearl comes to Hollywood as the first dance director for RKO, and there she creates the dances for *Rio Rita* and *Hit the Deck.* Charlie makes *Harmony at Home* for Fox. Joe, after graduating from the University of Pennsylvania, goes to work in RKO's story department writing synopses of screenplays.

1930–31   As radio and "talking pictures" become hugely popular, vaudeville moves into the movie theaters. Doris dances in "stage shows" up and down the West Coast and eventually gets a role in the chorus of the Eddie Cantor movie *Whoopee,* her last appearance in a movie (until a 1999 cameo appearance in *Man on the Moon* with Jim Carrey). Mary goes to London to star in the musical *Folly to Be Wise.* The careers of all the Eatons begin to stall as the depression sets in.

1932   Doris returns to New York as a specialty dancer in the Hollywood restaurant and club of Nils T. Granlund. Mary sadly ends her career after starring in an abbreviated version of *Sally,* playing four-a-days in movie theatres along the West Coast. Mary and Pearl, both married, leave show business for good. Charlie joins Doris in New York to try vaudeville.

1933   Doris does stock company work on Long Island and for the Thatcher stock company out of Hartford. Charlie teams with Buster West for a short-lived vaudeville act.

1934–35   Doris has a minor role in *Merrily We Roll Along,* with Walter Able and Mary Philips. Doris and Charlie try a vaudeville act, which doesn't succeed.

1936   Charlie, at twenty-five, makes his final appearance on Broadway in *Lady Luck.* Doris goes to work for Arthur Murray in the New York studios, initially teaching tap dancing.

1938–1968   Doris builds a chain of eighteen dance studios throughout the state of Michigan.

BIBLIOGRAPHY

Berliner, Louise. *Texas Guinan: Queen of the Nightclubs.* Austin: University of Texas Press, 1993.

Blum, Daniel. *A Pictorial History of the American Theatre.* 3d ed. New York: Greenberg, 1956.

Burke, Billie. *With a Feather on My Nose.* New York: Appleton-Centre-Crafts, 1949.

Feinstein, Michael. *Nice Work if You Can Get It: My Life in Rhythm and Rhyme.* New York: Hyperion, 1995.

Goldman, Herbert G. *Banjo Eyes: Eddie Cantor and the Birth of Modern Stardom.* New York: Oxford University Press, 1997.

Gottfried, Martin. *In Person.* New York: Harry N. Abrams, 1985.

Granlund, Nils Thor (with Sid Feder and Ralph Hancock). *Blondes, Brunettes, and Bullets.* New York: D. McKay Co., 1957.

Grossman, Barbara W. *Funny Woman: The Life and Times of Fanny Brice.* Bloomington: University of Indiana Press, 1991.

Kahn, Roger. *A Flame of Pure Fire: Jack Dempsey and the Roaring Twenties.* New York: Harcourt Brace, 2000.

Kashner, Sam and Nancy Schoenberger. *A Talent for Genius: The Life and Times of Oscar Levant.* New York: Villard Books, 1994.

Laurie, Joe Jr. *Vaudeville: From the Honky Tonks to the Palace.* New York: Henry Holt and Company, 1953.

Loney, Glenn. *20th Century Theatre, Volume I.* New York: Facts on File Publications, 1983.

Mattfeld, Julius, comp. *Variety Music Cavalcade, 1620–1950: A Chronology of Vocal and Instrumental Music Popular in the United States.* New York: Prentice-Hall, 1952.

McCabe, John. *George M. Cohan: The Man Who Owned Broadway.* Garden City, N.J.: Doubleday & Company, 1973.

McNamara, Brooks. *The Shuberts of Broadway: A History Drawn from the Collections of the Shubert Archive.* New York: Oxford University Press, 1990.

Mordden, Ethan. *The American Theatre.* New York: Oxford University Press, 1981.

Salwen, Peter. *Upper West Side Story.* New York: Abbeville Press Publishers, 1989.

Sobel, Bernard. *Broadway Heartbeat.* New York: Hermitage House, 1953.

Sobol, Louis. *The Longest Street: A Memoir.* New York: Crown Publishers, 1968.

Swindell, Larry. *Spencer Tracy . . . A Biography.* New York and Cleveland: The World Publishing Company, 1969.

Taylor, William R., ed. *Inventing Times Square: Commerce and Culture at the Crossroads of the World.* New York: Russell Sage Foundation, 1991.

Toll, Robert C. *On with the Show.* New York: Oxford University Press, 1976.

Ziegfeld, Richard, and Paulette Ziegfeld. *The Ziegfeld Touch: The Life and Times of Florenz Ziegfeld, Jr.* New York: Harry N. Abrams, 1993.

ACKNOWLEDGMENTS

From the very beginning of this book project, we have had the help and encouragement of Nils Hanson, the administrator of the Ziegfeld Girls' Club in New York and a good friend. He read the first draft of the manuscript and made a number of useful suggestions. He also coordinated every trip to New York during the seven-year gestation period of this book. Bill George, the chef and man Friday of the Travis Ranch, has also been a constant help, doing whatever was needed to advance the project, from occasional typing to scanning photographs to suggesting certain additions to the text. Joseph Eaton Jr., contributed his computer expertise along with his enthusiasm and his willingness to help out. Professor J. Madison Davis read the manuscript and generously gave his advice and criticism. Adele Hoving also read the manuscript, ferreting out grammatical lapses as only an English teacher can. Carol Burr, of *Sooner Magazine,* provided the cap-and-gown portrait by Gil Jain for the book's back cover. Finally, John Drayton, Director of the University of Oklahoma Press, paved the way for publication of the book in a cooperative arrangement with Ed Marquand, of Marquand Books, Seattle. To them and their talented staffs, we are deeply grateful.

"J. R. Morris, Provost Emeritus and Regents Professor Emeritus of the University of Oklahoma, is coauthor of this story of my family. After finishing the manuscript and finding a publisher, we celebrated my ninety-ninth birthday, in March of 2003. So what did we do? We DANCED!" (Photograph by Carolyn Glad)